GHOSTS

GHOSTS

Edited by Morven Eldritch

With material written by Lily Seafield,
J Aeneas Corcoran and Patricia Godwin

LUCEM LIBRIS DISSEMINAMUS

GEDDES &
GROSSET

Published 2005 by Geddes & Grosset,
David Dale House,
New Lanark, ML11 9DJ

Edited by Morven Eldritch

Text written by Lily Seafield,
J Aeneas Corcoran and Patricia Godwin

ISBN 1 84205 532 1

Printed and bound in Poland, EU

POLSKABOOK

Contents

Contents

Introduction

In this volume, a number of stories are related that refer to the existence of ghosts and ghost-like phenomena. They are not ghost stories in the sense that they are inventions, but neither are they true in that they definitely happened. We don't know what happened for sure. All we can be sure of is that they are reported in good faith as being a description of things that appear to have happened and that offer no other rational explanation. They include some that are well documented, those that seem a little bit far-fetched and others that are more likely to be folklore since the only evidence that now exists for their veracity is that handed down through the generations, either orally or by third person accounts. These older stories usually have a more fanciful flavour, probably derived from the fact that they have often been repeated and embellished over the years. Others, which usually tell of more recent occurrences, are often quite mundane and have no interest apart from the fact that they indicate the presence of unexplained phenomena. These have often been related to the reporter first-hand and are therefore less easy to dismiss as being the result of imagination, stress or autosuggestion. It is interesting, however, that the types of phenomena reported have not changed that much over the years, so that the kinds of ghost that are the subject of recent sightings bear more than a passing resemblance to those reported long ago.

Categories

In the previous paragraph, the term 'ghost' has been used to include a whole variety of phenomena that cannot be explained. Although there is no totally satisfactory explanation for any of the occurrences, they do fall into well-documented types. The categories also overlap on occasion, and the distinctions may be academic; however, in brief, they are:

- *Replays* or *playbacks* or *recordings*: ghosts that exactly enact previous events.

- *Presences*: strange feelings in the observer that seem to emanate from a certain place or object.
- *Poltergeists*: ghosts that disturb objects, usually in the presence of a particular person.
- *Interactive ghosts*: ghosts that often appear with a message or respond to the observer in some way.
- *Time slips*: these occur when a person seems to be transported to another time.
- *Living ghosts*: *doubles* occur when the same person is observed (by different people) at various locations simultaneously; *doppelgangers* occur when two images of the same person are observed, usually adjacent and carrying out the same acts; *vardogers* are spirits that precede the observer. Hence, when the observer first goes somewhere there is evidence that he or she has been there before.
- *Fairies and phantoms*: fairies, banshees, demons and other manifestations.

Replays, Playbacks or Recordings

These occurrences seem to replay events that have happened in the past. A characteristic of these sightings is that they often relate to highly emotional events that must have been traumatic for those involved. We have all experienced walking into a highly charged atmosphere at work or at home, and even somewhere neutral, such as a shop, and known that something was afoot. It is thought that replays or recordings are similar but the event was so highly charged that it remained imprinted on the environment only to return when similar conditions were favourable. It is all too easy to dismiss such theories. However, it is well known that a violin sounds better the more it is played because the vibrations somehow change the structure of the wood and make the next note clearer than the last. Could something similar be taking place with replay occurrences?

A typical example of such an occurrence would be the sighting of a figure as it moved, say, through a room or along a road. Such a figure does not react to the viewer and can on occasion 'walk through' the observer since it is merely passing the same way that it did at the time that it was charged with its spiritual energy. For the same reason, these apparitions are reported to walk through walls, the explanation being that at the time of the trauma the obstruction did not exist or a door has subsequently been bricked up. The image conjured up is similar in nature to that of a hologram. It may speak to itself or someone else in its own time and make noises by, for example, stepping on creaking floorboards but will not respond to anything the viewer does.

Some of this type seem to appear at about the same time of year and are consequently referred to as anniversary ghosts. This makes some sense if the explanation that the trauma was somehow imprinted onto the environment is accepted. It would then be reasonable to assume that the time of year would play an important part in the reconstruction of conditions suitable to the reappearance of the apparition.

Presences

In the description of replays, the example of entering a room only to become aware of 'something going on' was used to explain how these might work. This same explanation is much more appropriate when used in relation to presences. This is when a person senses that something is present in a particular place but has no explicit way of proving its existence. The feeling the presence produces in the observer may be anything from a familiar benevolence to one of dread and oppression. It may 'feel' like the presence of an identifiable person or even an animal to the observer. As before, these 'sightings' should not be readily dismissed, especially when the presence is reported independently by more than one person.

Poltergeists

Poltergeist means 'noisy ghost' in German. This is an apt description since the phenomenon is often made manifest by sound. This can be smashing, banging or scraping as made when dragging something heavy across the floor. The poltergeist can also make things move, even heavy pieces of furniture, and can be very destructive. These phenomena are usually associated with people rather than places, and the events that poltergeists cause seem to happen only when a particular person is present. They can be experienced by others if they also happen to be present at the same time.

Interactive Ghosts

These include messages and contacts from the dying and those under extreme stress. Interactive ghosts in some way intentionally make their presence known to the observer. The evidence for their existence is mostly in the form of some message, and usually the ghost is seen only by the recipient of the information. Often the ghost is someone whom the observer has known quite well, such as a relative or friend, who has since died. The ghost might foretell some piece of news, such as a birth or death, unknown to the observer or, indeed, which had not happened at the time but subsequently turns out to be true. The message may be transmitted by the ghost speaking to the observer, by pointing or by some other means such as making a sound.

This might appear to be conclusive proof of the existence of such ghosts, but statistically the chance of such dreams or imaginings happening is actually much higher than is generally recognised. How many times have we all imagined a happy event such as, say, the birth of a child to a sister? If you then dream of such an event, only to be informed the next morning that you are about to become an uncle or aunt, does that make you a mystic? What are the chances, then, of any one person in a sizeable town having a predictive dream on a particular day? I expect the chances are quite high.

However, interactive ghosts are different from this in one important aspect since they appear to the observer while he or she is fully conscious. As you will see from the stories in this volume, the chances of some of the details observed being imagined are extremely slight. One major question for the sceptical investigator is why the ghost seems to appear only to that one person.

Deathbed messages are a type of interactive ghost in which the apparition appears only at the time of the trauma and not some period afterwards. The interaction is also all one way. There are many stories told about contacts from dying people, and these contacts are usually in the form of messages to loved ones. Sometimes it is just to inform the observer that the spirit has died. At other times there may be warnings of some danger in the future. Sometimes they might predict the death of the observer many years hence.

The phenomenon known as an 'out-of-body experience' is well documented. It is widely accepted that people have genuinely thought that their spirit (for how could it be anything else?) has looked down on their body from some suitable vantage point. Such experiences almost always take place when the subject is in a highly traumatic state, such as being on the point of death. We know this because subjects who have subsequently recovered have been able to relate things that happened at the time of their trauma, even in other rooms, when they were in fact unconscious and being medically monitored. It seems reasonable to assume that those who do not recover also have these experiences.

This seems to be evidence of some autonomous spiritual existence between full consciousness and death. If this existence is transitory, the possibility opens up that while in this state the spirit would want to communicate some important information to loved ones. There is also the possibility that what is happening is purely some form of telepathy or coincidence, as mentioned above.

Another type of sighting is so common in form that it deserves a mention, that of the phantom hitchhiker. These are apparitions that seem to haunt roads. Typically, they are seen by motorists and are sometimes the cause of accidents as drivers try to avoid hitting them. Sometimes, when the driver stops, the apparition is no longer there and one can conclude that these are replay-type ghosts. At other times, the driver may give the spirit a lift, only to discover later on that it is no longer in the car. These are like interactive ghosts in that they respond to the observer.

Time Slips

In the film *The Man who Fell to Earth*, there were many fine tricks and effects used to portray the story of an extra-terrestrial being who takes a human form. In one scene, the protagonist, who has become very rich, is being driven along a road in the Appalachian Mountains in the United States in a 'stretch limo'. He looks out of the window at a field, empty apart from a few cows enclosed by a wood. In the blink of an eye, instead of the empty field, he sees a very poor family staring back at him from their farmyard but against the same wooded background. The odd thing about the scene is that the family seems to be from a previous century, obviously before the invention of cars. The scene lasts only moments in the film and does not otherwise figure in the plot, leaving the audience wondering if they really saw it! This is a good representation of what it must be like to witness what happens when a time slip takes place. It is as if the observer has been suddenly transported to the same place but at a different time. The place, with its buildings, objects and people, appears just as it would have at that time. The only difference is that the observer seems to be there too!

In the previous description of ghosts that are interactive, some doubt may have been cast on their existence because the experiences are rarely reproduced. The same can be said of time slips. However, some checks can be made by research into what a certain place was like at the time the slip occurred and the door to the past opened. Could the 'man who fell to earth' have checked in his local library to see if there was a farm at the same place in years gone by? As with interactive ghosts, despite the lack of corroborative evidence, the stories in this volume are believed to have been related in good faith by the people who observed them.

Living Ghosts

Have you ever seen someone you know in a particular place and then remarked to him or her later on that you had seen him or her at that place and time, only to be told that you were mistaken? Usually you rationalise this to yourself – perhaps you were mistaken, or the person you saw just looked like your friend. Possibly your friend had some ulterior motive for denying that he or she was in that place at the time you reported. But how do you rationalise it if you had a conversation with your friend, who in turn has witnesses to say that he or she was somewhere else at that particular time? Even then, you might say to yourself that your friend has a long-lost twin, or you got the time wrong or some such explanation. But if you can prove that the time, date and location are accurate, what is happening? When you have exhausted all the rational possibilities, you might then consider the possibility that the person you saw and spoke to was actually your friend's double.

There are other similar phenomena. The well-known term, 'doppelganger', is often used in everyday language to refer to someone who looks extremely like the subject. However the term, if used accurately, refers to a double who is simultaneously carrying out the same actions as the subject but in a different location. Another less well-known term is that of 'vardoger'. This phenomenon occurs, for example, when a person goes somewhere for the first time only to find out that the people, whom he or she thinks of as strangers, all seem to know him or her. What has happened is that the vardoger has been there first and the people who seem to know *you* have actually been talking to *him* or *her*!

Fairies and Phantoms

A whole host of fairies, banshees, demons, ghosts, green ladies and other manifestations – the nameless supernatural 'types' that were thought to visit the world of mere mortals, influencing them and sometimes playing havoc with their lives – are to be found in the folklore of Ireland and Scotland. Ireland's fame as a land of fairies and other 'little people' is great – not only in a host of well-remembered stories and legends, but also in a vast number of actual sites such as 'fairy raths', fairy hills, and such-like. The memory of an earlier, vanished race is preserved and, on the whole, respected. The devil has also been associated with many of the ghostly tales of evil deeds and strange occurrences after death that have been told over the years.

Where or why stories of the supernatural began no one can be certain, but they have entertained audience and teller alike for many long years and continue to do so. Whether such stories have any base in fact is a matter for debate, but there will always be those who believe that they have some truth attached to them.

Ghostly Encounters

Ghost: Alexander Agnew
Place: *Glenluce, near Dumfries, Scotland*
Date: *c.*1655

The household of Gilbert Campbell, a weaver in Glenluce, was disrupted in or about 1655 by poltergeist activity. The spirit appeared to be closely connected to the children in the family, in particular to Campbell's son, a young student at Glasgow University.

The first indication of trouble to come was given when Campbell's daughter, Jennet, began to complain of strange noises in her ears. The noises were shrill, like whistling. Then Jennet was heard to utter the words of some unseen spirit: 'I'll cast thee, Jennet, into the well.'

After that, the house was subjected to continual bombardment with stones. Clothing was hurled from drawers, clothes were ripped to shreds, and sleepers were woken as the bedclothes were dragged off them by an invisible force.

Much alarmed, Campbell moved his children out of the house for their own safety. The disturbances ceased as soon as the children had gone. The children moved back into the house with the exception of the eldest son, who was studying in Glasgow. For a while things were quiet, but then Campbell's son returned to the house and the trouble started again with renewed vigour. Stones were hurled around, belongings were damaged, and at one point the house caught fire.

The affair caught the attention of the church, and various attempts were made by ministers to exorcise the spirit. The spirit was apparently quite communicative and claimed to have Campbell's son in its power. It claimed to have been sent by Satan from hell to torment the occupants of the house.

While the spirit was willing to communicate with the religious men, it was nevertheless resistant to all their attempts to banish it from the house. It continued to torment the family, beating the children as they lay in their beds, starting fires around the house, hiding the family's belongings or hurling them through the air.

The family showed remarkable courage, remaining in the house throughout all this. Then, without warning, the activities of the malevolent force stopped, and the family was left in peace.

Although no one could be certain as to the cause of the fearful disturbances, one theory connects them to a beggar who had turned up at Campbell's house some time previously. Campbell had sent him away without giving him a penny, and the beggar had angrily threatened to avenge this cold-hearted treatment. It was said that the man was a certain Alexander Agnew, who was eventually accused of crimes against the church and was hanged some miles away in Dumfries. His death apparently coincided with the sudden return to harmony at Campbell's house in Glenluce.

Ghosts: The Amityville Ghosts
Place: *Amityville, Long Island, New York, USA*
Date: Late 1970s

This is one of those stories in which the truth is hard to determine. Many of the events could be put down to coincidence, others to imagination, while some have more than a semblance of truth to them.

The site on which all this is centred is Amityville, a small, middle-class community on Long Island, New York. The story of the Lutz family was told in a book by Jay Anson and it was later made into a film called *The Amityville Horror*. The Lutz family lived in their house for only one month, so frightened were they by their experiences there. The house had three storeys and was built in the style used by early settlers, with columns supporting a balcony that overlooked a large lawn, which was smoothly inclined towards a lake's edge. There was even a boathouse. The Lutz family were not rich and had been able to afford the house only because the asking price was so low and no one else seemed to be interested. The only snag was that the reason it was so cheap was because a few years before it had been the scene of a grisly murder.

The house had been previously occupied by the Defoe family, who had all been drugged and subsequently shot by the eldest son, Ronald. In his defence, Ronald claimed that he had been acting on the insistence of voices. The judge was not impressed, and Ronald was sentenced to six life sentences to run consecutively, one for each member of his murdered family.

George Lutz and his wife, Kathleen, were down-to-earth people and did not scare easily. Nevertheless, either because they were devout Catholics or because they were taking out a little insurance, the Lutzes employed the services of the local priest to bless the house. And that is when things started to become a little strange. As the priest conducted his small blessing ceremony, he passed from room to room repeating his liturgy and flicking holy water, but in one of the rooms a deep voice sternly ordered him to 'Get out!' He looked about him for the source of this voice but found he was entirely alone in the room.

In his book, Jay Anson goes on to narrate various outstanding events. From the first, the house seemed to be full of unexplained noises and bumps, but on the third night they were awakened by a loud crashing coming from the front porch. George Lutz ran downstairs to find that their heavy front door had been torn from its hinges. What's more, it had been forced from the inside against the anti-burglar plate that had been fixed around the door opening. Only someone exceptionally strong could have performed such a feat. Other events took place: doors and windows seemed to have a life of their own, smashing open and shut at will. The banister was torn from its fixings. But these were as nothing compared to what followed.

About three weeks after moving in, George was woken up by some unusual movement in his bed. He was horrified to find his wife floating above the bed. He switched on the light and pulled her down beside him but was devastated to find that this was not his wife but an old hag. But he was wrong, for she snatched a glance at her reflection in the mirror and cried out in alarm to her husband that the image that they could both see was not her. She took a full six hours to return to normal. It must have been a long night.

The Lutzes were obviously stoical people because they did not evacuate their new house even after this horrendous experience. They stayed on for more and apparently got it! They witnessed two staring red eyes at the window and when they went outside to investigate, found cloven hoof prints in the snow! This was the last straw, and they decided to leave immediately; but the house was not through with them yet. As they packed their bags, green slime seeped from the ceiling and black stuff dripped through the keyholes.

This is such an extreme and unusual case that one cannot help asking whether green slime and black stuff have more to do with selling books and films than with fact.

But the ghost or ghosts that were the protagonists in the film also seemed to have inveigled themselves into the lives of those making it. Typical of these stories are those concerning James Brolin, the star of the film. He is said to have be convinced of its presence, apparently because on the first day of shooting he was trapped in a lift, admittedly a frightening experience, and also on the second day he twisted his ankle at the studio – not a totally unusual event for most of us. The writer of the original book also tells of other events surrounding the manuscript.

He gave some early chapters to a woman who took them home to read, but that night she was consumed in a fire and all but the manuscript perished in the flames.

The photographer who went to take pictures of the Amityville house delivered these to Anson, but when he went back out to his car he found it in flames, even though he was sure that the engine had been turned off. Fire also consumed the car of Anson's editor when he went to Anson's office. Someone else put the manuscript in the boot of his car, only to drive through a puddle that turned out to be 3 metres deep – the manuscript was bone dry!

The only thing connecting all these events is the manuscript and, of course, Anson. There is one further twist to the story. The house at Amityville is now owned by James and Barbara Cromarty, and they say it isn't haunted!

Ghosts: Marie Antoinette and Others
Place: *Petit Trianon Within the Grounds of the Palace at Versailles, France*
Date: August 1901

This story is about a well-documented time slip and was originally published in 1911 by the two observers and called 'An Adventure'. The two observers were women in their thirties, well educated and not likely to be given to fantasy. Miss Moberly was a principal of St Hugh's College, Oxford, where Miss Jourdain had been a distinguished scholar.

Versailles lies 8 miles from Paris and was transformed in the 17th century by Louis XIV from a bucolic chateau into possibly the world's most extravagant series of buildings, set in over 55 square miles of sculptured park and woodlands. Along with innumerable fountains, statues, stretches of water and formal gardens, there were a number of smaller chateaux scattered throughout the grounds. One of these, built as a private retreat for Louis XIV, was called the 'Grand Trianon'. Later, Louis' son, Louis XV, built an extremely charming residence for his mistresses and called it the 'Petit Trianon'. Later still, in the 18th century, it was occupied by Marie Antoinette. While she and her courtiers played at Versailles, the rest of France was gripped by the severe economic troubles of the time. The French people laid much of the blame on her, and she became a hated figure known as Madame Deficit. She was beheaded in 1793, towards the end of the revolutionary upheaval of those years.

To get back to the story, Eleanor Jourdain had a flat in Paris where she ran a kind of finishing school for young ladies. The two women were introduced with a view to their working together in Oxford and shortly after this, made a visit to Versailles in early August 1901. Neither had been there before, and after viewing the main sights of interest, they decided to take a look around the grounds. They walked past the Orangerie in order to visit the famous Petit Trianon, which is quite close to the main house. They passed the Grand Trianon and, as they thought, up the path that led to the small (by Versailles standards) house.

As they walked, they came across another small, pleasant-looking path, which branched off through the trees.

Despite the fine day, the women became strangely dejected and glum. All seemed rather dull, uncommonly silent and lifeless. They soon came across a house and assorted outbuildings. Miss Moberly saw a woman shaking out a white tablecloth. (Later Miss Jourdain could remember no people present.) They continued on their way and came across two men, apparently gardeners, working with a wheelbarrow. The men were dressed in the clothing of a previous era and wore the three-cornered hats common a century before. The women asked directions to the Petit Trianon and were silently pointed in the right direction. A little later they came across a small cottage in front of which were standing two women, also dressed in old-fashioned clothing. This time it was Miss Moberly who later could not remember the scene.

Farther on, they came across a small summerhouse, thought to be the Temple de l'Amour, beside which stood a man of repulsive appearance. They could see him but apparently he could not see them. At this point they realised that something was wrong. While they were wondering which way to turn, a young man came running up to them, again dressed in old-fashioned clothes. He advised the correct way to the house and then ran off.

The women followed his directions, which took them over a narrow bridge and into the formal garden of a charming house. They were apparently in the back garden of the Petit Trianon. By the house, Miss Moberly noticed a beautiful woman dressed in an elegant dress working at an easel. She looked up as they passed by, but again Miss Jourdain saw nothing. At that point, a rather cheerful young man arrived and guided them through the house to the front where he quickly left them. As they emerged from the front of the house, the 'spell' was suddenly lifted from them. They found that they were in a group of other chattering people, their feelings of depression were suddenly gone, the birds were singing and the day had come alive again.

The two women realised that they had been part of something extremely odd, and some time later they decided individually to write down a description of their experience. They decided to return to

Versailles and on that visit found things very different from the first occasion. For example, the narrow bridge was no longer there. In their research they found out that the bridge had existed in 1789 but had since been removed. Similarly, other things that they had seen on their first visit were also found no longer to exist although, again, research revealed that they had been there in 1789. The date is significant because shortly afterwards Versailles was ransacked by the mob of the French Revolution.

In their investigations, the two women discovered that other people had had similar experiences – always in August. They further discovered an account of an event that happened on 10 August 1789, which described how Marie Antoinette had been sketching in the sun-kissed garden when a messenger arrived with news that the mob was approaching. The mob, in fact, did not arrive until October of that year. The two women speculated that through all the personally traumatic times ahead, Marie Antoinette cast her mind back to the moment when she realised that the dream had finally ended. Such was her distress and anguish at that particular moment that it had imprinted itself on her surroundings.

Probably because the events that may have taken place are so well documented by the people who witnessed them first-hand, they are widely discussed in the literature surrounding the subject of the paranormal. Despite the scholarly character of the observers, however, and the meticulous care that they took in checking their recollections by further visits and noting their experiences in 'An Adventure', the events are still a matter of dispute. For example, Hilary Evans maintains in his book, *Visions, Apparitions and Alien Visitors*, that on balance the events probably did occur as the two women related. However, Michael Coleman in *The Ghosts of the Trianon* concludes, after the most careful and detailed consideration of 'An Adventure', that the two women were overcome by the heat of the day, possibly after a glass of wine (or two) at lunch time, and what they witnessed was merely some kind of pageant.

Ghost: A Haunted Antique Chest
Place: ***Stanbury Manor, Morwenstow, Cornwall, England***
Date: Various

Stanbury Manor contains a chest that is thought to have come to this country with the Spanish Armada. The owner had bought it from an antique shop whose proprietor was glad to be rid of it, as he was convinced that it was haunted. When the chest was first taken to the manor it was placed temporarily in the armoury. On the morning of the day following delivery, the owner, passing through the armoury, saw six guns, which had been held to the walls with heavy wire, fall to the floor. Neither the wire nor any of the fixings were broken. The chest was moved to the bedroom one day and on the same evening, the owner was in an adjacent room hanging pictures on the wall, when one of them fell and struck him on the head. The picture was quite heavy but there was virtually no force behind it when it hit him, as though it had been controlled by some mysterious force.

The next day, three more pictures fell to be followed by four more two days later. These last four were in the drawing room adjacent to the bedroom where the chest stood. The day after this another picture fell in the drawing room, and on none of these occasions were the wires or fixings damaged in any way. On hearing, two days later, of the death of a relative the owner thought that there might have been a connection between this and the falling pictures, as there were no further incidents in connection with the chest.

These strange events were reported in the press and the following tale was told by a former curate, someone familiar with the phenomenon. The chest was once owned by two elderly ladies who lived nearby. Both were deaf and would communicate by writing notes. They kept themselves to themselves and were hardly known to their neighbours or to other local people. They had amassed a large collection of furniture during their lives, and the curate went to look at the pieces when the women put them up for sale, but bought nothing as he found the continual writing and passing of notes too frustrating. He discovered some time later that the sisters had both been struck deaf one morning when they had gone to stay with friends. They had arrived late at night and gone to bed without unpacking and had, next morning on waking, seen the lid of a chest which was weighed down by others opening of its own accord. On looking into the chest they saw something so dreadful that they were both struck deaf on the spot.

In another story, a surgeon, in the Midlands, went to stay with a friend. His bedroom was large but drab and had a large carved wooden chest standing in a corner. His curiosity made him open the top and he was confronted with the corpse of a man lying with his throat cut from ear to ear. In his shock he let the lid of the chest fall closed, but on recovering his composure, re-opened it to find the chest empty. The next morning he mentioned this terrible experience to his host who, astonished, told him that a previous occupant of the room had killed himself and the body had been in the chest covered in blood.

Ghost: The Ballechin House Ghost
Place: *Ballechin House, Dunkeld, Perthshire*
Date: 1892

A Jesuit priest, Father Hayden, stayed in Ballechin House, just outside Dunkeld, for a few days in 1892. One night, when asleep, he was awakened by loud noises. He moved to an adjacent room and found that the noises had followed him and he told of hearing sounds like those of 'a large animal throwing itself violently against the bottom of the bedroom door.' The noises were accompanied by bangs and screams. Next year he met, by chance, a woman who was an ex-governess at Ballechin House, who told him that she had left her employment there because she had been frightened by strange noises which had kept her awake at night. As she elaborated on her story, it became obvious to Father Hayden that she had occupied the two rooms that he had used during his visit.

The house was rented in 1896 for twelve months, to a family who left after eleven weeks thus losing more than nine months rent which they had already paid. They were driven out by mysterious groans, rattling noises, bangs and footsteps. On one occasion clothes were pulled from beds and an icy chill descended on the house.

Father Hayden had told Lord Bute of his experiences. Lord Bute rented the property and arranged for two investigators to live in the house and try to explain the phenomena. The investigators were greeted on their arrival by a 'loud clanging sound' which echoed through the building and was repeated for two hours. They too reported voices, dragging and pattering sounds, bangs and knockings.

A ouija board was used in an attempt to communicate with the spirit or spirits and during one session, someone with the name of Ishbel told the investigators to go at sunset to a valley nearby. When they did so they saw, against the white background of newly fallen snow, the figure of a woman wearing a nun's habit which moved away from them and vanished under a tree. The same figure was seen on subsequent occasions and was heard to cry and talk 'in a high note, with a quality of youth in her voice.'

The mystery has never been resolved.

Ghost: Marc Baus
Place: *Anger, Brittany, France*
Date: 1951

In August 1951, John Allen set out from Calais on what was to be a cycle tour through France. When he was just outside Anger in Brittany, he had a puncture and, as he had no spare inner tube, he had to spend some time in pouring rain trying to effect a repair. This proved to be unsuccessful, and he started to push his bike, hoping to reach a village before it became dark. After two hours on the deserted road, he at last saw a house in the distance and approached it, hoping to find assistance or, if not that, at least shelter. The house, when he reached it, turned out to be a deserted and run-down farmhouse with the ground floor windows solidly boarded shut but the door left unlocked. The house was very damp and smelled of decay, and the furniture, which no one had bothered to take away, was green with mould.

Cold and tired, John decided to light a fire in the old fireplace. He managed to find some dry wood, which he placed in the grate before going to the entrance hall to fetch some paraffin from the saddlebags on his bike, which he had left there. Suddenly he was petrified with fear as he saw a wet trail showing up against the dust on the hall floor. Following the trail into the living room, where he had intended to light a fire, he found that it ended on an old settee on which lay a few pieces of rotting cloth – the remains of a pair of pyjamas. As he lifted them from the settee, a wave of disgust and nausea made him sway on his feet.

He considered the situation and came to the conclusion that a combination of tiredness and hunger had affected him, and, although he found the farmhouse very unsavoury, he decided to spend the night there and to move on the next day. He lit his fire, which was immediately blown out by a sudden gust of wind.

Then he heard a noise, the sound of something wet falling on the hall floor outside, but when he went to investigate there was nothing to be seen. He was trying to re-light his fire when he heard the noise again. This time when he looked in the hall he recoiled in fear. The floor was now soaked in water, which moved towards him, slid through the doorway and reached the old pyjamas, which began to take on the shape of a man as water ran from them. John had had enough and ran from the house until he reached a bar where the owner, seeing him in such distress, poured him a glass of cognac and told him to drink it. Eventually, he was revived enough by the spirit to tell his story and noticed that no one else in the bar seemed worried or surprised. Exhausted, he rented a room, and having been assured that his belongings would be safe in the house where he had left them, he went to bed and fell asleep.

Next morning, over breakfast, he discovered the terrible secret of the farmhouse. During the Second World War the farmhouse had been the home of a collaborator, an artist whose name was Marc Baus, who had betrayed many Resistance fighters. Arrested and tried in 1946, Baus was found guilty but sentenced to only two years in prison, from which he returned to his home in 1948. One night his house was attacked by a crowd of people, and the next day, fearful for his life, Baus disappeared, to be found dead two months later, wearing his pyjamas, in a shallow pond behind the farmhouse. When his body was discovered it was taken into the house and laid on the settee, where its ghost was seen by John Allen.

Ghost: Captain Bayliss
Place: *France and Britain*
Date: 1915 and Later

In March 1915, Captain Terence Bayliss was the adjutant to the 39th Gharwal Rifle regiment. The regiment was heavily engaged in the vicious fighting around Neuve Chapelle in Flanders in the First World War. In one of the many almost suicidal attacks on the German trenches, during which the Indian troops won many honours, Captain Bayliss was killed. His regiment felt his loss deeply as he was a much respected and courageous officer who had greatly helped his men to come to terms with the horrors of the war. As the war went on, most of those who knew him were themselves killed, until the regiment was comprised mainly of replacements who had never met him and he was gradually forgotten – until one day in September 1915.

On that day, shortly before the battle at Loos, the regiment had attacked enemy positions on a hillside and had been stopped by machine-gun fire 50 metres from the German trenches, unable to go forward or to retreat, when the figure of a British officer riding a white horse appeared through the smoke. The figure waved the troops on towards the enemy positions and, although shells burst all around it, remained unhurt and encouraged the troops to advance. The soldiers were convinced that the apparition was that of Captain Bayliss and, being more frightened of the ghost than anything else, they charged at the enemy lines and after a fierce battle won the day. They looked for the figure on the white horse but it had gone.

Then, two years later, on a night in 1917, a very frightened sergeant told a story to his orderly officer. The officer had left the mess to inspect the regimental guard. He was accompanied by an NCO, and together they walked through the woods to the parade ground where the regiment was camped. As they reached the parade ground, he gave the password, expecting to have a response from the sentry, but none came. Disturbed by this breach of discipline, the officer went to the parade ground and found the guard assembled in two ranks as though awaiting inspection. The troops were talking quietly to each other and glancing around fearfully while their sergeant looked over a wall that bordered the field in which they stood. When summoned, the sergeant told his story, to which the officer listened incredulously.

Shortly before the arrival of the officer, the sergeant had heard someone challenged by the sentry and had been told, on asking the sentry who it was, 'Orderly Officer's rounds.' The sergeant had ordered the guard to turn out for inspection and saluted the officer, who was riding a white horse. The sergeant's salute was returned and the mounted figure, without dismounting, had carried out a critical inspection of the guard before, without warning, leaping his horse over the wall. The parade ground was searched but no trace of the mysterious officer was found, not even a hoof print.

The strange officer reappeared to inspect the guard again. This was one week later, and this time he spoke 'in a voice faint and hollow', ordering the sergeant to put on report a soldier, one of whose tunic buttons was not done up. He then disappeared again over the wall, but not before he had been recognised as the dead Captain Bayliss. He then appeared so often that there was soon hardly a man who had not seen him.

Long afterwards, when India gained its independence, the regiment was being disbanded and just at sunset as the Union Jack was lowered and the sounds of the Last Post were heard, the figure of the dead captain appeared on his white horse, wearing a uniform from thirty years before.

Ghost: The Bealings House Ghost
Place: *Bealings House, Woodbridge, Suffolk, England*
Date: 1834

In 1834, Bealings House was occupied by Major Edward Moor, FRS, who had retired from the East India Company and returned to Britain. Major Moor returned home from church on Sunday, 2 February 1834, to be told by his servants that the bell from the dining room had rung on three occasions when the room was empty. The next day the same thing happened, and at the last ring the Major was at home and heard it himself. He was out on business the following day and, on his return in the late afternoon, he heard that all the service bells had rung violently all day long. As he listened to the story a bell rang in the kitchen. There were nine bells in the kitchen each connected to a room in the house by means of a wire pull so that a servant could easily be summoned. The bells were hung about three metres from the floor in the kitchen.

Major Moor's cook told him that the bells that had been disturbing the household were the five on the right of the row which served the dining room. These served a drawing room over the dining room, a bedroom next to the drawing room and two attics above. As he looked at these bells, the five on the right suddenly rang with such force that they almost fell from the wall. Major Moor's son was with him this time and told his father that he had heard the bells ring on a previous occasion. The bells then sounded fifteen minutes later and four more times in the next hour before falling silent.

That evening, the Major and his son were having dinner in the breakfast room when the bell for that room rang once although neither of them had touched the bell pull. As the meal proceeded, the five bells that had sounded before rang every five minutes and did so until eight o'clock that night when, for no apparent reason, they fell silent.

The following day, Wednesday, 5 February, Major Moor, his son and his grandson were in the breakfast room and most of the servants were in the kitchen, when the five bells rang out again. The Major went to the kitchen to find his staff terrified. Five minutes later the bells rang again, and again one of them rang with such vigour that it struck the ceiling before settling into silence.

Although the Major was convinced that no human hand was responsible for the bell ringing, he could find no other explanation. The bells continued to ring day after day, when there was no one in the room or the passageway concerned, and all became convinced that something other than a human force was responsible.

The bells rang from 2 February until 27 March 1834 and then stopped. The cause was never discovered and the bells still hang, disconnected, in the kitchen at Bealings House.

Ghost: Cardinal Beaton
Place: *Ethie Castle, Arbroath, Scotland*
Date: *c.*1546 and Later

Ethie Castle, about 5 miles from the town of Arbroath, is now the home of the Forsyth family. The castle as it stands today dates from the early 15th century, but there was undoubtedly another building on the site before the present one was constructed.

Cardinal Beaton, Abbot of Arbroath in the 15th century, commissioned the building of the present castle, and his ghost is said to haunt the place still. He lived at Ethie for several years, and Marion Ogilvy, his mistress, also lived there.

Cardinal Beaton was a powerful figure in the Catholic Church and a fierce persecutor of those of the Protestant faith. He had many enemies. His life came to a violent end in St Andrews on 29 May 1546, when he was brutally murdered by Protestant nobles in the castle there.

The ghost of Cardinal Beaton parades slowly round Ethie Castle, particularly in the area close to his bedchamber. The sound of his footsteps is quite unmistakable – his gouty leg thumping and scraping as it drags along the passageways of the castle.

Ghosts: The 'Beasts' of Tuamgraney
Place: *Tuamgraney, County Clare, Republic of Ireland*
Date: Around Halloween

By Tuamgraney in County Clare is a wooded hollow that is said to be haunted, especially around the end of October, when Halloween is near. At that time, the residents used to avoid the area, but one young man, either sceptical or forgetful, went walking there in late October. It was a peaceful autumn day. Carrying a stout stick, he walked downhill among the trees. There did not seem to be anything threatening in the quiet woodland but despite this, a sense of acute foreboding came upon him quite suddenly – a combination of fear and a strange, deep sadness. He paused for a moment, and almost decided to turn back, then dismissed the feeling as imagination and pressed onwards. But he went more cautiously now and was unable to rid himself of the sense of being on forbidden and dangerous ground. The trees seemed more numerous and more densely packed than he remembered.

Walking softly along the indistinct and overgrown path, he saw ahead of him that the wood was bathed in a dim, unnatural light. Thoughts and memories came to him, of how groves like this were used in past times for pagan rites and ceremonies. Perhaps blood sacrifices had been offered up here, in this place that was now so still, so ominously breathless and silent. As he made his way slowly along, there was a movement in the bushes ahead and he saw a dog among the leaves – a black dog, its size hard to gauge in the shadows, but with an expression of malevolence in its red eyes. Some stray, he said to himself, but his heart was beating wildly. The creature's abrupt disappearance did nothing to allay his fears. Then he jumped with fright as something sprang into his path. It was a hare, a big, black hare, and red-eyed like the dog. For a moment it looked at him, and again he felt a current of malice flow towards him. The hare bounded away into the undergrowth, and now a cat appeared, the colour of straw. It faced him on the path – its back arched, fangs bared, eyes glaring – before it too retreated into the shadows. He would have turned and fled, but now the ground beneath his feet was rising upwards, and he felt it was quicker to press on than to go back. But his experiences were not yet over.

The way led into a clearing. Oncoming evening made the sky here almost as dark as the forest cover had been, but he saw that the clearing was occupied. Two animals were struggling there, one a deer hind, the other a black ram with ferocious eyes and massive curled horns. The deer sank to its side, wounded and exhausted, and the young man caught what seemed to be a look of appeal in its eyes. Brandishing his stick, he ran forward and attempted to beat off the ram. But as he struck, he found his blow connected with nothing but empty air. Yet when the ram turned on him, he felt a savage buffet as the massive horned head butted him. He fell to the ground, winded, and blacked out for a moment. When he came to, the scene was deserted; also, to his surprise, there were only a few trees instead of dense woodland surrounding the clearing. But as he got to his feet, his sides were still aching from the ram's horns, and he made his way slowly home.

At home, he told his story as if it had been a dream, but an uncle of his confirmed that others too had stumbled into beasts of the phantom forest around that time of year.

Ghost: The 'Bell Witch'
Place: *Robertson County, Tennessee, USA*
Date: 1817

John Bell lived with his wife, four sons and a daughter on a farm in rural Tennessee. Betsy, the daughter, became the focus of the hauntings of a spirit now referred to as the 'Bell Witch'. The disturbances started in 1817 and were, initially, no more than the sound of scratching and the occasional knock. Soon, however, bedclothes were being pulled from people as they slept and there were odd noises as though of someone choking. Furniture began to move, stones were thrown and then the spirit started to slap Betsy across the face. She would hear the noise of a blow and her face would redden in the pattern of a hand. On many occasions her hair was pulled violently and painfully. Obviously now the target of the spirit's malevolent attacks, Betsy was soon tired out and eventually John Bell sought help for his daughter from a neighbour, James Johnson, who was a much liked and respected lay preacher. Johnson very quickly came to the conclusion that it was not practical jokes that were being played, and he decided that the only thing to do was to try to contact the spirit.

It became apparent after a while that the spirit was trying to communicate, and according to one account, 'It commenced whistling when spoken to, in a low, broken sound, as if trying to speak in a whistling voice, and in this way progressed, developing until the whistling sound was changed to a weak, fluttering whisper uttering indistinct words. The voice, however, gradually gained strength in articulating and soon the utterances became distinct in a low whisper so as to be understood in the absence of any other noise.'

Now that it could form words, it started to tell stories that were sometimes contradictory. It was the spirit from a body that was buried in the surrounding forest; it came from a settler who had hidden his fortune in the woods and had died before he could retrieve it; and it was an evil conjuring by a local woman, Kate Batts, who had the reputation of being a witch.

Then John Bell started to suffer attacks. The ghost declared that it would give him a dose of such a medicine that he would die from it.

His jaw then swelled, and he suffered violent spasms and convulsions, until one day he fell into a coma from which he never awoke. When he eventually died, the spirit filled the house with cries of triumph that were repeated at his funeral a few days later.

For a short period after this, the remaining members of the Bell family had peace, and then, in 1821, one evening as they sat around the supper table, a large smoking sphere rolled from the grate and gradually vanished as it turned into smoke. The spirit's voice cried out, 'I am going and will be gone for seven years.' It never returned.

Ghost: The 'Big Grey Man' of Ben MacDuibh
Place: *Ben MacDuibh, the Cairngorm Mountains, Scotland*
Date: 19th Century Onwards

Ben MacDuibh in the Cairngorms is a magnificent but lonely place to experience a ghost. Upper slopes of the mountain have snow on them for several months of the year and make an awesome sight, but even in summer the landscape possesses a certain power. The mountain is one of Scotland's 'Munros' – hills over 914 metres high – and is popular with walkers and climbers, but in spite of that it is still very isolated. It is quite possible for the solitary walker to spend several hours on the mountain without coming into contact with another human being. On occasion lone walkers have found that they have company after all – not human company but that of *An Fear Liath Mhor* – 'the big grey man of Ben MacDuibh'.

Sightings and sounds of the big grey man have been reported by several people for more than a century now. The ghost is not only seen on the mountain itself but also in the surrounding area of the Cairngorms, in the Lairig Ghru and in Glen Derry, for example.

Several common elements link the stories that have been told by various witnesses. One of the first reported experiences was that of Professor Norman Collie from London. He was climbing back down from the summit in 1891 when he heard something behind him in the mist. It sounded as if something or someone was following him down the mountain, taking one step to every three or four of his. Professor Collie was unable to make out anything in particular, as visibility was very poor, but he was sufficiently frightened to take flight, risking a fall rather than be caught by his pursuer.

Other witnesses in the years that have followed have told stories that have strikingly common elements about them.

Often the first thing that the witness notices is the sound of footsteps; the footsteps are heavy and slower than those of a walker of average stature. This leads the witness to conclude that what he or she is hearing is probably a very large person. Sometimes this is all that the witness has experienced. Other witnesses, however, have also seen something – generally a very large, upright figure in the distance. People who have seen the figure and have tried to follow it have seen no trace of footprints. Descriptions of the figure vary slightly, but it is usually described as being grey, very tall, human in form, but somehow not quite right – unnatural.

In 1943 a man called Alexander Tewnion was on Ben MacDuibh. He was a naturalist with considerable experience in the mountains. As he climbed, he became aware of the sound of heavy, slow footsteps. After a while a large figure rushed at him out of the mist. Tewnion shot at the shape three times but seemed neither to hurt it nor scare it off. He turned and fled and eventually managed to shake off his sinister follower.

The figure on Ben MacDuibh, whoever or whatever it might be, certainly seems to be a malign presence and its manifestations have succeeded in inspiring great fear in even the most hardened mountaineers.

Ghost: The 'Black Lady' of Broomhill
Place: *Broomhill House, Larkhall, Scotland*
Date: Early 20th Century

The case of the ghost of Broomhill House was given a great deal of publicity in the 1960s when a television documentary was made on the subject. The house stood on a site that had been inhabited for hundreds of years, buildings of various forms having been successively built and destroyed during the course of time. The house in its final form was the home of the McNeil-Hamilton family at the turn of the 20th century, and the last of the family to live there was Captain Henry Montgomery McNeil-Hamilton. The ghost that haunts the ruins, the 'black lady', is well known to locals in Larkhall, in the area of South Lanarkshire in Scotland where the ruins of the house stand. The house has attracted the interest of clairvoyants and ghost-hunters alike, and much research has been carried out by psychic investigators and other interested parties to find out who the black lady was and why she haunts the place.

The ghost is a sad one, it would appear, and she has been seen and has been making her presence felt since quite early on in the 20th century.

Captain Henry McNeil-Hamilton was a military man and served in South Africa during the Boer War. It is thought that the black lady was in fact an Indian woman who, having been taken to South Africa, found herself working for the British Army there. She was possibly brought to Scotland by McNeil-Hamilton to live as his mistress. There are stories of such a lady living at Broomhill, who seemed to disappear in mysterious circumstances, and some people believe that she may have met a violent end.

Broomhill suffered from a fire in the 1940s and was badly damaged. The McNeil-Hamilton family sold the house and land in 1954. The house, already in a desperate state, fell further into ruin and very little remains now. Nevertheless, in spite of attempts at exorcism over the years, the black lady is still said to be there, her appearances characterised by an overpowering feeling of melancholy and a smell of spices and perfume.

Ghosts: The 'Blue Man' and Other Ghosts of Arundel Castle
Place: *Arundel, Sussex*
Date: *c.*1700

The ancestral home of the Dukes of Norfolk, Arundel Castle, although mainly of the 19th century, is probably built on foundations dating from the 12th century or earlier and has four ghosts: a white bird, a dandy, a boy and a girl.

The white bird, a portent of ill tidings or evil, is found fluttering against the windows of the castle when the death of one of the family is nigh.

The figure of a dandy has been reported since the days of King Charles II and is known as the 'blue man'. The figure has been seen, on many occasions, looking at books in the library and dressed in blue silk, hence his name, but nobody knows what he is looking for, or why, or if he ever finds it.

A former kitchen boy, ill-treated by the head cellarer some two hundred years ago, haunts the great kitchen of the castle, and his ghost has been heard, but not seen, cleaning pots and pans as though his very life depended upon it.

A young girl, dressed in pure white, is seen on still, moonlit nights in the vicinity of a tower on the brow of a hill. The tower is named Hiorne's Tower, and from it the girl is said to have thrown herself to her death in desperation because of unrequited love.

Ghost: Anne Boleyn
Place: *Blickling Hall, Norfolk and Elsewhere in England*
Date: 1985 and Later

Anne Boleyn was brought to the court of King Henry VIII when she was quite young. Although married to Catherine of Aragon, the king became enamoured with Anne but found that she was not to be won except by marriage. The king was desperate for a son, and although the queen had borne him a daughter, he resolved to replace Catherine and to marry Anne. After Archbishop Cranmer pronounced the marriage to Catherine null, Henry married Anne in a private ceremony, and shortly afterwards she bore him a daughter, later to become Elizabeth I. Henry was obviously very fickle, because not many months later Jane Seymour had attracted his attention. In order to get rid of Anne, Henry, willingly aided and abetted by Cranmer, brought Anne before a special court on trumped-up charges of treason. The alleged offence was not merely adultery but incest. Needless to say, Henry got his way and Anne was duly sent to the Tower of London, where she was beheaded on Tower Green in 1536. Henry's one gesture of humanity was in allowing her to be beheaded by a French expert from Calais, using a special sword, rather than one of the usual executioners.

There are stories of Anne's headless ghost being seen at the Tower, near the Queen's House, where she stayed while awaiting execution, the ghost being identified by its fine clothes, and also at Hampton Court, where she would have stayed many times with the rest of the court.

There are also many stories of her being seen in the corridors of her family home, Blickling Hall in Norfolk, of which two are well documented. On one occasion, in 1985, Mr Steve Ingram, who was employed in the management of the house by the National Trust and lived on the site, had a strange experience in the middle of the night. He awoke to hear the footsteps of a woman approaching down the corridor and across the carpet towards the foot of his bed. He had experienced the sound many times before since it sounded just like his wife, but she was lying beside him. He immediately switched on the light, only to find no one was there. He would probably have put this down as an odd but 'ordinary' ghost-like occurrence but for the strange coincidence (if that is what it was) that the date happened to be the anniversary of Anne's death.

The other well-documented occurrence happened to another of the administrators working in the building. Sidney Hancock was looking out of the kitchen window when he saw a young woman wearing the clothes of a bygone age. She wore a long grey dress with a white cap and collar, similar in style to those popular in Tudor times. She was strolling in the grounds down by the lake. Intrigued, but at the same time mindful of his duties, Hancock went into the garden to confront the woman and see if she was lost. He asked if he could help, to which the woman replied with words that sounded like, 'That for which I seek has long since gone.' Hancock's attention was momentarily distracted and when he turned back she was gone. This happened in an open space with nowhere to hide.

The figure that Hancock saw may or may not have been Anne. If it was, her message may have referred to the building because the house she had lived in was replaced on the same site by another house, one hundred years after her death. But as has been mentioned before, ghosts are known to haunt buildings long after they have been altered or replaced.

Ghost: Charles Bonner
Place: *The* Discovery, *Discovery Point, Dundee, Scotland*
Date: *c.*1901 and Later

Discovery Point, berth of Captain Robert Scott's ship, *Discovery*, is now a tourist site of which the city of Dundee can be justifiably proud. The vessel was built in the city at the end of the 19th century, and it is a testament to the fine workmanship of its construction that it survived the rigours of its service as a royal research ship in the polar regions.

On the British National Antarctic Expedition in 1901, *Discovery* saw two tragic deaths among those who sailed on her. Just as the ship was leaving New Zealand, a seaman called Charles Bonner fell to his death from the crow's nest of the vessel. The other death occurred some months later in Antarctica when another seaman was killed onshore.

It is the ghost of Charles Bonner, the first to die, that is thought by some to be the most likely cause of strange noises that haunt the vessel. The noises are heard above the officers' wardroom, just below the spot where the seaman fell to his death. Some visitors report a feeling of distinct uneasiness in the wardroom, as if there is a sinister presence there.

Ghost: Theophilus Brome
Place: *Higher Chiltern Farm, Chiltern Cantelo, Somerset, England*
Date: 1670 and Later

The skull of Theophilus Brome is kept in a cabinet in the hallway, above the main door, of the farmhouse at Chiltern Cantelo near Yeovil in Somerset. It remains at the farmhouse because the owner in life of the skull requested that on his death, his head should be removed from his body and be kept there. The motive for such an extraordinary request was formed by Theophilus' experiences in the Civil War that was particularly hard fought in the West Country. Theophilus had originally been a Royalist but was so disgusted by the ritual impaling of their enemies' heads that he actually changed sides and became a Parliamentarian. He developed such a fear of this vile treatment that he made his sister promise that after he died, she would see to it that his head was removed and kept at their farm so that even if some enemy wanted to dig him up and impale his skull on a stake, they could not do so.

Over the years, any subsequent attempts to remove the skull from its resting place have been thwarted by unseen spirits. On those occasions when the skull has been removed, the house becomes haunted by the eerie screams of a soul in torment, which continue until it is replaced. One occupier of the farm tried to reunite the skull with the body and even got as far as starting to exhume the body. This endeavour was abandoned, however, when the spade that was being used broke in two even though it was not being exposed to undue stress.

The spirit of Theophilus is said to be benevolent to those who respect it. A Mrs Kerton, who lived at the farm in the 1970s, reported that before moving in she was inspecting the farm with her fiancée when Theophilus warned her that she was about to step on her coat. She had thought that she was only about to walk over a shadow but his call directed her attention to a dark shape. She found that far from being a shadow, the darkness was in fact caused by an old well shaft. Another step and she would have fallen to her certain injury if not death. This incident could obviously have been a lucky coincidence but Mrs Kerton credits the ghost of Theophilus with her salvation.

The skull became a bit of a celebrity in the 1970s and was the subject of at least two television programmes. One of the programmes involved the comedian Dave Allen, who was so disturbed by the visit that he swore never to go there again. On another occasion the television crew witnessed the sudden appearance of a well in the garden. This was put down to Theophilus, and Mr Kerton explained that the spirit was trying to tell the crew something. However, exactly what this was could never be discovered.

Theophilus was not, apparently, too good at communication. As well as being paranoid, he was obviously also illogical, since he would have been less likely to have had his head impaled if he had remained a Royalist. Also, by keeping his head constantly 'available', he made possible impalement by an enemy so much easier than if it had been buried in the first place!

Ghost: A Bronze Age Warrior
Place: *Bottlebush Down, Dorset, England*
Date: 1924

Some of the stories in this volume are quite recent but this one takes pride of place as being about a very ancient apparition. The ghost in this story has been estimated to be over 2,000 years old. How do you estimate the date of a ghost that is over 2,000 years old? Well it helps if you are an archaeologist and you can draw on that expert knowledge to place all the clues together.

The archaeologist in question was named R. C. Clay. He was working on a dig, a Bronze Age village near Christ church, and was returning to his home in Salisbury, Wiltshire, when he came across the spirit. As he was driving along, he saw a horseman riding at full speed across the fields. The horse was quite small and it was obvious from the rider's position that it had neither bridle nor stirrups and the man was riding it bareback. It must have crossed Clay's mind that it was a boy from a local Gypsy encampment or something of that ilk. Anyway, it was apparent that if they both maintained their respective courses they would soon collide, so Clay slowed down to avoid an accident but when the rider got about 35 metres away he veered off and rode parallel to the road. For several seconds the rider and car travelled together, long enough for Clay to get a good look at the man.

Clay described him as wearing the clothes of another era with bare legs and a long flowing cloak. He was waving some kind of sword or other weapon over his head. Clay glanced back at the road and when he returned his gaze, the horseman had vanished.

Clay stopped the car to regain his composure and had a cursory look around but could see nothing. Since dusk was gathering and it was a very isolated spot, and probably because he was feeling rather insecure after being witness to such an event, Clay decided to return home. He did not let the matter drop there, however, and the next day he went back to the same spot to see if he could find any evidence for what he had witnessed the day before. He found nothing whatsoever but what he did discover seemed to him to be significant. On the spot where the vision had disappeared, he found the remains of an old burial chamber that he was able to date as being very roughly of the same age as that of the horseman. Clay went back to the place many times after that, even at exactly the same time of day, but he never saw the horseman again.

Clay never saw the horseman again but many others have done so both before and since. On one occasion, he was seen by two schoolgirls out riding their bikes. The area where the horseman appears is littered with burial mounds and standing stones, some quite substantial. The two girls were pedalling home to Sixpenny Handley when the horseman appeared from out of the blue and kept ghostly company with them for several seconds before disappearing as quietly and quickly as he had arrived.

Ghost: Marion de la Bruyere
Place: *Ludlow Castle and Churchyard, Shropshire, England*
Date: 12th Century Onwards

Ludlow Castle occupies a strategic position on the border between England and Wales and was the last to surrender to the Parliamentary forces in 1646. The castle dates from the 11th century but its haunting stems from the days of Henry II when it was in the midst of many border skirmishes. One of the occupants, Marion de la Bruyere, had a lover who sided with the enemies of those in the castle and one night, when the castle's custodian, Joce de Dinan, was absent, she lowered a rope to let him visit her. On this particular evening he did not, as usual, pull the rope up after him but left it hanging, thereby allowing 100 men to climb up, open the gates, and take the castle. When she realised that she had been used and betrayed, she slew her lover with his own sword and then killed herself by jumping from the walls of the Hanging Tower onto the rocks beneath.

Although her ghost was, for many years, said to have been seen below the tower from which she leapt to her death, walking amongst the ruins of the castle now fallen into disuse and disrepair, all that is now heard is the sound of sighing or breathing which seems to come from the tower itself. This could be the breathing of the knight who betrayed Marion, or her own, as she killed him.

A local resident has heard the sounds on many occasions and has said that the noises could be those of someone in a deep sleep but that they are so clear and loud that they seem to come from the top of the battlements. On first hearing the sounds, he took his wife to the castle without telling her of them and, on arriving below the tower, she mentioned the strange noise which seemed to come from the castle. The same man, although hearing the same sounds on many occasions, had never found any rational explanation for them and has discounted the noise of the wind or that of nesting birds.

The parish churchyard at Ludlow is also said to be haunted. An elderly and tall woman, wearing a long drab robe, has been seen outside the rectory and strange footsteps have been heard by some people living nearby. The same figure has been seen to walk around the gravestones.

Ghost: George Bullock
Place: *Abbotsford, Home of Sir Walter Scott, in the Scottish Borders*
Date: *c.*1818 and Later

Sir Walter Scott had a keen interest in the supernatural, and during his lifetime he witnessed a ghost in his own home. George Bullock, a Londoner, was appointed by Scott to take charge of many of the building works at the writer's home, Abbotsford. George Bullock died in London in 1818, while work was still in progress at Abbotsford, fourteen years before the author's own death.

On the night of Bullock's death, Scott told of being woken by violent noises in the house. Although it was the middle of the night, it sounded as if builders were at work. Scott got up to investigate, but as he made his way through the house apprehensively, sword in hand, he could find nothing to explain the disturbance. The house was quiet again, and there were no signs of any disturbance.

Later, Scott was to discover that the bizarre events coincided with Bullock's death in London. The ghost of Bullock is said to have put in an appearance at Abbotsford on a number of occasions since then.

Ghost: Jenny Cameron
Place: *East Kilbride, South Lanarkshire, Scotland*
Date: Between 1772 and *c.*1966

The following story can be found in a book by Maggie Craig called *Damn Rebel Bitches*, which describes the history of the Jacobite Rising of 1745–46 by recounting stories of the fascinating women caught up in those turbulent times. Many lurid stories were written about Jenny Cameron, about whom we actually know very little for certain. We do know that she came from Glendessary, a very remote part of the Highlands at the head of Loch Arkaig, and that she was a fervent Jacobite who led about 300 of her fellow Camerons to the Raising of the Standard at Glenfinnan in 1745. Most of the stories told about her were invented by English hacks who were out to demonise anything Scottish. The pamphlet writers of Fleet Street described the Scots as a dirty, violent and deceitful race and Jenny was depicted as a spoilt child who went to the bad in Edinburgh, bedding all-comers and ending up having several children from an incestuous relationship with her brother. The emergence of Jenny Cameron on the scene must have been a godsend to them; now they had sex to write about as well as violence. They naturally went on to assert that she was the mistress of Bonnie Prince Charlie although there is no evidence for this.

As is well known, the rebellion was finally crushed by the Duke of Cumberland and his army at Culloden. After that battle, Cumberland systematically set about clearing any supporters of the Bonnie Prince from even the most remote parts of the Highlands and Jenny Cameron was forced from her home. She eventually settled in South Lanarkshire, at East Kilbride, although at that time it was open countryside. She obviously managed to bring some of her wealth with her for she bought a fine house called Blacklaw. Jenny renamed the property Mount Cameron and started a school for orphans of the '45 rebellion. She became a respected and well-liked member of the local community and despite the fact that she was a Catholic she attended the local Protestant parish church. She died in 1772 and her last wish was that she be laid to rest at Glendessary, but in those days it would have taken many days to reach such a remote part and, instead, her relatives buried her in the grounds of her house in South Lanarkshire.

East Kilbride was the first of the so-called 'new towns' to be built in Scotland during the 1950s and 1960s, and Jenny Cameron's estate was eventually cleared to make way for a golf course, although her grave was preserved. On several different occasions in the evening, when the light had started to fail, golfers are said to have witnessed a strange light hovering around the grave. Was this the spirit of Jenny, restless at being in this place so far from home? We don't know for sure, but we do know that the lights are no longer seen.

The area around her grave is now a children's play park surrounded by a housing estate. Jenny lives on in the memories of local children; they learn of her part in those violent times and her story plays an important part in local history. Two of the local schools are called Blacklaw and Mount Cameron, and the streets around the play park have names such as Glendessary, Mount Cameron Drive, Glen Nevis, etc, all names with which she would have been familiar. Far from being more disturbed by the presence of such a modern creation as a housing estate, Jenny seems to be quite at home there, and in 1995, on the 250th anniversary of the uprising, a new stone was erected on the site. As Maggie Craig says in her book, 'She may not have reached the Highlands, but they have been brought to her.'

Ghost: Mary Cameron
Place: ***Inverawe House, Taynuilt, Argyll and Bute, Scotland***
Date: ***c.*1660**

In the 17th century, Mary Cameron's family lived at Callart House, which is an old tower house by the shores of Loch Leven, quite near the famous Glen Coe. She was engaged to be married to Diarmaid Campbell, who lived at Inverawe House, situated at the foot of Ben Cruachan, near the main road to Oban from the south. But, although engaged, she was not too old to be punished and on one occasion, she was locked in her room for crossing her father. While she was locked up, a Spanish ship arrived in the sea loch to trade with the locals. But along with its fine goods, the ship also brought the plague and everyone at the great house was infected and died as a result. Meanwhile, Mary remained locked up, wondering why the house was becoming quieter and quieter.

Eventually a man was sent to burn down the house in the hope that the pestilence would die with it. When he arrived he was just in time to find Mary still alive. She pleaded with him to help her but the man was afraid that she carried the disease and would contaminate him. He agreed, however, that he would take a message to her fiancé at Inverawe before he set fire to the place. Diarmaid came with all speed and rescued Mary but when he returned with her to Inverawe, his father refused them entry, fearing for the health of his household. The two were forced to take refuge where they could in the open countryside, but after a lengthy quarantine, Diarmaid's father let them back into Inverawe. They were eventually married and had many children. Mary died some time after Diarmaid, who was a victim of the Montrose army at Inverlochy in 1645.

The spirit of Mary lives on at Inverawe. It is said to be a friendly ghost and is locally called 'Green Jane' since she appears to be slightly green in colour whenever she appears.

Ghost: The Virginia Campbell Poltergeist
Place: *Sauchie, Between Tillicoutry and Alloa, Scotland*
Date: 1960

There are many who believe that poltergeist activity is associated with a single person rather than attached to a place, like so many other manifestations. This view is supported by a typical poltergeist case that took place at the beginning of the 1960s in Central Scotland.

Dr William Nisbet of Tillicoutry was the family doctor of the Campbell family of Sauchie. He was called in by Mrs Annie Campbell to attend their 11-year-old daughter, Virginia, in November 1960. Unfortunately there was little the doctor could do because the patient had nothing physically wrong with her. The doctor was a significant figure of authority within the community, and it was on this basis that he had been called in to witness the strange occurrences that always seemed to take place near Virginia; there were unusual knocking sounds that could not be explained and objects, even heavy ones, moved when she was close by.

The doctor consulted several local worthies. One was his partner, Dr William Logan, and another was the local minister, the Rev Thomas Lund. They were obviously perplexed but came up with a couple of theories that they tried out. They suspected that the bewildering occurrences had a direct connection with the girl and thought that her mind might be so disturbed that somehow she was responsible for the phenomena.

One theory was that the girl was terribly upset because she had been forcibly separated from her dog when the family moved from Ireland some months before. They thought that Virginia was so missing her pet that this had affected her mind. Dr Logan decided to lend his dog to Virginia to see if this would help. Unfortunately it had no effect.

They next tried drug treatment. Dr Nisbet was reported in the local paper, *The Alloa Advertiser*, on 9 December 1960, as saying: 'The girl was hysterical all the time that the phenomena were appearing.

We decided to try sedation. Virginia was given a mild tranquilliser to quieten her. If the phenomena were being conjured up by her own imagination they would no longer appear if her brain was dulled. But even though the brain was not working normally the phenomena still appeared.'

They then decided to eliminate the house from their investigations. Dr Nisbet continued, 'The next thing we tried was a change of environment. Virginia was moved to the house of a relative in Dollar (nearly 3 miles away) for two nights. The manifestations still appeared.' Dr Logan and his wife, also a doctor, attended the girl here and witnessed many rapping noises that seemed to be concentrated around Virginia. Mrs Logan, who was sceptical at first, became convinced that the noises were certainly not being generated by anyone in the room. They also witnessed Virginia talking in a most un-childlike manner to some unseen person as if her voice had been taken over by some spirit; she seemed to be in a trance.

They next tried to insulate her from any outside influence. As Dr Nisbet recalled, 'She was brought back to Sauchie and we tried isolation. The child was put to bed and left on her own to get to sleep. But still the phenomenon appeared and made itself heard. From a room below we could hear the child screaming and sawing and bouncing noises.'

On Thursday, 1 December 1960, Virginia's ordeal practically came to an end. The Rev Lund brought in two of his colleagues from the Church of Scotland and held a short service in the house. As Dr Nisbet recalled, 'When Virginia went to bed, a short service was held at her bedside. We all prayed. Since that night nothing has happened. I believe the cure is now complete.' He went on, 'In any case we have on record, by ciné-camera and tape recorder, what has happened; a moving linen box, the lid of the box opening and closing, rippling bedclothes, moving pillows and bouncing noises. The tape and film will be available to any person who is interested in this case.'

Virginia's most frightening experiences lasted about a week. She was then allowed back to school. After that, other strange things happened while she was around but these gradually petered out, and in any case were almost benign when compared to the violent things that had upset her so much in November. For example, in January 1961 her teacher at the local Sauchie Primary School, Miss M. Stewart, reported that a bowl of hyacinths moved slowly across her desk when Virginia was standing nearby. These minor events continued until March 1962 when they finally stopped for good.

Ghost: Evelyn Carew
Place: ***Potter Heigham, Norfolk, England***
Date: 1742

Every year, at midnight on 31 May, a phantom coach races from the Hall at Potter Heigham to its destruction on the three-arched bridge in the village. In the 18th century, Lady Evelyn Carew was married to Sir Godfrey Haslitt. The marriage ceremony took place on 31 May in Norwich Cathedral but the wedding had been made possible by the bride allegedly contracting with the Devil, saying that she would be his if only she could first marry Sir Godfrey. Midnight struck, the bride was abducted from her new home and carried to a waiting coach. The Devil had demanded his due. The coach, pulled by four black horses and occupied by four skeletons, raced down the driveway and took the road to Potter Heigham.

The night was quiet but a few people still abroad saw the coach with its terrified passenger race down the road until it reached the bridge in the village, where it swung across the narrow road and, smashing into the parapet, broke into pieces and fell – horses, coach and passengers – into the river below.

Ghost: The Mary Carrick Poltergeist
Place: *USA*
Date: 1867

Mary Carrick emigrated from Ireland to the USA in May 1867. Illiterate but bright, and in good health, she quickly found a job as housemaid with the Willis family. Mr H. A. Willis himself told the story in a report for the *Atlantic Monthly* of August 1868, which he titled 'A Remarkable Case of Physical Phenomena'.

After Mary Carrick had been six weeks in the Willis house, the kitchen bells began to ring at intervals through the day, even though no one was pulling the cords. The bells themselves were some three metres up on the kitchen wall. When disconnected, they continued to ring, but only when Mary was in the room or the room adjoining. The rings were violent, as if the bells were being tugged hard. Then came rappings, on doors, walls and windows close to where Mary was at work. She herself grew nervous and hysterical as a result of the happenings. She feared dismissal and pleaded with the Willises, 'Please don't send me away.'

She had no friends or contacts in the USA to turn to. Some local spiritualists, hearing of the case, showed interest, but Willis, convinced there must be some rational physical cause, would not admit them to the house. The happenings grew more violent. Chairs were tipped over, crockery flew across the room, and tables were lifted and tilted. A heavy stone washing-slab rose up, fell back, and broke. Things came to a climax in August, with pails tipping and spilling, the washtub emptying itself, and heavy furniture turned over, while furious raps and bangs were heard on the wall. Mary was sent away for a rest and peace returned to the household but when she came back it all broke out again. On 12 September, Mary suffered a nervous collapse, and was taken away to a nearby asylum. She briefly returned to work for the Willises but preferred to go back to the asylum, where she worked as a maid for the rest of her life.

Willis's own explanation for the attacks was that in some way they involved electricity. When he put glass insulators under Mary's bed and the kitchen table, these remained still whilst other objects continued to move. But he could not establish what kind of process it was, nor could he explain how Mary herself became clairvoyant for the duration of the attacks.

Ghost: The *Castel a Mare* Ghost
Place: Castel a Mare, *Torquay, Devon, England*
Date: 1920s

In 1920, the writer Beverley Nichols, his brother, and a friend, Lord Saint Audries, went to a house in Torquay one evening. The house, *Castel a Mare*, was said to be haunted by footsteps and horrible shrieks that had been heard since someone was murdered there. With a candle to guide them they went from room to room, each one of which was more dilapidated than the last. Plaster had fallen from the ceilings, wallpaper was hanging from the walls and the rooms were cluttered with rubbish. The house had such an effect on them that they spoke in whispers as they climbed a narrow staircase to the top floor.

Beverley Nichols, disappointed that nothing odd had occurred, was in front of his friends and waited for them alone on the top floor, when he realised that his mind and body seemed to have slowed down and that even his thinking had become laboured. As though under the influence of a drug, he started to lose consciousness but managed to crawl to a window and fainted. When he awoke, his first reaction was to leave the place as quickly as possible but his friends, who had not had the same experience, decided to investigate further and when they had spent more time in the building, including the room near which Beverley Nichols had felt the strange influence, they came to the conclusion that the house was empty and completely benign.

Lord Saint Audries decided, once his friend seemed to be recovered, to look around again on his own after agreeing that he would whistle every minute to let the others know that he was safe. For 20 minutes, carrying a candle for light, he roamed the building and was heard as he passed across the upper hall after he had climbed the stairs. His friends whistled and the sounds were replied to although, oddly, the whistles from the house seemed to get louder.

Suddenly Beverley Nichols and his brother had the impression of something leaving the house and passing them, without making any noise. They heard a terrified, pleading, shout from Lord Audries. From upstairs they heard the noise of a violent struggle and then the dishevelled, plaster and dust-stained Lord Audries came from the house into the garden and collapsed beside them.

When he was sufficiently recovered and could talk sensibly he said that, while he was in the house, his attention had been continuously drawn to the room near which Beverley Nichols had had his terrifying experience. After sitting in the corridor for a time, he suddenly saw a greyish light in the darkness of the upper hall coming from the room. As nothing happened, he decided to leave and report to his two friends outside but, on standing up and turning to descend the stairs, something black, silent and man-shaped rushed from the room and knocked him to the floor. An overwhelming sense of evil overcame him and he struggled to keep his sanity as he forced his way down the stairs through the blackness to his friends outside.

The three discovered later that there had been two murders in the house. A mad doctor had killed his wife and their maid and the murders had been committed in a bathroom, the small room outside of which Beverley Nichols and Lord Saint Audries had had their horrifying experiences.

Ghost: The Castletown House Ghost
Place: *Castletown House, Celbridge, County Kildare, Republic of Ireland*
Date: 18th Century

Castletown House at Celbridge, County Kildare, was built by William Connolly, Speaker of the Irish Parliament, in 1722. The house was inherited by his nephew, who married Lady Anne Wentworth, daughter of the Earl of Stafford. It was she who one day saw the figure of a tall man standing in the upper gallery, who proceeded to walk down a non-existent staircase, past a big window, taking little steps as though each stair was quite shallow. It paused and laughed a high, cold, arrogant laugh, as though it were the rightful owner of the place mocking at the people who lived there.

Ten years later, a staircase was built in exactly the location in which Lady Anne had seen the figure. More than twenty years after that, Lady Anne's son, Thomas Connolly, now the owner of the house, was walking in the garden with his wife and recalling the strange story of what his mother had seen in the hall. A few days after that, he was out riding with the Kildare Hounds and a wild and stormy November day it was. Many of the hunt gave up and went home, for the fox was proving to be tricky and elusive. Only Connolly and a handful of others were left, when Connolly noticed that a newcomer seemed to have joined them. Mounted on a fine black horse that looked as fresh as if it had just come out of the stable door, he was a long, tall fellow, dressed in grey, with great thigh-boots.

'Good day to ye,' called out Connolly. 'A poor day for sport, though.'

The man merely grinned, showing large, discoloured teeth, then set his horse to the slope of the hill and went galloping up. At that same moment, the hounds began to bay, as if they were closing in on their prey. Connolly followed the other horseman up the hill, but when he got to the brink, he reined in, astonished. The hounds were not to be seen, but the stranger stood there, dismounted from his horse, and with the bloody carcass of the fox held in both hands high above his head. He grinned again at Connolly, then lowered the fox's body to the level of his mouth, and in one swift bite with his great teeth, cut away the brush. Dropping the carcass he held it out to Connolly, still grinning.

The young squire of Castletown turned away in disgust but the man then spoke.

'Connolly, if you will not take the brush, will you offer me a cup of something hot in your great house?'

The Connollys had always maintained a tradition of hospitality, and Thomas did not refuse, though there was something about the man, his leering smile and his high voice, that turned his blood.

'There is hot rum punch at my house for all who want it,' he said.

The stranger entered the house at Connolly's side, and Connolly saw him pause and survey the great entrance hall, and the staircase that came sweeping down from the gallery, past the window, and he heard a sound of hissing laughter from the man's lips. The stranger took a chair by the fire, and stretched out his legs as the other huntsmen were doing, but when a servant came up, to help take his riding boots off, he waved the man away.

'Leave me be,' he said. 'I am sleepy and don't choose to be disturbed.'

He closed his eyes and appeared to settle down for a comfortable nap. Coming more closely to get a good look at him, Connolly was amazed to see that the stranger was as hairy as an animal. Coils of hair matted on the backs of his hands and more emerged at his cuffs. Tufts of coarse hair sprang from his ears. Beginning to have suspicions, Connolly told two of the servants to take off one of the sleeping stranger's boots. As they cautiously worked it off, a thickly haired leg appeared, terminating in a great black hairy hoof.

Hastily, as all the company retreated from the fire, Connolly sent a man to ride for the parish priest. As the priest arrived, the stranger awoke, glanced at his feet and saw one boot had been removed. With a snarl he rose up and placing himself against the mantelpiece, right in front of the roaring fire, he laughed the same high-pitched, spine-chilling laugh that Lady Anne had heard all those years ago in the same room. The priest, as terrified as anyone, mumbled an incantation, but it had no effect except to provoke further demoniac laughter.

At last, the priest in desperation threw his missal at the figure. It missed its target and struck the mirror above the fireplace, which shattered. But, at the threat of being touched by the holy book, the figure leapt high in the air and vanished, leaving only a greasy boot in the room and a great crack in the stone fireplace.

Ghost: John Chiesly (Johnny One-Arm)
Place: *Dalry, Edinburgh, Scotland*
Date: *c.*1688 and Later

The ghostly figure of John Chiesly was known as 'Johnny One-Arm' to the people around Dalry in Edinburgh. He haunted the streets of the area, scaring grown-ups and children alike, for more than 300 years.

John Chiesly lived in the middle of the 16th century, an unhappily married man until he finally sought a divorce from his wife in 1688. He then became an unhappily divorced man. The Lord President of the Court of Session, Sir George Lockhart, had pronounced that John Chiesly should pay his wife a substantial sum annually in settlement. Feeling the sum awarded to be entirely unreasonable, being out of all proportion both to his wife's needs and his own means, John Chiesly decided to vent his anger upon Sir George. He followed him to church one Sunday morning and, catching up with him in Old Bank Close, he shot him. Sir George died and the full weight of the law descended upon John Chiesly. He was tortured cruelly to establish whether he had acted alone or with the help of others. Then his right arm was cut off while he was still alive as fitting punishment for its part in the crime – his right hand had held the murder weapon. Finally, John Chiesly was taken to the gallows and hanged. His body was left hanging on the gallows as an example and a gruesome warning to all. Then someone – nobody knew who – took the body down and secreted it away. Had it been buried? Nobody could, or would, tell.

Ghostly happenings began to be reported in Dalry. Several people reported seeing the anguished figure of a man in the streets around the area. The ghost had one arm missing. It screamed. It laughed maniacally. It gave the neighbouring children nightmares. The ghost appeared, again and again, over the next 300 years.

In 1965, builders started work in a cottage in Dalry. On removing part of the floor they were surprised to find the skeleton of a man. The skeleton was cracked and broken, as one would expect the skeleton of a tortured man to be. Most significantly, however, the skeleton had only one hand. It could only be John Chiesly. The remains were removed from the house and re-interred in another place. The streets of Dalry are at peace now, for Johnny One-Arm no longer has cause to haunt them.

Ghost: Lady Clanbrassil
Place: *Killyleagh Castle, Strangford Lough, Northern Ireland*
Date: Middle of the 17th Century

In the middle of the 17th century, when Oliver Cromwell was making his notorious way through Ireland, he met an unexpected check at Killyleagh Castle on the shore of Strangford Lough. This was the home of the 1st Earl of Clanbrassil, a supporter of King Charles I in the Civil War against the Parliamentarians. The Earl had raised a force to try to relieve Carrickfergus Castle, held by Cromwell's troops, but his effort failed. His little army scattered and all had to flee to find safety where they could. Clanbrassil could not get back to Killyleagh. At that time, it was little changed from the old Norman keep and courtyard that had been built in the 12th century. The Earl's wife, Anne, summoned all his tenants and retainers, brought them into the castle, and issued them with weapons. The gates were barred, ready to withstand the inevitable siege. Soon enough, the Cromwellians arrived.

A castle commanded by a woman should have been no great problem for such seasoned troops. But they were forced back by the determination of the defenders. They returned and tried to batter down the great wooden doorway. But the Earl's wife had seen to it that the gate was solidly reinforced from behind. When the soldiers attempted once again to storm the walls, every manner of missile from arrows to kitchen furniture forced them back once again. It was only when food supplies ran out and her faithful garrison was beginning to starve, that a signal offering truce was sent out. It was accepted by the besiegers. The makeshift garrison was allowed to make an honourable exit from the castle, led by its commander. Cromwell imposed a fine of £10,000 on Clanbrassil, but the lady, by ardent pleading, got him to reduce it by half. Not only that, she obtained a pardon for her husband.

Killyleagh, still standing above an inlet of the Lough, was much altered and rebuilt in the mid-19th century. But its great hall is still said to be patrolled by the figure of a woman in 17th-century costume. No one who knows the history of the place doubts that this is Anne, Countess of Clanbrassil, whose spirit still defends the castle she so bravely held against the might of Oliver Cromwell.

Ghost: 'Corney' – a Poltergeist
Place: *Dublin, Republic of Ireland*
Date: Not Known

One Dublin poltergeist actually used to speak to the family whose house it inhabited. They referred to it, or him, as 'Corney', and he answered to the name. His voice was said to sound as if it came out of an empty barrel. The servants, who slept in the kitchen, were afraid of Corney and asked to sleep in the attic instead. However, the first time they slept in the attic room, the doors of its cupboard burst open and Corney said: 'Ha! Ha! You devils, I am here before you. I am not confined to any particular part of this house.' He was seen only twice, once by someone who apparently died of fright as a result, and once by a seven-year-old boy, who described the figure to his mother as that of a naked man, with a curl on his forehead, and 'a skin like a clothes-horse'.

Corney had a somewhat warped sense of humour: his first manifestation was by mimicking the sound of someone on crutches when one member of the household had to temporarily go on crutches with a sprained knee. He would not allow anything to be kept in one of the kitchen cupboards, tossing out whatever anyone tried to put in there.

On one occasion, he announced he was going to have 'company' that evening, and if the residents wanted any water out of the soft-water tank, they should draw it before going to bed, as he and his guests would be using it. Next morning, the water was a sooty black, and there were sooty prints on the bread and butter in the pantry. When a clergyman came to investigate him, the crafty Corney kept quiet, and on being asked later by the servants, 'Corney, why did you not spe ak?' he said, 'I could not speak while that good man was in the house.'

Corney made life so lively for the family that they resolved to leave the house and sell the remainder of their lease. But each time someone came to look over the house, his antics speedily drove them away, until at last the lady of the house appealed to him to stop troubling prospective buyers. Corney relented. In fact, he said 'You will be all right now, for I see a lady in black coming up to this house, and she will buy it.' Within half an hour, a widow had called and agreed to take over the lease, and the family thankfully left Corney behind.

Ghost: Lady Mary Crawford
Place: *Crawford Priory, Fife, Scotland*
Date: 1833 Onwards

In spite of the ecclesiastical sound of the name of the place, Crawford Priory has no connections with the church whatsoever. It was built as a private home in 1813 by Lady Mary Crawford. Its architecture harks back to much earlier times, inspired as it is by the Gothic religious style. On a gloomy day its impressive facade looks undeniably grim; in fact, it looks as if it ought to be haunted. The imaginative visitor could quite easily conjure up a picture of sinister cowled figures moving around the grounds or the headless spectre of some unfortunate figure from the past. Such a vision would certainly fit the appearance of the building but is far removed from the truth.

Crawford Priory is haunted, but the ghost is free of any malevolence or unhappy history. Lady Mary was an eccentric figure by all accounts, a determined and sometimes fierce spinster who, having indulged her fantasy in the building of Crawford Priory, chose to share her life with a menagerie of animals upon whom she doted. She kept many animals and birds, both wild and domestic, at the priory and seemed to prefer their company to that of human beings. Lady Mary demonstrated her great concern for their welfare even after her death. In her will, she left instructions regarding the euthanasia of her brother's horse, which she had been looking after. She wanted the beast to suffer as little pain and distress as possible.

Lady Mary Crawford died in 1833, and her funeral was quite an impressive affair. She is buried in the family mausoleum nearby, but her ghost remains at the priory, wandering around the grounds, beckoning her beloved creatures to come to her.

Ghost: Abraham Crichton
Place: *Sanquhar, Dumfries and Galloway, Scotland*
Date: 18th and 19th Centuries

In the 18th and 19th centuries, the kirkyard at Sanquhar in Dumfries and Galloway achieved notoriety on account of the ghostly activities of a man called Abraham Crichton. Abraham Crichton died in 1745 in a particularly unpleasant manner after a colourful life.

Crichton was a wealthy man, laird of Carco and the owner of several properties in the area as well as a great deal of land. However, much to the suspicion of various local people, he was declared bankrupt in 1741. His properties and land were sold off bit by bit, but rumours were circulated that Crichton was not in the dire straits that he would have people believe. He had, somewhere, secreted away a great deal of money. This, combined with the manner of his death, made it hardly surprising that his tortured soul would be unable to find peace.

There was a disused church in the district, which had been the kirk of a former parish, that of Kirkbride. For some years there had been a dispute as to what to do with the building. Some locals wanted to tear it down; whilst in the opinion of others such an act amounted to sacrilege. The story goes that previous attempts to demolish the church had been unsuccessful and that those who had taken part in the exercise found themselves the victims of considerable misfortune as a result. In the eyes of those who believed in such things, these happenings had been manifestations of the wrath of God.

Abraham Crichton was having none of this. He wanted the church to be brought down. He engaged a group of workmen to accompany him to the building to start demolition. They set to work, but hardly had they done so when an almighty storm blew up, preventing them from getting any work done. Forced to abandon their efforts until the next day, they all set off for home.

Whilst riding back from Kirkbride, Abraham Crichton met with disaster. A bolt of lightning caused his horse to rear up in panic and

Crichton was unseated. A tumble from a horse is bad enough, but one of Crichton's feet had become wedged in the stirrup and as the horse bolted, he was dragged along in its wake. The horse galloped off at a great rate, and it did not stop, nor even slow down, until it reached Dalpeddar. When the frightened beast finally drew to a halt, its owner lay by its side, lifeless and bloody.

It seemed as if the death of Abraham Crichton was divine retribution. Not only had this man been dishonest in his financial dealings, said his critics, but he had also been guilty of sacrilege. He should never have tried to tear the church down. The locals shook their heads and tut-tutted self-righteously as preparations were made for Crichton's funeral.

They had not seen the last of Abraham Crichton, however. Not long after he was buried in the graveyard at Sanquhar, he returned in ghostly form, causing great consternation in the district. He would pursue passers-by in the fields next to the churchyard. He would appear suddenly in the churchyard itself, frightening the life out of anyone who happened to be there. Always, he seemed to be trying to speak to those whom he followed. His hand would stretch out in entreaty, but none dared to take it. The kirkyard at Sanquhar became a place much feared in the hours of darkness. Locals would take detours in order to avoid passing close to the church as a longer walk was considered well worth the effort if it meant avoiding the ghost of Abraham Crichton. News of the haunting spread, and Sanquhar became a topic of heated debate amongst those who had any interest in matters paranormal.

At length it was decided that something had to be done, the ghost was causing too many difficulties. A minister by the name of Hunter was appointed to deal with Crichton's troublesome spirit. The bold minister took himself to the kirkyard one dark night with a Bible and a sword to await an encounter with Crichton. He insisted on carrying out his vigil alone, and no one saw what came to pass in the course of the night. When morning came, however, the minister left the churchyard, tired but in confident mood. He never related precisely what happened during those long hours of darkness. He was, however, able to give his assurance that Abraham Crichton's ghost would wander no more.

The ghost was never seen after that, but, just in case, the people of Sanquhar secured his tombstone in its place over the grave with very sturdy chains.

Ghost: Lady Crichton of Frendraught
Place: *Frendraught House near Huntly, Scotland*
Date: 17th Century

Frendraught House, as it stands today, was constructed in the 17th century around a much older castle. The property stands in beautiful surroundings close to the town of Huntly and is haunted by a ghost whose story starts in 1630.

In 1630, the laird of Frendraught at the time, Sir James Crichton, killed Gordon of Rothiemay in a dispute over land. As a consequence of this, he was ordered by the Marquis of Huntly to pay compensation, or blood money, to Gordon's son and namesake.

Some time later, Crichton became involved in a feud with Leslie of Pitcaple. Fearing violence from Leslie, Crichton sought the services of the Marquis of Huntly's son, Viscount Aboyne, and the new laird of Rothiemay, as part of an armed guard to protect him.

The men were lodged in a tower of the house for the night. A terrible fire broke out and several people were killed – Viscount Aboyne, Gordon of Rothiemay, Colonel Ivat, English Will and their servants.

It was agreed that the fire had probably been started deliberately – Lady Crichton was the one upon whom most people's suspicions fell – but an official investigation that took place at Frendraught in 1631 was unsuccessful in finding enough evidence to blame any one individual, and the laird and his wife escaped any form of retribution.

The Lady of Frendraught apparently was troubled by her conscience after death, for she has returned to the scene of the crime several times since then. Her ghost, reportedly dressed in white, is traditionally never seen or heard by any laird of Frendraught, but other people, either living in the house or visiting it, have witnessed the presence of something supernatural, either seeing the figure of a lady or hearing loud sounds of raised voices and banging, which have no rational explanation.

Ghost: The 'Death Coach' of Ballyduff
Place: *Ballyduff, Republic of Ireland*
Date: Not Known

An anonymous correspondent from Clonmel passed this story to T. C. Croker, who included it in *Fairy Legends of Southern Ireland*.

This was the experience of Michael Noonan, who lived near Ballyduff. One fine evening in summer, he was walking to Ballyduff to collect a pair of mended brogues from the shoemaker there. His way, on foot, took him by the river, past the derelict Hanlon's Mill. To his surprise, as he came by the mill, he heard the sound of hounds and huntsmen in full cry, yet there was nothing to be seen of them. Furthermore, he knew that the Duhallow hounds were out in quite another quarter of the countryside that day. His surprise turned to fear when he heard the 'clack, clack' of the mill's mechanism at work, for the place had been abandoned for many a day. He positively ran the last of the distance to Ballyduff.

When he got to the cobbler's shop, his fear subsided. There he found an old friend and near neighbour, Darby Haynes, a carrier by trade. Darby Haynes was waiting in town for his nephew to arrive, and he asked Michael if he would drive his cart home for him. Michael was pleased to agree, not fancying a return along the footpath that day, with the dark coming on.

He drove home slowly under a clear sky, knowing that the old horse had had a long day of it already. The moon rose, past a quarter towards the full, shedding brightness across the land. Lying back in the cart, Michael was idly watching the moon's reflection in a long pool that ran by the road's edge, when he saw it suddenly blanked off by a shadow. Wondering where the cloud had come from in that cloudless sky, he looked round, and saw a sight that chilled his blood.

Drawing close alongside him, in utter silence, was a great black coach, drawn by six black horses. The coachman, high on his box, was draped in black. But the terrible thing was that neither he, nor his horses, had heads. The coach came abreast and passed rapidly by, the horses raising their hooves in a smart trot; the headless coachman laying the whip across their backs, and the wheels spinning round without a sound. The only noise came from his own horse and the squeaky axles of the cart that needed greasing. In a moment, the black coach had disappeared in the darkness of the next clump of trees. Michael Noonan, trembling, continued home, unharnessed the horse, put it out in the field, and put himself to his bed. Next morning he was standing by the roadside, still perplexed and alarmed by the events of the previous day, when he saw Daniel Madden, huntsman to Mr Wrixon of Ballygibblin, come riding down the road at a mad pace. Stepping out, he waited for Dan to come up to him.

'For the love of God, don't stop me!' gasped the rider.

'Tell me what's the matter,' said Michael. Madden gasped out the news that his master had taken a fit during the night and now lay close to death. He was riding to fetch the doctor. But maybe Michael could run across the fields and tell Kate Finnigan, the midwife, for she had medical skills that might help till the doctor got there. Michael went, as fast as he could go. But he already knew, and so it proved to be, that it was too late. The death coach had already claimed its latest passenger.

Ghost: The Derrygonelly Farmhouse Ghost
Place: *Derrygonelly Farmhouse, near Enniskillen, Northern Ireland*
Date: Late 19th Century

The farmhouse at Derrygonelly was a typical farmhouse of the later 19th century, with a living room and two smaller rooms off it, which were used as bedrooms – and, of course, with no electric light. It was situated near Enniskillen, County Fermanagh, and occupied by a family of six, which included the farmer (widowed), his son, and four daughters.

The eldest child was one of the girls, Maggie. She was almost twenty at the time that the hauntings began, and it seems that they had some connection with her. Unlike the great majority of rural cases, this one came to the attention of some high-powered ghost-watchers, including Sir William Barrett, a former President of the Society for Psychical Research (SPR) and also a distinguished scientist and Fellow of the Royal Society. The first signs were noises – rapping and scratching sounds that sometimes continued through the night. These were succeeded by moving objects. Some items were found right outside the cottage after thumps and bangs in the dark of the night. Lamps and candles seemed to be the particular target of whatever was the source of the noises. It became impossible to keep any of these in the house overnight.

The farmer was a Methodist, and was advised to leave an open Bible in the room occupied by Maggie and her younger sisters, with its pages weighed down by stones. This had no effect and indeed the stones were removed and pages from the holy book torn out.

Sir William Barrett visited the cottage with Mr Thomas Plunkett from Enniskillen. His report, quoted by Peter Underwood in his *Gazetteer of Scottish and Irish Ghosts*, runs in part:

> After the children, except the boy, had gone to bed, Maggie lay down on the bed without undressing, so that her hands and

> feet could be observed. The rest of us sat round the kitchen fire, when faint raps, rapidly increasing in loudness, were heard coming apparently from the walls, the ceiling and various parts of the inner room, the door of which was open. On entering the bedroom with a light, the noises at first ceased but recommenced when I put the light on the windowsill in the kitchen-cum-living room. I had the boy and his father by my side, and asked Mr Plunkett to look round the house outside. Standing in the doorway leading to the affected bedroom, the noises recommenced; the light was gradually brought nearer, and after much patience I was able to bring the light into the bedroom while the disturbances were still loudly going on. At last I was able to go up to the side of the bed, with the lighted candle in my hand, and closely observed each of the occupants lying on the bed. The younger children were apparently asleep, and Maggie was motionless; nevertheless, knocks were going on everywhere around, on the chairs, the bedstead, the walls and the ceiling. The closest scrutiny failed to detect any movement on the part of those present that could account for the noises, which were accompanied by a scratching or tearing sound. Suddenly a large pebble fell in my presence on the bed; no one had moved to dislodge it, even if it had been placed for the purpose. When I replaced the candle on the windowsill of the kitchen, the knocks became still louder, like those made by a heavy carpenter's hammer driving nails into flooring.

Barrett came three more times to the cottage on consecutive nights, with other members of the SPR, and each time the noises repeated themselves.

Prompted by the farmer, who said that the ghost in the house could answer questions by means of raps, Sir William tried the experiment of asking mentally for a certain number of raps to be done. Immediately, the ghost rapped to order. He repeated this four times, with the correct number of raps being made each time.

One of Barrett's companions, the Rev Maxwell Close, read some passages from the Bible, to the accompaniment at first of a terrific din. This gradually ceased, and by the time the minister came to recite the Lord's Prayer things had calmed down. After that, the hauntings at Derrygonelly came to a stop.

Ghost: The Double of an Elderly Friend of a Mr and Mrs Parker of Hereford
Place: *Hereford, England*
Date: Unknown

Mr and Mrs Parker were out shopping in Hereford when they were hailed by an old friend. He was 80 years old and now quite frail but had once been a captain in the armed forces. Since there was a chill wind blowing, Mrs Parker suggested that they meet a little later in a local coffee shop. Mr and Mrs Parker waited for some time at the allotted time in the coffee shop but the captain did not arrive. They assumed that he had forgotten but sent him a note anyway, apologising, just in case he had arrived after they had left. They suggested that they meet up at another time.

They received a note back from the captain saying that he did not recall their meeting in Hereford on the day indicated in Mrs Parker's note. He said he did have a vague memory of meeting her somewhere, but it could not have been that day since he had been in his bed all morning recovering from a dinner party the night before.

When the two eventually met they discussed the morning's events in detail. They were able to confirm the date and checked with the captain's housekeeper that he did not rise until late that morning. Mr and Mrs Parker were adamant that they had met with him and Mrs Parker recalled that she had even been touched by the captain, when he took her arm.

Ghosts: The Doubles of the Rev Spencer Nairne and Miss Wallis
Place: *Aberdeen, Scotland*
Date: 1859

The Rev Spencer Nairne was walking with a fellow passenger, John Chambers, on their way to join a ship for Norway when Nairne saw an acquaintance of his walking towards him. It was Miss Wallis, who had worked for his extended family as a governess. There was no doubt that it was she for they had known each other for over 20 years, since he was a young child. He made towards her and returned her smile of recognition, but just as he was about to address her, she completely disappeared even though they were within touching distance of each other. Nairne looked around for her thinking that he must have been distracted or something, but although he searched in nearby shops she was nowhere to be found.

Nairne went on his trip but some weeks later in London, he came across Miss Wallis talking to members of his family. He was about to ask her about their encounter in Aberdeen when Miss Wallis good-naturedly remonstrated with him for cutting her in the street. Nairne explained that, although he had seen her and she had obviously seen him, she had disappeared as he was about to address her. She said that this was extraordinary since that was exactly as she had seen the event. She had remarked to her brother and companion at the time that that sort of behaviour was most unlike Nairne.

Some time later, they were discussing the strange event again when the question of dates came up. Miss Wallis claimed that she had been in Aberdeen with her brother sometime towards the end of July. Nairne knew exactly when he was there from his itinerary – 31 May. They had obviously seen the double of each other and that was why each had disappeared so suddenly.

Ghost: Lady Jean Drummond
Place: ***Newton Castle, Blairgowrie, Scotland***
Date: 14th Century and Later

Newton Castle, Blairgowrie, dates from the 14th century and is haunted by the ghost of 'Lady Jean'. Her story is well known. She was Lady Jean Drummond, and she fell desperately in love with a local laird. He had dallied with her for a while but had become distracted by another woman. In order to win back the affection of her beloved, Lady Jean did her very best to make herself attractive. She dressed in finest silks and satins, wore shoes with silver buckles and adorned her braided hair with pearls and precious stones. The transformation in her appearance, however, was not enough to bring the heartless scoundrel back. She took to spending her time singing mournful songs of lost love as she sat alone in a tower of the castle.

Eventually she sought the advice of a local witch. The witch told her that her fine clothes were no good. She must dress in 'the witchin' claith o' green'. In order to do this, she must cut some grass from the churchyard, take a branch of a rowan tree from the gallows-knowe and bind them together with a plaited reed. Then she was to take them as darkness was falling to the Corbie Stone by the Cobble pool and sit there and wait.

This the Lady Jean did. After waiting for some time, she became aware of the sound of laughter. She could feel a strange sensation, as if something was pulling at her clothes. She fell asleep, and when she awoke at dawn she was dressed all in green.

The magic of the witch had worked, for Jean married her great love, Lord Ronald, still wearing the 'witchin' claith'. Her new husband was quite besotted with his bride in her strange green dress. The wedding ceremony had hardly taken place, however, than disaster struck. Lord Ronald looked at his bride and saw that something was far wrong. He took her hand in his, but it felt deathly cold. Then, to his horror, Jean let out an unearthly scream, fell to the ground and died. Her lifeless body was laid out on the bed where the wedding couple were to have consummated the marriage

Lady Jean was buried nearby, and her gravestone is said to turn round three times each Halloween. Then the sound of her sad singing comes wafting from the tower at Newton Castle.

Ghost: Granddad Duggan
Place: *Basildon, Essex*
Date: 1995

This story was related by Carol Vorderman on her TV programme, *Mysteries*.

After a family day out the Duggan family went to bed early as they were all tired. At about midnight Pauline, the mother, woke up and realised the room was full of smoke. She shouted to her husband, Larry, to get up and get the kids out. She herself grabbed their baby, Nicola, and started down the corridor shouting at her three older children to get out. At that point Nicola collapsed and Pauline realised she had to get her out quickly and rushed down the stairs followed by her two sons, Paul and Steve.

Larry, who was groggy with smoke and sleep, started to check the children's bedrooms. First he checked the room of Michelle, their nine-year-old daughter; it was empty. Then he checked the boys' room; that also was empty. He logically concluded that everyone was safe outside, and by then he was starting to be overcome by the thick smoke, so he too escaped. When he eventually got out he was confronted by his family who as one shouted at him, 'Where is Michelle?'

At that point one of the boys saw Michelle at the window. He shouted at his parents to get her out. 'If you don't get her out, she won't be here tomorrow!'

Larry attempted to get back into the house but by now the flames had taken hold and it was impossible to get inside. There was only one thing for it; Michelle would have to break the window and jump out. The whole family implored her to jump. Larry promised to catch her. Pauline ordered her to break the window, pretending to be angry. All their pleas seemed to be in vain until the window was suddenly broken by a china ornament: a blue and white elephant. Moments later the elephant was followed by Michelle who, as her mother put it, 'Came out like a dart. She just floated through the window!'

Minutes later the Blue Watch at Basildon Fire Station arrived at the scene. John Moss, the Acting Sub-Station Officer found the family safe but completely overcome with emotion. It was part of his duties to ensure that everyone was out and find out how they achieved this. He asked each member of the family how they had got out. When he came to Michelle he was surprised that she had managed to get out of the first floor window. He reported that at the time, he thought to himself, 'She must be mistaken; there's no way she could have got out of that window.'

'How did you manage to get out of such a high window?' he asked, only to be told by Michelle that her granddad had helped her. This rang alarm bells inside Moss's head because there was no old man with the family and this had been the first mention of him. He thought that he must have missed one person and asked for details of him. Pauline told him that the old man had been dead for several months!

Later, Moss went inside to inspect the cause of the fire and check out Michelle's story. He found that the window was quite high up and there was nothing that Michelle could have climbed up. This confirmed his belief that she must have been mistaken, but the whole family had seen her fly out of that window.

Did Michelle really get help from her grandfather? This is her story: 'I woke up coughing and went to the toilet. I had had a cough that day and was very tired after our day out so thought nothing about it. When I came out of the toilet, I collapsed and couldn't breathe. I thought I was going to die. I felt something cold and when I looked up I saw what looked like a shadowy figure standing over me. When it started talking I realised it was Granddad. He was wearing the same jacket with the yellow patches on it that he was wearing when he got buried. He said, "Don't give up Michelle, I'm going to get you out. Remember, you were always my favourite." He told me to go to the window and pick up the elephant and break the window. I did not want to because I thought Mum and Dad would be cross. They were shouting at me but then this hand forced me to throw the elephant. It broke the window and I thought, "I can't get out of that small hole." He just lifted my body and threw me out.'

Ghost: Viscount Dundee ('Bonnie Dundee')
Place: *Killiecrankie, Scotland*
Date: *c.*1689

Two stories have been told about the death of John Graham of Claverhouse, Viscount Dundee or 'Bonnie Dundee', the persecutor of the Covenanters who was killed at the Battle of Killiecrankie in 1689, a landmark battle in Scottish history.

The night before the battle, it is said, as Graham slept, he was disturbed by two things. First, he saw a strange red glow in the darkness, which could not be explained by human activity. This same glow has reportedly been seen by visitors to the site on the anniversary of the battle in years since. Ghostly lights are quite a common phenomenon, as has already been mentioned, both as signs of approaching death (death candles) and as spectral 'markers' of places where bloodshed and death have occurred.

The second thing to trouble Graham happened towards the hours of dawn, we are told. He saw a vision of a man by his bed, blood dripping from a head wound. The terrible figure pointed at Graham and cried, 'Remember Brown of Priesthill!'

Brown of Priesthill was a man called John Brown, a Covenanter who was killed for his beliefs. It is said that when the men in the firing squad saw Brown's steadfast courage and unfailing religious conviction in the face of imminent execution, they faltered, and Viscount Dundee himself fired the fatal shot.

Graham was greatly disturbed by the spectre of Brown of Priesthill. Thinking (hoping) that what he had seen had not been a ghost but instead some devious trick by his enemies, he got up and inquired of the sentry whether there had been intruders in the camp. The guard outside, however, said that all had been quiet and that nobody had approached Graham's tent.

The figure that Bonnie Dundee had seen had been a sign – its appearance, along with the eerie red glow, foretold his death in battle the next day.

Another person, many miles away, had a vision to tell him of John Graham's death. He was Lord Balcarres of Colinsburgh, unable to join his acquaintance in battle because he was under arrest on the orders of Parliament. On the night after the battle, he was roused from sleep by a sound next to his bed. He looked up and saw his comrade, Viscount Dundee, standing by the bed. He rose to greet him but the figure turned away and then disappeared. It was only later that Lord Balcarres found out that Viscount Dundee had been killed in battle that very day.

Ghosts: An Elizabethan Lady and Baby
Place: *Littlecote, Wiltshire*
Date: 1575 and Since

There is a story from Elizabethan times, when the Manor House, the seat of the Darrell family, was occupied by 'Wicked' Will Darrell, who murdered a newly born child in 1575. In a deathbed confession, a midwife told a story about how she was once asked on a dark night, to go in secret to a woman who was about to give birth, and was induced to do so by a large sum of money. The midwife was blindfolded and taken to a house that was not known to her. The blindfold was removed and the child safely delivered only to be snatched from her by a man who quickly threw it into the fire and crushed it under his boot until it was dead. The poor midwife was terrified but managed to cut a piece of fabric from the bed hangings, and counted the number of stairs she was led down, blindfolded again, before being taken home and sworn to secrecy.

Her confession led to Darrell being suspected and he was arrested when the piece of fabric was found to match a hole in the bed curtains surrounding a bed at Littlecote. The number of stairs coincided with those leading to a bedroom in the house. Darrell was tried but acquitted, and the house was made over to the judge who presided at his trial. Darrell died in 1589 when out hunting. It is said that as he approached a spot on his estate, known to this day as 'Darrell's Stile,' the ghost of the infant appeared in front of him and startled his horse, which shied and threw him, breaking his neck. To this day horses still shy away from the spot where he died.

The ghost of the baby's mother has been seen in the house on many occasions, sometimes carrying a child, and terrible screams have been heard in the early hours of the morning, from the room where the child is said to have been murdered.

Darrell had many mistresses – his own sister was one, and the identity of the mother of the child has never been discovered. He himself appears in the house and where his apparition is seen, woodwork on the floors rots away no matter how often it is repaired.

Ghost: Margaret Ellis
Place: *North Wales*
Date: 1983

Although some mediums have had a bad press and are often portrayed as charlatans and fraudsters, this story helps to redress the balance. The Rev J. Alwyn Roberts tells the story of how a gentle ghost was helped by a medium in his book *The Holy Ghostbuster*.

Two of his parishioners, an elderly couple who did not want to be named, came to seek his help with an unusual problem. They knew he was interested in the spirit world and thought that a ghost was resident in the house into which they had recently moved. They described the presence of a spirit at the top of the stairs outside their bedroom. When they stood at that point they were overcome by a feeling of great misery and the temperature seemed to be distinctly colder at that spot. The priest advised them to put up a crucifix and say some prayers as that might calm the ghost.

When he saw them after church a few weeks later, the couple told him that although they had done as he had suggested, the spirit was still in residence and that it filled them with such a sense of foreboding that they had taken to sleeping downstairs. The Rev Roberts suggested to the couple that he be allowed to investigate the phenomenon with a friend of his who was open to the spirit world and was also a medium. The medium very quickly established that there was something present at the top of the stairs. He also sensed that the spirit was female, non-threatening and extremely depressed about something.

The medium decided to attempt to make contact with the spirit and during these sessions the full story came tumbling out. The ghost was that of a spinster of the parish, Margaret Ellis, who had lived in the house during the 19th century. While still quite young she had been courted by a local worthy, Ernest Johnson. Unfortunately he was married. In those days, this was an extremely risky position for a young girl to be in, but the situation got worse when she realised that she was pregnant with his child. Ernest was extremely incensed when he heard this and seemed to blame poor Margaret, telling her to get rid of the child. Despite her youth and the mores of the time, Margaret insisted on raising the child herself. In response to this stubbornness, Ernest decided that the only way he would be rid of the embarrassment would be to do away with the child and he hired two drifters to kill the infant. This they did by throwing the baby down the stairs. When Margaret told the police what had happened, they did not believe her, preferring instead to assert that she had carried out the crime herself. They could not prove this however, and Margaret spent the rest of her days as an outcast in her own village.

The story has a happy ending though. During one of the séances, the couple were able to tell Margaret that they, at least, believed her version of the story. Having them on her side apparently did the trick because from that time on, Margaret never returned to their house. The Rev Alwyn Roberts goes on to say that he checked the church records and found out that a Margaret Ellis had lived in the house up until the time she died in 1873.

Ghost: Elizabeth Elphinstone née Pittendale
Place: *Morningside, Edinburgh, Scotland*
Date: *c.*1720

Morningside today is a pleasant ‘leafy’ suburb of Edinburgh, but at the time of this story, in the early part of the 18th century, it was largely rural. At the north end of Balcarrres Street, which runs from Morningside Cross to the playing fields of George Watson’s School, stands what was once considered to be a large country house. In 1712, the house was acquired, on his retirement, by Sir Thomas Elphinstone, a former governor of one of the American colonies. Sir Thomas must have looked forward to many peaceful and enjoyable years in his new home. The only sadness in his life was the fact that his wife had died some years before, while giving birth to his son, now a young man who no longer lived at home. Sir Thomas was not a man to leave things to chance, and he was taking steps to resolve the potential loneliness in his life by paying court to a local beauty, Elizabeth Pittendale. Her family seemed pleased with the match and they encouraged her to marry such a well-placed gentleman, despite the fact that he was nearly 40 years her senior.

Sir Thomas’s age was one consideration but there was an even greater deterrent to the marriage from Elizabeth’s point of view; she was already involved in an intimate relationship with a young army officer who went by the colourful sobriquet of Jack Courage. Elizabeth finally gave way to the entreaties of her family and at last told Jack that she was to marry, and could therefore see him no more; in any case he was soon to be posted abroad.

The marriage duly went ahead and with his new house and wife Sir Thomas found the contentment he had sought. Some months later that contentment turned to delight when he learned that his only son was to return from abroad. Sir Thomas set about celebrating the event with a large party that provided an ideal opportunity to introduce his son to his new wife. The happy couple stood by the door greeting their guests. Sir Thomas proudly introduced his son, John, to his wife but in the excitement of the occasion, failed to notice that the two were acting very strangely towards one another and hardly speaking. This was perhaps not unreasonable since John was none other than Elizabeth's former lover, Jack Courage.

Jack and Elizabeth managed to keep up the pretence that they were strangers for some time, but it was clear that they still had strong feelings for each other. One day Sir Thomas came into a room unexpectedly and found them kissing. He was understandably outraged and in the ensuing fracas, Elizabeth was stabbed through the heart. A heartbroken Sir Thomas later killed himself and husband and wife were laid to rest in the family vault.

John could not live in the house after that and leased it to a friend, and it was he who witnessed a strange and sad vision. He reported seeing a lady, obviously in some distress, walking slowly down the corridor to the bedroom previously occupied by John where she collapsed in tears on the bed. As the new tenant approached the lady she vanished before his eyes. Despite the fact that the ghost was not threatening in any way, he did nevertheless find it very disturbing so he employed the services of a spiritualist to see if there was some way in which the house could be freed of her spirit. Elizabeth's spirit communicated with the medium and told her that she would continue to haunt the house while she was laid beside the man who had killed her. John, now in charge of the family's affairs, carried out Elizabeth's wishes and when he died himself, left instructions that he should be laid to rest beside her. Elizabeth never haunted the house again.

Ghost: The Enfield Poltergeist
Place: *Enfield, Middlesex*
Date: Between 1977 and 1979

The case of the Enfield poltergeist is exceptionally well documented. The well-known psychic investigator, Maurice Grosse, worked on the case full time and collaborated with another famous investigator, Guy Lyon Playfair. The latter wrote a detailed account of the affair called *This House is Haunted*. The house in question was very ordinary: a three bedroom semi-detached house in a typical home counties' suburb. The house was occupied by a single parent, Mrs Peggy Hodgson, and her four children.

The events started quite gently with Janet, aged eleven, becoming aware of a shuffling noise coming from her bedroom. This was later followed by knocking noises that could not be identified. But the manifestations soon became more alarming when the whole family witnessed a heavy chest of drawers sliding across the room. This was just the start of the extraordinary things that the family and others, including the police, witnessed over the next few days. Articles flew across rooms, doors slammed open and shut, the toilet flushed itself and more knocking sounds were heard. This was not just frightening for the children but also extremely dangerous. One of the small boys received a blow on his forehead from a hairbrush that was thrown violently about. Despite being very frightening, there was absolutely nothing anyone could do to make the poltergeist stop.

A policewoman called in to investigate, WPC Caroline Heaps, was witness to a chair floating in the air about a metre off the ground. Matters became even more serious when the poltergeist started to attack the children. On one occasion the sheets on Janet's bed tried to strangle her and it was only her muffled cries that caused her mother to come to her aid. Peggy's nine-year-old son, Billy, had a narrow escape when a heavy iron grate landed on his bed as he lay sleeping.

The strange events at the house became notorious around the town but many locals thought they were all the work of the children playing tricks on their poor mother, although they were at a loss to explain how it was that this was taking place. The phenomena eventually came to the attention of the Society of Psychical Research who treated the case with much more seriousness. They were asked to investigate and they appointed one of their leading members, Maurice Grosse, to head up the inquiry.

The events continued and became even weirder. Apart from objects flying through the air that by now were almost commonplace, two of the children, Janet and Margaret started to speak in tongues, sometimes uttering obscenities. More accurately, strange deep voices, which a child could not keep up for any extended period, emanated from their bodies. Electronic equipment would occasionally refuse to work inside the house but operated perfectly as soon as it was taken outside. Pools of water would suddenly appear and part of a wall was damaged. Janet was held fast by her leg and, on another occasion, dragged down the stairs. She levitated on one occasion right through her bedclothes. A grey-haired lady, an old man and a small child appeared as apparitions. There was a case of spontaneous combustion. All in all, over 1,500 separate phenomena occurred and were witnessed by many people.

It is quite common for poltergeists to be associated with people. In this case the person that the poltergeist seemed to concentrate on was the child Janet. This theory is supported by the fact that strange happenings also occurred when the family were staying in a caravan by the seaside. Along with her sister Margaret, it was Janet who threw some small but inconsistent light on the subject. While still asleep, Margaret was witnessed bouncing up and down on her bed shrieking, 'Go away, you ten little things.' When asked, she continued to give details of what she could see in her sleep. There was an elderly man, whom she described as having died in the chair downstairs, and named him Frank Watson, along with his wife and a number of children. At the same time, Janet started to make the aforementioned deep-throated noises. Maurice Grosse interviewed her while she was in this strange state and the voice identified itself as Bill Hobbs from Durant's Park Graveyard. He said he was 72 years old and had come to the house to see his family but was disappointed to find them gone.

Why did Mrs Hodgson put up with such trauma? She tried to move house but being a single parent, she could not afford to re-house her family and they were forced to endure it. In the end, the poltergeist activity ceased as suddenly as it had begun.

There is a codicil to this story. Maurice Grosse was convinced that he had been 'chosen' for this investigation. Two years before, his 22-year-old daughter had died in a car crash and he was sure that the events in the Hodgson case were an attempt by his daughter to make contact with him. There were a number of unusual coincidences that led him to believe this, which he noted to the Society of Psychical Research.

Ghost: Harry Evans
Place: *Dulwich, London, England*
Date: January 1967

Harry and his sister Kitty had lived together in the same house in Dulwich since their mother had died 50 years previously. Now in their 70s, they were well known in the neighbourhood. One of their neighbours was Mrs Cynthia Aspinall. She was well acquainted with things psychic, as were her family, and they had witnessed many phenomena over the years.

Mrs Aspinall had been away for Christmas with friends and returned to her home near the Evans' house in the January of 1967. She saw her neighbour Harold standing in his garden, but strangely clad for the time of year, in just his shirtsleeves with no coat, even though the temperature was close to freezing. He seemed preoccupied but Mrs Aspinall greeted her friend cheerfully. Harold Evans ignored her greeting, however, and just morosely stared straight ahead. Mrs Aspinall was slightly taken aback by this and although she did not want to intrude on his deliberation she was rather concerned for his wellbeing on such a cold day, so she gently suggested it might be better if he put on a coat and went about her business.

A couple of days later Mrs Aspinall was having coffee with Harry's sister and another neighbour. The conversation turned to holidays they had taken and where they would like to go in the future and Mrs Aspinall said that she knew of just the place in Scotland for Kitty and her brother to go. This casual remark had a devastating effect on poor Kitty for she at once dissolved into tears. Mrs Aspinall was distraught to learn that it was her remark that had been the cause of her friend's distress and inquired why it had been so offensive. She was told by the other neighbour that almost a month previously, while Mrs Aspinall had been away, Harry had died of leukaemia.

This strange event was investigated by Andrew MacKenzie and, together with Mrs Aspinall, he put together what he thought seemed to be a plausible explanation of what may have happened. After 50 years of living together, the two siblings had become extremely close.

After Harry died, Kitty thought about him often. The bereaved often comment that after someone close dies they can still *feel* them. It is speculated that such was the intensity of this feeling that Kitty managed to project Harry onto the surroundings and this is what Mrs Aspinall saw in the garden.

Ghost: Michael Faraday
Place: *The Royal Institution, London, England*
Date: 1962

Each Christmas, the Royal Institution puts on a series of lectures that are aimed at fostering an interest in the sciences among children. These days they are also shown on television and include a number of experiments and demonstrations that are very visual in nature and are able to involve the children. These lectures were started by Michael Faraday when he was in charge of the Institution. He started work there under another famous scientist, Sir Humphry Davy of Davy Lamp fame, and became director of the laboratory in 1825. He was subsequently made Fullerian Professor in 1833; so the lectures have a long history.

To be asked to give the lectures, even though they are aimed at children, is quite prestigious and in 1964 the honour fell to Dr Eric Laithwaite, Professor of Heavy Electrical Engineering at Imperial College, London. The subject of his lectures was naturally concerned with electricity, and this was most appropriate because Faraday is famous for the early work he did in the field of electromagnetism and electrolytic cells – he formulated Faraday's Law.

At one point in the lectures, Laithwaite carried out a demonstration that involved passing an electric current through a dish containing a ball. If performed correctly, the ball would leap up in the air in a dramatic fashion; however if the switching on of the current was mistimed it would merely bobble around in the dish. Laithwaite tried the demonstration twice without tremendous success; this was not unusual as the odds against a jump were quite high. However, what happened next was highly unusual. Laithwaite is said to have felt the presence of a man who, for some reason, he was convinced was the grand old man himself. The spirit of Faraday told him that this time the demonstration would be successful and that he should announce this, in advance, to his audience. So confident of success was Laithwaite that he did just this and sure enough, the ball jumped out of the bowl!

Faraday's spirit was felt by many others on different occasions but always in the same place, near the front of the main lecture hall. After his encounters with Faraday (the one described above was merely the most dramatic) Professor Laithwaite is reported as commenting to the effect that, just because one could not understand or measure every phenomenon, that did not mean that such happenings were not real.

There is an ironic twist to this story. In life, Faraday was a deeply religious man who never failed to attend the Sunday services conducted by the Sandemanians (or Glassites) sect. He was a man who kept his science and religion rigidly separate, so how would he have explained the activity of his spirit?

Ghost: Catherine Ferrers
Place: ***Markygate, Hertfordshire, England***
Date: 16th Century

The old house at the centre of this ghostly encounter was named Markygate Cell after a hermitage built by a 12th-century monk from nearby Saint Albans. In the 17th century Catherine Ferrers married, at the age of 13, a 16-year-old member of the local Fanshawe family. The marriage was not a success and Catherine, probably as a result of boredom and frustration, took to a life of crime that was to lead to her being known as 'the wicked Lady Ferrers'. She became a highwayman and had a cupboard built into a chimney in the kitchen in which she kept her costume of hat, breeches and cloak. The cupboard was reached by a stairway (which still exists) and having dressed, she would descend the stairs and ride off on her black horse to rob and kill travellers and coach passengers.

She was shot one night while attempting to rob a coach, and although she managed to get back to her home, she died on the doorstep leading to the secret stairway. Following its discovery, the doorway was bricked shut for almost 200 years. It was soon after her death that her ghost began to be seen riding over the treetops in the surrounding countryside, and swinging in the branches of an oak tree beneath which she is reputed to have buried the money and jewels from her robberies.

Over the years there have been many sightings of the ghost of Catherine Ferrers. On one occasion, when there was a serious fire at Markygate Cell, she was seen by people trying to put out the flames under a tree in the garden. After the fire the current owner decided to open the bricked up doorway, but could not induce any local people to do the work because of the odd noises so often heard there. Workmen were eventually found in London and when they broke through the brickwork, they discovered a narrow staircase that led to a heavy door of oak. The room behind the door was empty.

Ghost: The *Flying Dutchman* (Ship)
Place: *In the Southern Oceans*
Date: Since *c.*1800

This story refers to the many sightings of a traditional, square-rigged sailing ship from the era of the East Indiamen, which is often seen off the Cape of Good Hope. The various sightings may, of course, be different ships but, if so, they have been seen by several people at the same time and all of them seem to disappear unexpectedly. The name comes from two assumptions about the vessel. The 'Flying' part comes from the fact that the vessel is always seen under full sail – an impressive sight indeed, and a ship with all its canvas set would at least be flying metaphorically. The 'Dutchman' part comes from the legend attached to the ship; the captain is said to be Dutch, variously called Van der Decken or sometimes Bernard Fokke.

Whatever his name, the story is that the ship was struggling to get around the Cape of Good Hope in mountainous seas and that the crew were pleading with the captain to put in to Cape Town until the storm abated. But the captain was a fearless man with an evil reputation and swore to his men that as long as he was in command nothing could destroy the ship, not even God Almighty! Apparently, God was so annoyed at this foolish statement that he condemned the ship to sail the seas until Judgement Day without ever being able to make port. The story continues that whenever the spectral ship is sighted, some misfortune will follow closely in its wake.

There have been several well-documented accounts of a sailing ship being seen despite the rather romantic nature of this story – for, even if true, how would anyone be able to recount it? Probably the best known of these happened on 11 July 1881 when a 16-year-old midshipman and others on board the Royal Naval ship, *Inconstant*, sighted a ghostly-looking ship while steaming off the Australian coast. The ship was described by the midshipman as being 'bathed in phosphorescence'. Although seen at night, the weather was described as calm and clear, with good all-round visibility. The officer of the watch sent the midshipman foreword to the forecastle to get a better view, but by the time he arrived after no more than a minute, there was no sign of any unidentified ship but a clear view to the horizon. The *Inconstant* was sailing in convoy at the time and the phantom ship was also seen by other ships in the convoy.

There are two codicils to this story. The midshipman on the *Inconstant* was the Prince of Wales, later to become George V, and the sailor who had first seen the ghostly vessel fell to his death from the crow's nest only hours later. Although the Prince of Wales saw the Flying Dutchman off the coast of Australia, most of the sightings have been in the seas around the Cape and in March 1939, almost 100 people saw something very odd. They were enjoying an Easter break on Glencairn Beach in False Bay, to the southeast of Cape Town, when they witnessed a fully rigged sailing ship looming out of the heat haze. Despite the presence of only light airs the ship was 'flying'. There is no doubt that the appearance of such a vessel would have caused quite a stir on the beach since the days of sail had long gone and everyone would have been watching it intensely. It is therefore all the more remarkable that, as they watched, the ship suddenly disappeared.

Three years later, in September 1942, the same, or at least a similar craft was sighted heading into Table Bay by four people who had a good vantage point from the terrace of their house at Mouille Point. They watched for several minutes but, before the vessel could reach the bay, it disappeared. The story of the Flying Dutchman has inspired several books and the famous Wagner opera of the same name.

Ghost: King George II
Place: *Kensington Palace, London, England*
Date: 1760

George II was born in Hanover in 1683, the son of an electoral prince, and remained there, apart from some time spent fighting during the war of Spanish Succession, until 1714 when he was 31 years old. He remained there long after the Act of Settlement in 1701 had placed him in succession to the throne of Great Britain, and after he was made Duke of Cambridge in 1706. He arrived in England to join his father and became king on his father's death in 1727. His reign was not a quiet one. There were many conflicts in Europe in which he was personally involved, right up until 1743 when he was 60. There were also the colonial wars in North America going on at the same time.

Against this background, it is not surprising that George II's thoughts often returned to the time of his youth in Hanover and it was widely known that he would like to return one day. He was thwarted in this by his bad health and had to content himself with news of his native city. As he lay on his deathbed in 1760, waiting for news from home, he constantly asked, 'Why don't they come?' The messengers in question could not get through because the weather was so bad that all continental ships were confined to port. King George took to staring out of the window at a nearby weather vane repeating the same question. News of his city never came and he died on 25 October 1760.

Since that time, many people have reported seeing the his face at the window staring towards the weather vane and some even claim to have heard him repeat the question, 'Why don't they come?'

Ghost: A Ghostly Apparition, Identity Unknown
Place: *Pitlochry, Perthshire, Scotland*
Date: Turn of the 20th Century

Whilst a young man, the writer and expert in the supernatural, Elliott O'Donnell, spent some time in Pitlochry, a particularly charming town in that most lovely of counties, Perthshire. He took lodgings at Donald Murray House, in the home of a spinster of the town, Flora Macdonald.

During his stay O'Donnell, a keen cyclist, made an excursion to nearby Loch Tay, a round trip of about 50 miles. He arrived back at Pitlochry at about ten o'clock in the evening and stopped at a crossroads just short of the town to admire the last moments of the dying day. The sky was a deep crimson and the moon was bright in the sky. O'Donnell was standing soaking up the atmosphere when he suddenly became aware of a presence in the shape of a ghostly column of light in the middle of the road. That was frightening enough, but as O'Donnell watched the apparition, two figures on a hay cart arrived at the same spot. On seeing the spectre, the two passengers, a farmer and a boy, became very fearful; they seemed to recognise it. The boy pleaded with the farmer to keep the thing away from him, crying out that it had come to get him. At that point, the horse, which had previously been brought to a halt by the phantom, took fright and bolted down the road with the spectre in hot pursuit. As it flew down the road, the phantom became more shapeless, except that it formed tendrils that seemed to reach out to the couple.

At this point, O'Donnell was in such a state that he jumped on his bike and flew down the road himself, but in the opposite direction! When he reached the safety of his digs, he breathlessly told his landlady, Flora, of his weird encounter. She looked slightly sheepish and told O'Donnell that she should have warned him of that spot as the spectre had been seen there several times.

She said that any person touched by the thing would die shortly afterwards. She went on to say that, as a girl, she had been driving home with her father along that road. They had been to a croquet party at the Blair Atholl house of Lady Colin Ferner and on reaching that spot the horse had suddenly bolted. It had been startled by the same thing that O'Donnell had seen. Her father was also very scared, a novel sight for Flora, and instead of trying to calm the animal seemed to be encouraging it in its flight. She saw nothing at first but turned to see it chasing them down the road. It followed them with great bounding leaps, and as it overtook them, seemed to reach out towards her father and touch his arm with an eerie gentleness. He died later that year.

She went on to relate what she thought to be a story linked to that of the crossroads ghost, which was told to her by her mother. In her youth, her mother's family had been friendly with the family of Sir Arthur Holkitt, who lived in a house quite near to the crossroads called the Old White House. Flora's mother and grandmother often visited the house. The older people would play cards while the youngsters did their own thing. If their visit to the family was going to extend beyond about ten in the evening, it was their custom to stay over.

One evening, however, Flora's mother visited the house alone, because her mother had taken to her bed with a bout of 'flu. The Holkitts were having a dinner party, and it was likely to be a lively occasion and so the mother insisted that her daughter should go without her. Flora's mother planned to return home that night, but during the evening, there was a heavy fall of snow and she, along with numerous other guests, was forced to stay the night. The next morning the snow had not lifted, and it was several days before they could contemplate risking the journey. On her last night at the house, there was a remarkable occurrence that shook Flora's mother to her core. She, and the elder of the two daughters of the house, Margaret, were making their way upstairs to bed when the other daughter, Alice, called to them to come into the room of the maid, Mary. They found Mary in a state of deep shock. She was shaking and crying inconsolably. Mary told them that she had finished turning down the bed of one of the guests but when she tried to blow out the candle, no matter how hard she tried, she could not blow it out and this had frightened her greatly.

Margaret, the oldest of the three, was rather scornful of the young maid and told her to stop crying and stay where she was. They would extinguish the candle. When they got to the room, the three were not feeling quite as brave as they had been a few moments earlier. However, Margaret managed to pluck up her courage and was just about to cross the threshold when the door swung closed in front of her, shutting the three girls out. Margaret turned the handle but there seemed to be a weight behind the door. The three put all their strength into opening the door without any success, when suddenly it opened and Flora's mother fell into the room.

No sooner was she in the room than the door slammed shut behind her, leaving her alone. Again the door could not be budged. She immediately sensed some evil presence in the room, which seemed to emanate from the candle, which was burning with an uncanny glow. She reasoned that if she could blow out the candle the spirit would leave, but no matter how hard she tried she could not do this. This terrified Flora's mother and she cowered away from the light. Through her fingers she saw that the candle seemed to be moving around, and finally approached and lightly touched her, whereupon she fainted. She woke up in bed surrounded by anxious faces.

The next day the snow had melted enough for the guests to go home. There are two interesting codicils to this story. When she arrived back home, Flora's mother found that her own mother had taken a turn for the worse and she died shortly afterwards. Was her encounter with the spirit just coincidence? The Old White House was vacated by the Holkitts a few years later, and because of its reputation as being haunted could not be sold and was eventually demolished. The house had been built on an ancient burial ground.

Ghost: A Girl in a Red Dress
Place: *The Carlingford Rectory, Republic of Ireland*
Date: 1935 Onwards

The rectory at Carlingford was built in the 17th century and was first occupied by the Stannus family, one of whom (an ancestor of Dame Ninette de Valois, the famous ballerina) extended the house. It was bought around the year 1870 by the Church of Ireland to use as the local rector's house. In 1960, it was a 22-room house, and had just been bought from the Church by the painter Ernest McDowell. In 1963, it was still empty.

About five o' clock one hot evening in early September, both Ernest McDowell and his brother were by the house, McDowell mowing the lawn and his brother cutting corn in a nearby field. Looking up, McDowell saw the figure of a girl in a red velvet dress moving towards the door. Before he could see her face, she disappeared. He identified the dress as belonging to the Edwardian period. Looking around him, McDowell now saw another figure – coming in at the gate was a clergyman, wearing a high, stiff collar. Even as McDowell looked at him, the figure vanished. He was convinced that there was some link between the two.

The rectory had some earlier records of strange happenings. A previous resident, Canon Meissner, had also seen the girl in the red dress, on this occasion inside the house. The canon's wife and daughter had both heard footsteps on the back stairs when no one else was in the house to make them; and his daughter had also once observed one of the dining-room doors vibrate, as if under pressure, and then burst open, and though apparently no one entered, her dog stared, raised its hackles, and finally fled away. Ernest McDowell was sensitive to psychic manifestations, and he too had heard footsteps. Although he felt sure there were presences in the house, they did not seem to him to be unhappy or disturbing ones.

The ghost hunter, Hans Holzer, took an interest in the house, and went to visit Canon Meissner and his family in 1965. They had lived in the rectory for twenty-five years up to 1960, and had noticed a number of odd things. Mrs Meissner had been told that the ghost of a sea captain, drowned at sea, had come back to the house, his original home; and on some summer evenings, she would feel the presence of something white and silent going by. On one occasion, when they had been visited by the sister of Ninette de Valois, a young man staying in the house as a guest had declared her to be the exact image of a ghostly figure he had seen in the guest room. Strangely, too, on being shown round the house, she had felt that she had been in the guest room before, although it was her first visit to Carlingford Rectory.

The spectral sea captain was never tracked down, but the researches of Holzer, who also used the services of a medium, Sybil Leek, to communicate with the spirit of the girl in the red dress, and of McDowell, convinced them that there had been some kind of romantic tragedy in the house during the mid-19th century, involving the girl and the clergyman, which kept their restless spirits still on the site.

Ghosts: The Glamis Castle Ghosts
Place: *Glamis Castle, Tayside*
Date: Various

Glamis Castle is one of maybe three or four structures that can lay claim to the title of the most haunted building in the UK. The castle is set in fine countryside beside the Dean Water about 15 miles north of Dundee and is the seat of the Earls of Strathmore and Kinghorne. The current Queen Mother is the daughter of the 14th Earl. She was formerly Elizabeth Bowes-Lyon and her daughter Princess Margaret was born in the castle. The castle is still used as the principal home of the family and the Queen Mother regularly spends time there. Although it is said to contain many ghosts, tradition has it that members of the Bowes-Lyon family are unable to see them.

To describe all the fascinating ghosts that are said to exist at Glamis would take a complete volume in itself, so here it has been decided to concentrate on just a few of them. One of the ghosts about which little is known is one that haunts the grounds of the castle on moonlit nights. His ghostly, but harmless, figure has been seen running across the grass and he is known as Jack the Runner. Maybe he is a forerunner of the 'streakers' that seems to haunt grassy spaces in modern times!

More sinister is the story of a ghost who appears to have a bloody mouth. No doubt a modern interpretation would include talk of vampires but although a more mundane explanation is widely accepted, it is no less grisly. It is said that the ghost belongs to a female servant of an early Earl who witnessed a brutal crime. In order to silence the woman for ever more, the miscreant cut out the poor maid's tongue and she died of the shock.

There is a little more detail known about the ghost called Earl Beardie. Some say he was the first Lord Glamis, others that he was one of the Earl's friends, a Lord Crawford. In any case he won his sobriquet by virtue of his long straggly beard. If it was the 1st Earl, that would place the events that are said to have led up to the haunting at about 1459. These days, the condition that the Earl suffered from would be well recognised as that of compulsive gambling. He was known to gamble with dice and cards and with anyone with the wherewithal, for long periods well into the night.

It is said that one night he was gambling with friends in one of the tower rooms at Glamis Castle. He was losing badly and as the evening wore on, became more and more bad-tempered, swearing and drinking to excess. In the end his friends could stand no more and told him that if he did not moderate his behaviour they would leave him. This made the Earl even angrier and he told them that they could do as they wished for if they would not remain with him he would play with the devil! At that remark, the devil himself is said to have appeared and demanded a game with the Earl. The Earl continued his losing streak and is said to have died a few days later. Since that night the strangled cries of the angry Earl can sometimes be heard in the tower. Some are reputed to have seen the ghostly figure with a straggly beard; a man condemned to play with the devil repeatedly.

Sometime around the early part of the 19th century, one of the Earls of Strathmore, Patrick, is said to have fathered a son who was born badly misshapen with an excess of hair on his body. Although the detail of his deformity and whether or not he was mentally retarded, is not known it is clear that in early Victorian times, such a misfortune in a family would have been a source of great shame. The shame would have been even more acutely felt if, as in this case, the child had been a first-born son and heir to a great title and estates. The Earl decided to keep his son hidden from the rest of the world and kept him locked away in a secret room within the castle. Only a few trusted servants knew of the secret or had contact with the poor unfortunate for the rest of his life, which some say lasted almost 100 years. The story might have been laid to rest there but, just like today, such secrets were bread and meat to the gossips of the time and rumours got around about the existence of the sad freak. No doubt fuelled by these rumours, stories started to emerge about visitors to the castle being accosted by a hairy vision.

In 1869 a Mrs Munro is said to have been woken by a hairy man and others tell similar stories about grunting sounds being heard during the night. Whether these are ghost stories or accounts about a real person is not all that clear since some, like that related above, took place while the person was still alive. Maybe the grunts were just someone snoring but whatever the truth, it is well guarded by the family. It is said to be known only to the Earl, his heir and the estate factor. It is also apparent that the secret is a source of immense sorrow to the family. When asked about the great secret, the 13th Earl is said to have replied that if the questioner knew what the matter was, he would thank God that it was not his own affair. The rumours suggest that when the poor man died he was placed in his coffin and was then bricked up in his secret room. It is said that the only trace of him left is that of his ghost exercising along a rooftop walk known as the 'Mad Earl's Walk'.

Ghosts of women often go by the name of 'Grey Lady' or 'White Lady' because that is how they appear to the observer; wraith-like, semi-transparent and colourless. Glamis Castle has both a White Lady and a Grey Lady. The Grey Lady is particularly interesting. She was seen in the castle chapel by the late Lady Granville, the Queen Mother's sister, and also by a previous Earl. The Grey Lady is said to be the ghost of Janet Douglas who became Lady Glamis, the widow of the 6th Earl, John. Later on, she was married to Campbell of Skipness in Kintyre. The king at the time was James V of Scotland who came to the throne when he was only 12 years old. His father had been killed at Flodden Field some years before. In the interim, various nobles effectively ruled Scotland, and even after he became king he was only kept in power by one noble or another. To make things worse, the auld enemy, the English, invaded in 1542.

All this must have made him feel pretty insecure and he was always on his guard against some insurrection both from within as well as without Scotland. During that period the Douglas clan was particularly powerful. A charge of trying to poison the king was fabricated by a distant relative, William Lyon and laid against Janet Douglas, Lady Glamis, her husband, Campbell of Skipness and Lord Glamis her eldest son. His motive was presumably the prospect of seizing the Glamis estate for himself. The king attacked the family at Glamis Castle, which was besieged and captured. The son was kept in gaol until James died in 1542, whereupon he was given back his estates and castle. His mother and her husband were not so lucky; she was accused of being a witch and taken from her cell onto the Castle Hill where she was covered in pitch and burned at the stake. Such was the distress of her husband who, with his son, was forced to watch the spectacle that he threw himself from the battlements the very next day. Lady Glamis' spirit found its way back to Glamis Castle where it is said to appear to warn the Bowes-Lyon family of impending disaster.

Also within the castle there is a room called the Haunted Chamber. It is now sealed up but is said to be the scene of a notorious deceit inflicted on a neighbouring clan by the Glamis family. The nearby Ogilvies were fighting with the Lindsays. On one infamous occasion, the Ogilvies were in full retreat and pleaded with Lord Glamis for sanctuary within the castle. He inveigled them into a secret room in the castle but instead of protecting them, he locked them in and then proceeded to starve them to death. The reason for such a disgraceful act is not known but it is said that on occasion, the cries of the starving men can still be heard.

Other haunted rooms include one called the Hangman's Chamber. It is haunted by the ghost of a butler who strung himself up there, and there are also said to be rooms where the furniture occasionally takes the form of that from a bygone age.

The castle has one further claim to fame; it is the setting of Shakespeare's famous play *Macbeth* in which, of course, there is a famous ghost. Shakespeare wrote the play in about 1605 but It is not known if that coincides with the beginning of Glamis Castle's notoriety.

Ghost: Gourlay (First Name Not Known)
Place: *Sanquhar, Dumfries and Galloway, Scotland*
Date: On Various Occasions

There was once a shepherd called Gourlay who lived near the town of Sanquhar in Dumfries and Galloway. He was smitten by a young woman who lived in a farmhouse a few miles away. The woman's name was Mary Graham, and she lived with her two brothers, Robert and Joseph.

One night the shepherd went to call on Mary Graham, but as he approached the farmhouse, he was alerted by the sounds of a struggle. Deciding that it was better not to risk going straight in by the front door, he crept up to a window and surreptitiously peeked inside. To his horror, he saw his sweetheart and her two brothers struggling with a man. It was hard at first to make out who the man was, but as soon as Gourlay caught a glimpse of his face, he recognised him as a pedlar who regularly plied his wares around the district. Within moments, Gourlay saw Mary Graham and her two brothers beat the poor man into submission and then strangle him.

Gourlay fled back home, all thoughts of romance gone. He was horrified at what he had seen – obviously the Grahams had been intent on robbing the pedlar. What were they going to do with his body? It was too terrible to contemplate. He told his mother about what had happened that night and swore her to secrecy.

The pedlar's horse was found wandering around in the woods close to the farmhouse the next day. There was no sign of the pedlar or his pack.

Gourlay stopped visiting Mary Graham. After some days had passed, she called upon Gourlay to ask him why his courtship seemed to have ended so suddenly. Gourlay was not quick-witted enough to think of any other response – he blurted out to her that he could not contemplate a relationship with her after what he had seen her doing on that terrible night. Mary turned on her heel and left his house in a grim silence. Gourlay had signed his own death warrant.

The Graham family did not wait long before they got rid of Gourlay and his big mouth. They ambushed him on his way home a couple of days later. He managed to run away but they chased after him. Gourlay fell into the river. He would have been swept away there and then but he managed to get a grip on a tuft of grass at the water's edge. The Grahams hurled stone after stone at him as he clung desperately to the bank. Finally, his fingers lost their grip, and he slipped back into the water and was drowned.

The Grahams thought that their secret was safe. They did not know that Gourlay had told his mother what he had seen. Shortly afterwards, Gourlay's battered body was recovered from the river, and his mother was filled with rage. Without hesitation, the old woman pointed the finger of blame at the Graham family. Unfortunately, the Grahams managed to escape into hiding and were never brought to justice.

The pedlar's body was found buried in moorland some years later. The ghost of Gourlay returned to the spot where he was killed by the Grahams to haunt the place. The cries of the poor man as he clung on to the banks of the river in the last moments of consciousness were heard in the same spot from time to time for a long time afterwards.

Ghost: The 'Grey Lady' of the Pannanich Wells Hotel
Place: *The Pannanich Wells Hotel, Ballater, Scotland*
Date: Various

Ballater is a beautiful town in Deeside, a spa town frequented in Victorian times by the rich and influential, who sought to benefit their health by taking the waters there. The Pannanich Wells Hotel in the town dates from the middle of the 18th century and was most favourably mentioned by Her Royal Majesty Queen Victoria in the journal that she kept.

As well as having the honour of being visited by Queen Victoria, the Pannanich Wells Hotel has another claim to fame. It is the haunt of a 'grey lady', the ghost of an elegant young woman dressed in a grey blouse and a long grey skirt. The grey lady has been seen both in and around the building by various people. Sometimes the ghost cannot be seen, but instead people have heard noises such as doors opening and closing without apparent reason. The grey lady is not a ghost that causes great alarm, and indeed she is regarded with a certain amount of affection by those who are familiar with the hotel.

Ghost: Lady Jane Grey
Place: *Beauchamp Tower, Tower of London, England*
Date: Many Times Since 1554

Lady Jane Grey was Queen of England for nine days. She was the great-granddaughter of Henry VII and a cousin of Edward VI. Henry VIII was her uncle. Beautiful and extremely erudite, she was much admired by the great scholars of the day. No doubt a little full of herself, she was persuaded to become involved in a project to alter the line of royal succession from the Tudors to the Dudleys, the family of the Dukes of Northumberland. To this end she was married to Guildford Dudley, the Duke's son, on 21 May 1553. The announcement of her accession to the throne was made on 10 July but her reign was brought to an abrupt end on 19 July with her arrest by the forces of Mary, the daughter of Henry VIII by Catherine of Aragon. She was sentenced to death and, along with her husband, was beheaded on Tower Hill on 12 February 1554.

Since that time there have been many reports of sighting of them both. The ghost of Guildford has been reported weeping silently in the Beauchamp Tower, where he awaited his execution, and Lady Jane has also been seen many times. One of the best documented sightings happened on 12 February 1957 when a guard at the Tower, called Johns, saw Lady Jane Grey on the battlement above the place where he stood. He called to his colleague who also saw the spirit. It was 403 years to the day since her execution.

Ghost: The 'Grey Lady' of Cleve Court
Place: *Cleve Court, Minster, Kent, England*
Date: Various

Cleve Court was bought in 1920 by Sir Edward Carson, who died in 1935. His widow, Lady Carson, although a very level-headed woman, was convinced early on that the house was haunted. Lord Carson tended to be sceptical about the origins of the occasional strange noises that were heard but there were some events that left even him mystified. One night when he and his wife were in their bedroom a light knocking was heard at the door. When Sir Edward called out 'Come in' there was no response and on opening the door he found no sign of anyone. Lady Carson herself heard many things: the sound of drawers being opened and closed, dragging noises and footsteps.

When children were in the house they often saw a mysterious grey female figure who walked in and out of rooms and never spoke. On one occasion the grey figure appeared beside the bed in which a child visitor was asleep and was eventually seen by Lady Carson herself. At about 1.30 a.m. she had gone downstairs with her dog who wanted to be let out, leaving a light on at the stair landing. She later went back down the stairs to let the dog back into the house and on her way past the light switch accidentally turned off the light.

She carried on to the bottom of the stairs in the dark and let the dog in only to see it run up the stairs and then stop in its tracks, whimpering and shivering, looking up to the landing at the top of the stairs. Lady Carson switched on the lights and saw on the landing a grey-coloured woman moving downstairs towards her. On reaching a half-landing the figure passed through an open door leading to an old part of the house. She saw the figure clearly and described it as that of a young woman wearing a grey dress reaching her feet, a matching cape on her shoulders and a white ribbon in her hair.

When the story became known, a woman who had been a housemaid at Cleve Court some years before, wrote to Lady Carson telling her that one morning, when she was fifteen, she had been working in the house and heard footsteps in a corridor. She had anticipated seeing another maid but had, instead, seen a woman in an old-fashioned dress who waved goodbye as she left the room.

When the Honourable Edward Carson, a future member of parliament and the only son of Lord and Lady Carson was six years old, he told his mother one day that a woman regularly walked in the corridor outside his room and that he neither knew nor liked her. Footsteps were heard for many years but after the night that Lady Carson saw the figure, the apparition never reappeared. Should there ever be children at Cleve Court again perhaps the 'grey lady' will show herself once more.

Ghost: Anne Griffith
Place: *Driffield, Yorkshire*
Date: Various

The Great Hall of Burton Agnes Hall contains the skull of Anne Griffith who died nearly 300 years ago. The property was owned at that time by Anne and her two sisters and they spent lavishly on improvements to the buildings and grounds. Anne, the youngest of the three, was obsessed by the work almost to the exception of anything else.

One day, after visiting friends, she was left for dead after being attacked and robbed. Found when barely still alive, she was taken to Burton Agnes Hall where she died a few days later but not before begging her sisters to preserve her head in the walls of the house. She told her sisters that should they not grant this, her final wish, she would do all she could to escape from her grave and return to the house. Her sisters told her that they would carry out her request but, after she died, they decided that it was too gruesome and probably only the result of her failing mind, and so her complete body was placed in the family vault.

A few days later the sisters heard loud, crashing noises for which they could find no explanation and then, one night, the whole household awoke to the sound of doors being slammed shut throughout the building. Night after night groans echoed through the corridors and at last the sisters, taking the advice of their vicar, decided to keep the promise they had made to their sister. Anne's corpse was disinterred and found to be in perfect condition except for the head which had been reduced to a skull. The skull was taken into the house and no further disturbances occurred. Some years later, however, a servant threw the skull onto a passing cart as a prank, but the horse stopped and stood sweating in terror. It was only when the skull was returned to the house that the cart driver managed to get the horse to move on.

Over time, different owners of the house buried the skull in the garden but thereafter had so much bad luck that they brought it back in. The skull of Anne Griffith is now built in behind a carved screen in the Great Hall, and a portrait of her hangs on the staircase looking down on the house she loved so much.

Ghost: Harry (Surname Not Known)
Place: *England*
Date: 20th Century

This more recent story concerns a couple in their late seventies who, as the year drew to a close, were both nearing the end of their life. Elizabeth was in hospital with terminal cancer and Harry was confined to their home. At the beginning of December, Harry's condition deteriorated to the point where he too had to be admitted to hospital. The family visited both of them each day but decided that it would be kinder if they did not tell Elizabeth of Harry's situation. Each day Elizabeth asked about Harry and sent greetings to her husband not knowing he was in the same building as her.

Again out of kindness, the family decided not to tell Harry that Elizabeth would not last long. She was very ill and was aware that she would soon die and was convinced that her death would occur on Christmas Day, her birthday. About a week before Christmas, however, it was Harry who died. This left the family in a bit of a dilemma over whether to inform Elizabeth of the sad news. Since she was so obviously close to death herself, it was decided to withhold the information in order to distress her no further.

The family continued to visit Elizabeth in the days before Christmas. It was melancholy to visit the old lady and pretend that Harry was still amongst them, but Elizabeth herself seemed to realise that something had happened for she suddenly stopped asking about her husband.

On Christmas Day the old lady passed away just as she had predicted. Elizabeth's daughter went one last time to the hospital to make the funeral arrangements and remarked to the ward sister that it was so sad that the old lady's husband had not been able to see her one last time. The sister said that was not the case. The old man had been in to see his wife each day that week and Elizabeth had drawn great comfort from his visits. Elizabeth's daughter said she was mistaken, for her father had died the previous week in the same hospital. The sister was more than a little surprised since he was definitely the same man whose photograph was on Elizabeth's bedside table. She said it was not just she who had seen Harry. There were several other nurses on the ward who had seen him, and on one occasion they even delayed the doctor's examination until he had left, realising that the old couple's time together was so short.

Ghost: Jack Hayson
Place: *Waterford, Republic of Ireland*
Date: The Late 19th Century

The Hayson family lived in Waterford, in the late 19th century. Their house was on the quay, just by the River Suir and the harbour. It was on Christmas Eve that Eli Hayson saw and heard the ghost of his twin brother, Jack. Jack was a seaman, and his ship, the *Thomas Emery*, was moored at Cork, some 50 miles away. But when Eli, just about to go to bed, heard the sound of running feet outside, and looked out of the window onto the moonlit quay, he saw Jack come running towards the house from the direction of the harbour. Eli was on the point of leaving his window to open the front door for his brother, when he saw three other figures pursuing Jack. He tried to shout, but could not make himself heard. Nor could he move, as he saw Jack, in his seaman's jersey and trousers, come right up to the house. But then the pursuing figures closed in on him. In the bright moonlight, Eli saw his brother's upturned face, and heard him cry, 'For God's sake, help me!' Still he could not move. Only when a cloud moved across the face of the moon and everything went dark, was the spell lifted. He hurried down and opened the door, but the quay was deserted.

Baffled, and believing he had had some kind of waking nightmare, Eli went to bed. But next day the Haysons received a message informing them that Jack had drowned after sleepwalking over the side of his ship. At the inquest in Cork, the twins' father affirmed that neither of his sons had ever been sleepwalkers. But several of the crew testified that they had seen Jack, on numerous occasions, get up from his bunk, dress, and walk about the ship's deck, still fast asleep. The verdict was one of accidental death by drowning. But, in the light of his strange vision, Eli and his family were by no means satisfied that the true cause of Jack's death had been established. As the years went by, it remained a mystery.

It was twenty years later that Eli discovered the truth about his brother's fate. He sometimes made business trips to Cork, and usually had a drink in the same bar each time. On one occasion, the barman gave him a message. An old man in the town wanted to see him, with some personal information. Going to the address given, Eli was received by an ancient man, Mr Webster, who welcomed him in. After some desultory talk, old Webster told his story. His own son, Tom, had been a night watchman at the warehouses on the quay at Cork. Tom had died shortly before, but had told his father something that had been on his conscience for a long time.

One Christmas Eve, he had been sitting half-dozing at his brazier, when he heard the sound of stealthy footsteps. Looking up, he was startled and frightened to see three grotesque figures pass along, close to the edge of the quay. Their bodies were those of men, dressed like sailors, but two of them had the heads of apes, and one that of a deer. Tom crept to the corner of a nearby shed and gazed after them in fear and wonderment. He saw the three figures going down some steps to the water then pulling away in a dinghy, bound for one of the ships moored in the river.

The moon was bright, and the ship was near. Venturing close to the water's edge, he was gazing intently over the moonlit water, when he was chilled by a scream of terror. A man appeared on the deck, and ran wildly along it, followed in a trice by the three bizarre figures. As they closed in on their quarry, the watcher heard him cry out, 'For God's sake, help me!' A moment later there was a splash. The young man had jumped overboard. Tom could hear him for a moment or two, flailing helplessly in the water, but he himself was frozen to the spot by terror. And then, there was only silence. But Tom was horror-struck to see the three pursuers raise their hands to their heads and, as it seemed, tear off their own faces, before they looked over the side. Then he realised they had been wearing masks.

'He went to the inquest,' said old Webster. 'But he was terrified that if he said anything, they would come for him too. So he said nothing. But it was always on his conscience that he had seen Jack Hayson die, and done nothing to stop it.'

Eli returned home, full of thoughts of that night, twenty years before, when he had seen his brother come running, in vain, to his home. What the motives of the assailants were – revenge maybe, or even only a vicious practical joke – he never discovered.

Ghost: The 'Hideous Hand' of an Unknown Lady
Place: *Littledean Tower, Maxton, Roxburghshire*
Date: 17th Century

Littledean Tower stands close to the village of Maxton in Roxburghshire. The building dates from the 15th centu ry. It has long been uninhabited, but it was at one time the stronghold of the Kerr family. One laird of Littledean, who lived in the tower in the 17th century, had a particularly bad reputation.

The laird was by all accounts a thoroughly unsavoury character. He drank heavily, mistreated his family and servants, and took great pleasure in playing an active part in the persecution of Covenanters in the district. He had a violent temper, and it is said that on one occasion he became so angry with a stable lad who had saddled and harnessed his horse improperly that he trampled the poor lad to death.

The laird enjoyed entertaining his friends – the only people who could bear his company were those who shared his liking for excess and bad behaviour – and they spent many raucous evenings drinking themselves incapable.

The laird's wife, Margaret, lived a miserable life. Her husband was undeniably cruel in his treatment of her. It seems, however, that she bore it all for the most part with remarkable dignity and stoicism. One evening, however, the laird overstepped the mark. He had, as usual, been drinking heavily with his companions, and one of them asked where Margaret was (it was her habit to keep well out of the way of her husband and his cronies at such times).

The laird dragged Margaret from her room and down to the dining hall where his visitors sat. He then proceeded to berate her and humiliate her in front of them. Margaret stood, confined by her husband's vicious grip on her arm, and suffered this treatment in silence.

At length the laird let her go, uttering as a final insult that he would rather be married to a woman from hell, for such a wife would have more warmth than the woman he had married.

It was a terrible thing to say, and Margaret finally broke her silence in response to it.

'You will live to regret these words,' she said, before quietly leaving the room.

The laird's friends bade him goodnight and left Littledean, but the laird was too fired up with drink and bad temper to settle. He saddled up his horse and rode off into the darkness. After some time, he came to a cottage in a clearing in the woods. The door was open and the laird could see a woman inside, sitting at a spinning wheel. He dismounted and approached. His horse seemed strangely agitated as the laird got to the cottage door, and he had to hold its reins very firmly to prevent it from bolting. Looking into the cottage, the laird thought that he could see shadowy figures moving in the corners, but it was too dark to make out what they were. He tried to speak to the woman. She did not respond in words to his greeting. Instead, she stopped spinning and turned to face him, still holding the newly spun thread between her fingers. With a maniacal laugh, she snapped the thread in two.

The laird saw no more, for at that point his horse took such fright and pulled him away with such force that he almost had to let go of the reins. He regained control of the animal at last, mounted and rode away. When he eventually arrived back at Littledean, he still had the picture of the woman in his mind. She had been the most beautiful creature he had ever laid eyes on.

The next day he found that in spite of himself he was preoccupied with the woman in the cottage. He set off to try to find her. He rode for most of the day, trying to find the same path through the wood that he had taken the night before, but in spite of many hours' searching he was unable to find any sign of the cottage where he had last seen the woman. He returned to Littledean, frustrated. As he approached his home, however, he caught sight of a graceful figure standing in a glade by the river – it was the very woman for whom he had been searching! She held out her arms to him in silence, and he went to her eagerly.

The laird's obsession with the woman grew. Every night at the same time, just before dark, she would appear at the same place by the river. His desire for her was so great that the laird ignored any need for caution. There, within sight of his marital home, he indulged his passion for this strange woman night after night.

It was inevitable that the affair would not remain a secret. The laird was seen with the woman and Lady Margaret was told about it. She confronted him and threw her wedding ring in his face. The laird merely turned on his heel and walked away.

Lady Margaret was ready to leave, but before she did she wanted to find out who her husband's mysterious lover was. Two men volunteered to go and search for the woman on her behalf. That evening they went to the glade by the river where the laird and the woman had been meeting, and after some time they caught sight of her. As they moved towards her stealthily, hoping to entrap her, she disappeared. A hare sped away from the place where she had been seen and ran far off into the distance.

The two men returned to Lady Margaret to find her in a state of great consternation. The laird was missing. There was little point in mounting a search at this late hour, for it was too dark. They had no choice but to wait.

It was far into the night when the laird's horse finally galloped up to the tower, carrying its master. The horse was sweating and exhausted; the laird was grim-faced and as white as a sheet. He was shaking as he told all those present what had happened to him. He had been riding towards home when he had caught sight of a hare running alongside his horse. Before long, the hare had been joined by several others, racing along beside him, in front of him and behind him. They leaped around the feet of his horse and jumped up to saddle height. The laird had been very frightened and had tried first to spur his horse on to outrun them, then to cut them down with his sword and trample them with the horse's hooves. His efforts were in vain until his sword struck the paw of one hare, cutting it clean off. The paw had jumped in the air and landed in his pistol holster. The pack of hares had then suddenly withdrawn.

By the time all this had happened, the laird had ridden all the way to the village of Midlem, a place notorious for witchcraft and many miles from his home. He had spurred his horse into a gallop and had neither stopped nor even slowed his pace until he reached the safety of Littledean.

'Devils,' he muttered through chattering teeth. 'Devils!'

When he had told his tale, the laird put his hand into the pistol holster to feel for the hare's paw. He screamed, quickly withdrawing his hand from the holster and throwing something down on the ground.

'It grabbed me!' he cried.

Lady Margaret looked down at the thing that her husband had thrown from his holster. It was not a hare's paw but the bloody severed hand of a woman!

The laird drew his sword and speared the hand. As he did so, it flexed, very much as if it were alive. The laird took it, still impaled on his sword, out of the tower and made for the river. When he reached the water's edge, he hurled the bloody hand into the river's murky depths with all his might. He was very close to the spot where he and the mysterious woman had been meeting, and when he had thrown the hand in the river, he turned around and saw her, crouching beneath a tree. She lifted her head to look at him. To his horror, the laird saw that her face had been transformed into a hideous, wizened countenance with an evil leer.

'You took my hand from me,' she rasped. 'Now it will be with you for ever!'

The laird returned to the tower, still shaking. He collapsed into a chair by the fireside and put his hand into his pocket. The hand was there again! He threw it from the window in disgust and stumbled up to his bedchamber, hoping to find relief in sleep. But when he got into bed, he realised that he could feel something beneath the pillow on which his head lay. Putting his hand under the pillow, he withdrew the hideous hand. By this time hysterical with fear, he threw the hand into the fire and hid himself beneath the covers.

The laird did not appear downstairs the next morning. After some time Lady Margaret sent servants up to wake him. Not a sound came from the laird's bedroom in spite of the servants' repeated knocking and calling. His door was locked, and they had to break it down to gain entry. When they finally managed to enter the room, they found the laird lying on the floor. He was dead. His face, far from appearing peaceful, had a look of unimaginable terror. His neck was bruised, and the bruises appeared to be the marks of fingers around the laird's neck. He had been strangled by the hideous hand.

Ghost: Lady Hoby
Place: *Bisham Abbey, Berkshire, England*
Date: 1840

Bisham Abbey was a preceptory of the Knights Templar and became, in essence, the building given to Anne of Cleeves by Henry VIII. Sir Thomas Hoby, at the time the owner of the property, was custodian to Princess Elizabeth, before she became Queen Elizabeth I. It is the ghost of his wife, the Lady Elizabeth Hoby, who is alleged to haunt the house.

The haunting of the abbey seems to be very much in line with Lady Hoby's character. She was a scholar who wrote in both Latin and Greek and composed religious treatises, and who had little patience with people of lesser intelligence and learning. Her son, William, was one such, in that his work was careless and untidy. His mother seems to have had a short temper and chastised him often and, one day, thrashed him so severely that he died.

Lady Hoby herself died soon after her son and her ghost was seen afterwards, coming from a bedroom washing bloodstains from her hands and clothes, using a basin that appeared to float in front of her without any means of support. The ghost resembles a portrait of her, which still hangs in the hall, but it always appears in the style of a photographic negative, black being white and white black.

An old woman dressed in black and sitting in a boat, was seen by two boys returning from an evening fishing trip. Both she and the boat disappeared as the boys approached. During the night various visitors to the abbey have been woken up by the sounds of footsteps and hysterical weeping, and the noise of someone moving along corridors that no longer exist.

When Admiral Vansittart lived at Bisham he scoffed at the idea of ghosts until, late one night, when playing chess in the room containing Lady Hoby's portrait, he finished the game and stood quietly looking out of the window. On turning to look at the painting, he saw that the frame on the wall was empty and that the ghost of Lady Hoby was in the room with him. He fled.

In 1840, workmen found copybooks hidden in a wall between the joists and the skirting under a 16th-century window shutter and these were some of the books used by the young William Hoby. The books were untidy and covered in inkblots.

Ghost: A Hotel Desk Clerk
Place: *Alberta, Canada*
Date: 20th Century

Sonya Fourché was a diabetic and her condition required that she inject insulin at precisely the same times each and every day. The first injection had to be made at exactly eight o'clock in the morning.

While touring one of the Canadian National Parks with her parents, she stayed in a hotel in southern Alberta. She asked for an early morning call and breakfast at eight o'clock. All went well for several mornings; first she received a telephone call and about five minutes later she would find her breakfast tray left outside her door.

One morning however, she received the telephone call as usual but on this occasion there was no breakfast. Thinking they were just a little late, she took a quick shower, gave herself her injection and again went to collect her breakfast; but still there was nothing there. She assumed that the staff had forgotten to bring her breakfast up and so decided to have it in the dining room with her parents, since they would be getting up soon anyway.

However, when she knocked on their door to see if they were ready to go down, her father was rather short with her and asked her if she knew what time it was. Instead of being just after eight, it was five o'clock. Sonya protested that it must be eight o'clock as she had just received her early morning call, but when she checked her watch she discovered that her father was correct.

In the morning, when the family complained to the desk clerk, he told them that they must have been mistaken since the desk was not staffed until eight, and the telephones were, in any case, turned off all night. As the clerk was trying to mollify the family, he suddenly realised that Sonya had been staying in room 6. He explained that guests in this room were occasionally disturbed by the ghost of a desk clerk who had died 'in harness' some years before. He then invited Sonya to place her observations in a book that he produced. Within, she found the recollections of several other guests who had had the misfortune of being in receipt of the ghost clerk's attentions.

Ghost: Charles Hutchinson
Place: *Dalkeith, Midlothian, Scotland*
Date: Since 1878

An attractive old house on the edge of Dalkeith, just outside Edinburgh, was the scene of some very sinister events early in the 20th century. On 3 February 1911, a large dinner party was held, after which several people fell dangerously ill and two lost their lives. A post-mortem examination showed that they had been poisoned. The two dead men were named as Charles Hutchinson and Alec Clapperton. The poisoner turned out to have been John, the son of Charles Hutchinson. He fled to the Channel Islands after the incident and when finally cornered by police there, he ended his own life by taking prussic acid.

A strange presence, thought to be the ghost of Charles Hutchinson, remains very much in evidence in the house nowadays, in the room where the dinner party took place. The family who live there testify to a strange atmosphere in the room and the family dogs are reluctant to enter it.

Ghost: Identity Unknown
Place: *Sampford Peverill, Tiverton, Devon, England*
Date: 1810 Onwards

The house, Sampford Peverill, has double walls with passages between them that may at some time have been used by wreckers or smugglers, who in turn may have been responsible for the strange noises heard there.

The property was tenanted in 1810 by John Chave, his family and their servants. They had decided to live there despite the fact that the apparition of a woman had been reported by a previous tenant. That year they became increasingly alarmed by strange and inexplicable occurrences which began in April of that year: 'The chambers of the house were filled, even in daytime, with thunderous noises and upon any persons stamping several times on the floors of the upstairs rooms, they would find themselves imitated, only much louder, by the mysterious agency.'

Women servants were often beaten at night, until they were covered in bruises. One night about 200 blows were struck on a bed with a sound resembling the blows of a strong man hitting it as hard as he could. Some servants reported being beaten so severely that they were bruised and sore for days afterwards and one, Ann Mills, was given a black eye and a blow to her cheek that swelled to the size of an egg. The servants who lived in the house, eventually refused to stay in their rooms at night and, in order to keep them, the Chaves offered to share their own accommodation with them.

Even this made little difference. Bangs, rattlings and the 'sound like that of a man's foot in a slipper' coming downstairs and passing through a wall, were heard. Objects were moved about in rooms, and the occupiers 'often heard the curtains of the bed violently agitated, accompanied by a loud and almost indescribable motion of the rings. These curtains, four in number, were, to prevent their motion, often tied up, each in one large knot. Every curtain of that bed was agitated, and the knots whirled and thrown about with such rapidity that it would have been unpleasant to be within the sphere of their action.

This lasted about two minutes and concluded with a noise resembling the tearing of linen. On examination a rent was found across the grain of a strong, new, cotton curtain.' On one occasion, when a door was being opened there was a loud banging on its other side but when it was fully opened there was nothing there. Sometimes noises in the house were so loud that the whole building shook.

The governor of the county gaol went to the house to witness the strange happenings. He laid his sword and a large folio Bible at the foot of his bed and awoke to see them both hurtle through the air to land against the bedroom wall some two metres away. Someone, roused by his cries of terror, ran to the room and, on opening the door, saw the sword floating in the air and pointing directly towards him before it fell to the floor.

It was suggested that the tenant was responsible for the strange events, hoping to frighten people away and buy the house cheaply. This story was eventually heard in Tiverton and sympathy for the tenants vanished; on some visits to the village Mr Chave was even attacked by a mob. He explained that he had no wish to buy the house and that he wanted to find another home at almost any price, so that he and his family could escape from the terror which they now experienced every day. Eventually he left with his wife and family, but the disturbances continued.

Ghost: Identity Unknown
Place: *Sandwood Bay, Sutherland, Scotland*
Date: Various

Sandwood Cottage has stood empty for many years and is now visited mainly by tourists and walkers, many of whom have returned with tales of inexplicable sights and sounds. Some campers who had pitched their tent near the cottage heard loud noises, the sound of doors opening and closing, and footsteps, and felt the building vibrate. On another occasion a local man, Sandy Gunn, stayed in the building and was awakened by the sound of someone walking about on the ground floor. When he investigated he could find no trace of anyone or anything.

A bearded figure, dressed like a sailor, has been seen in the surroundings of the cottage on at least three separate days and each time by different people. One afternoon, the figure was noticed by two crofters picking up driftwood on the beach nearby and they described a man who was wearing a dark coat with brass buttons, a seaman's hat and a pair of sea boots. An identical sighting was made by members of a fishing party, who, suspecting a poacher, chased the man until he disappeared behind some sand dunes. No one was found and there were no footmarks in the sand.

The apparition has been seen at the cottage itself by a fisherman, Angus Morrison, who slept there one night. He heard footsteps and a tapping on a downstairs window. On looking out he was presented with a bearded face and a man who looked, by his dress, to be a sailor. Angus opened the cottage door and searched outside but there was nothing to be found. He tells too of waking on another visit to feel himself being suffocated by some mysterious weight lying on him.

An Australian, who had grown to love the area and cottage while on holiday, died in his home country a few years before Sandy Gunn experienced the strange sounds. Is it possible that he has returned to a place that gave him so much pleasure in life?

Ghost: Ignatius the Monk
Place: *Elm, Cambridgeshire, England*
Date: Various

The vicarage at Elm is built on the site of an old monastery and is haunted by the ghost of a monk, Ignatius, who died about 800 years ago. One of Ignatius's many responsibilities had been to watch the water level in the nearby Fens and give warning to the monastery in times of dangerous floods. One night, while on watch, he fell asleep and did not give a warning as the water level rose and drowned some of his fellow monks, leaving him in guilt and disgrace.

A rector and his wife, shortly after they went to live in Elm Vicarage, were regularly awakened by the sound of footsteps during the night. Investigation found no reason for them or even their source. Soon after the footsteps began, the rector's wife met the ghostly monk, Ignatius, as she walked along an upstairs corridor one evening, and heard him say 'Do be careful.' With remarkable presence of mind she asked him who he was, to be told 'Ignatius, the bell ringer'. The ghost was wearing a brown monk's habit and sandals and was seen many times afterwards by the rector's wife, who eventually learned his history.

The rector's wife saw the ghost in many parts of the house. He always appeared initially as a faint outline, then gradually firmed into the figure of a man aged about 33 with dark curly hair and fine ascetic features. He was always dressed in an old, worn, monk's habit and appeared, usually, at dusk.

One night in September the woman decided to sleep, as she sometimes did, in a bedroom which was normally kept for guests. The family dog usually slept on her bed but on this particular night was distressed and ran whimpering from the room before being eventually calmed and persuaded to stay. The rector's wife fell asleep to wake up and feel something being tied around her throat. She switched on a light and found a tendril from a vine that grew outside the bedroom window lying across her neck. As she removed it she was picked up violently, thrown sideways over the bed, and became aware of a black shape leaning over her. A pair of gnarled hands appeared through a haze and gripped the terrified woman by the throat, gradually tightening their hold until she began to suffocate.

At this point Ignatius appeared and, coming toward her, reached for the hands and pulled them away, letting her fall back, exhausted, on the bed. Before she had time recover she was shocked again, this time by the sight of a vague creature with a huge head and red face bending over her and her dog snarling and fighting with something invisible. Somehow tearing herself free she rushed into her husband's room to discover that he had heard nothing.

The marks on her badly bruised neck were visible for days afterwards and the next time she spoke to Ignatius he told her that she had been attacked by a man who had been murdered in the room where she had chosen to sleep. However, some good had come from the affair. By saving the life of the rector's wife, Ignatius had completed his penance and could now be forgiven and allowed to rest.

Ghost: An Irish Policeman
Place: *A Police Station in Ireland*
Date: 1880s

In the 1880s, during a fine, moonlit night, two constables of the Royal Irish Constabulary were sent to walk with despatches to the next police station, some five miles distant. The air was still and clear, with a touch of frost. It did not take them long to reach their destination, and as they approached it, they saw another policeman appear on the road ahead of them. The police station was on one side of the road, and a whitethorn hedge at the other.

It was as if this third officer had stepped out from the hedge. He looked towards the two others, then stepped towards the station and disappeared into its shadow. The approaching policemen assumed he was on guard duty inside, and had simply come out for a breath of air. Both of them saw him clearly – a stoutly built, bareheaded man, with a pale, round face and mutton-chop whiskers, and his tunic open at the front.

However, when the two constables got to the station door, they found it was locked and bolted against them. It took prolonged knocking to rouse someone inside. When they were finally admitted, there was no sign of the whiskered constable, nor could he have got in and locked the door in the time they took to approach. They soon found that no one had been posted on guard, and realised that whoever or whatever they had seen, it was not a flesh-and-blood colleague. Fearing ridicule, they said nothing. It was only some years later that they learned that a policeman had been found dead in the snow, not far from the station.

Ghost: 'Pearlin' Jean'
Place: *Allanbank House, Berwickshire, Scotland*
Date: From the 17th Century up to the Early 19th Century

Allanbank House is now no longer standing, having been destroyed in the early 19th century, but the ghost that once frequented the house is well remembered. She is known as 'Pearlin' Jean' – the word 'Pearlin'' referring to the distinct pattern of the lace that she wore on her collar and dress. She was thought to have been the lover of the first Baronet of Allanbank, Robert Stuart, who lived in the 17th century.

According to some versions of the story, Jean was French and lived as a nun (presumably not in a closed convent) until she met Robert Stuart and became his lover. Some say that Pearlin' Jean actually returned to Scotland and to Allanbank with Stuart for a while. Whether or not this was the case, it appeared that Stuart did not see her as a suitable wife and, in time, he became engaged to another woman, leaving poor Jean in the lurch. Jean had sacrificed everything to be with Robert: her love, her respectability – virtually her life. She could not return to her former life; she had nothing more to lose.

Some versions of the story say that what happened next took place in Paris, whilst others place the incident at Allanbank itself. Wherever it happened, the consequences were tragic. Robert Stuart was driving out in his coach when the figure of Pearlin' Jean appeared in front of the carriage. She jumped up onto the carriage with the intention of confronting Robert and making him change his mind. Robert, on the other hand, was horrified to see Jean. He whipped the horses into a gallop, causing the carriage to move forward with a great jolt. Jean lost her grip and was thrown from her perch, falling under the wheels of the carriage. Whether by accident or by design, as the horses galloped on, Robert saw his former sweetheart crushed to death beneath the wheels.

It was Robert himself who first saw the ghost of Pearlin' Jean. He was returning to Allanbank one night when he saw her, a ghostly white figure perched at the gateway, her head covered in blood. He was rendered speechless with fear.

Pearlin' Jean continued to shatter the peace of the house long after her death, banging doors and clattering around the corridors. She was still seen and heard at Allanbank long after the death of Robert Stuart, but future inhabitants of the house were not threatened by her presence as he had been. She became a familiar sight and sound, regarded with something approaching affection. Visitors, however, were often startled by her antics and her bloody appearance. Since the destruction of the house, Pearlin' Jean seems to have gone, but she will be long remembered.

Ghost: Carl Jung in a Time Slip
Place: *Baptistry of San Giovanni, Ravenna, Italy*
Date: 1933

Carl Jung was a famous Swiss scientist who worked with Freud in the early development of psychoanalysis. He is particularly well known for his work on *dementia praecox* and the interpretation of dreams. In 1933, Jung visited the tomb of Galla Placida on two occasions. Nearby is the church of San Giovanni. On his second visit to the site, accompanied by his friend, he was particularly struck by four mosaics on the walls of the baptistry.

They showed scenes of perilous seas and ships being tossed around. The mosaics were constructed largely of various shades of blue and sea green and they gave a bluish hue to the baptistry. He was particularly surprised that he had not noticed them before. He seemed to recall that the first time he had visited the place there were windows there.

Jung continued on his way but not before attempting to buy some photographs of the beautiful mosaics. Unfortunately he could not find any. Some time later he asked a friend visiting Ravenna to see if he could purchase some pictures on his behalf. On his return Jung was astonished to learn that no photographs could be found of the mosaics because they did not exist. The location where Jung and his companion had seen the mosaics was now occupied by four windows.

On a historical note, in the 5th century, while on a stormy passage across the sea, the Empress Galla Placida, in fear for her life, made a promise. She vowed that she would build a church in honour of San Giovanni and decorate it with mosaics showing the hazards of the sea if she were safely delivered to dry land.

Ghost: Fanny Kent
Place: *Cock Lane, London, England*
Date: 1762

In 1762, a haunting was reported in a house in Cock Lane in Smithfield. The property had been occupied since 1759 by the parish clerk of Saint Sepulchres Church, Richard Parsons, his wife Elizabeth and their daughter of the same name. A William Kent, whose young wife had died in childbirth five years before, rented rooms there and was joined by his sister-in-law, Fanny. They lived together at Cock Lane and eventually made wills in each other's favour. William and Fanny left Cock Lane after Parsons had borrowed money from William but was unable to repay it, and moved to Clerkenwell where Fanny died in 1760. It was before they left that the strange happenings occurred which made the house famous.

Fanny and Elizabeth were left alone in the house one weekend when William went to a wedding. The child, Elizabeth, shared a bed that weekend with Fanny who did not want to sleep on her own. The next morning Fanny complained to Mrs Parsons that she and the child had been unable to sleep because they had been kept awake by bumps, rappings, knockings and scratchings on and around their bed. Mrs Parsons tried to mollify her by suggesting that the noises probably came from their neighbour, a cobbler, who sometimes worked throughout the night. However, when the sounds continued next evening, a Sunday, Fanny, became terrified and was convinced that the noises foretold her death. Fanny died 18 months later but during this period there were no further manifestations.

Shortly after she died, the manifestations began again but this time terrifying Elizabeth, who shivered in terror at the sounds around her bed and which surrounded her when she left the house to visit neighbours. As news of the hauntings spread, crowds would gather to gaze at the house and pester Elizabeth with questions. Contact was made with an entity that answered simple questions by using the old method of one knock for yes, two knocks for no and three knocks for unsure. By this means it was established that Fanny was responsible for the noises, and she managed to make it known that she had been poisoned by William Kent who had used arsenic to kill her.

Various séances were held, one of which was attended by Oliver Goldsmith. Goldsmith later published a pamphlet on the affair defending Kent who was increasingly distressed by the continuing allegations made against him. It was at this juncture that official inquiries were made by the authorities. During a series of séances, conducted with Elizabeth suspended in a hammock with her arms and legs spread wide, she was found to be hiding a little piece of wood and a small board under her dress with which rapping noises could have been made. She said she had been told that her father would be jailed in Newgate Prison unless the real culprits were found. William Kent then accused the Parsons and their servant, Mary Frazer, of slander. They were found guilty and had to pay large damages to Kent, in addition to which Parsons was sentenced to one year's imprisonment.

In 1845 Fanny's coffin was opened and her corpse was found to be untouched by decay or putrefaction.

Ghost: The Killackee Cat-spirit
Place: ***Dower House at Killackee, Ireland***
Date: 1968

In 1968, the old dower house at Killackee was bought by the artist, Margaret O'Brien, and her husband, Nicholas. There was much that needed doing to the house, and they had a team of workmen engaged on renovation and redecoration. When the workmen began to complain of a strange presence in the house – a big, black cat – Mrs O'Brien dismissed the story. But one day she saw it herself, inside the house when all doors to the outside were locked – a huge, jet-black cat, about as big as a medium-sized dog. The beast vanished, but soon afterwards one of the workmen, Thomas McAssey, at work in a room by himself, felt the air suddenly grow cold. He looked around but saw nothing. From beyond the open door, however, came a sound of low and threatening growls. Then a dark figure appeared in the doorway. He spoke to it, but a growl was the only answer. Mrs O'Brien had the house exorcised, which appeared to get rid of the cat-spirit, though other manifestations were said to trouble the place still.

Ghost: The Kinsale 'White Lady'
Place: *Kinsale Military Fort, Republic of Ireland*
Date: From 17th Century Onwards

The military fort at Kinsale was begun in 1677, and reinforced and extended several times afterwards. From quite an early stage in its history, the story of the 'white lady' has been associated with it. Accounts of the precise circumstances in which she met her end vary, but the common factor is the suicide of a young bride on the very day of her wedding. Her father was the colonel in charge of the fort, named as either Warrender or Browne, a strict disciplinarian with a violent temper. The girl, whose name has been handed down as the rather curious 'Wilful', was engaged to a young officer, Sir Trevor Ashurst.

On the evening of their marriage, they were strolling along the battlements, which rise above the cliffs. Looking over the wall by one of the sentry-posts, she saw some wild flowers growing, and said she would like to have them. To please the new bride, the sentry volunteered to climb down and pick the flowers; and Sir Trevor jovially said he would take the sentry's musket and stand guard while he was gone.

The evening was getting chilly, and Wilful went inside. The sentry seemed to take a long time to return with his nosegay. Sir Trevor, tired and none too serious about his role as a sentry, sat in the sentry box and dozed off to sleep. The soldier never came back – perhaps he had never planned to; perhaps he fell to his death on the crags. When the stern colonel came round inspecting the sentry-posts, he only saw a sleeping man inside. Enraged, he drew his pistol and fired, with the intention of scaring the fellow awake. But, in his haste, he failed to aim away and the bullet passed through the heart of his new son-in-law.

When the bride learned what had been brought about by her casual wish, she rushed out and threw herself off the battlements. The colonel, distracted by guilt and grief, shot himself that night. Such is the burden of one day's tragic happenings.

In the years around 1820, the officer in charge of the fort was Major Black. One summer evening, he saw the figure of a young woman dressed in white appear at the doorway of his own quarters and go up the stairs. Thinking at first it was a lady who had come in by the wrong door, he moved to speak to her, but something held him back. He saw how noiselessly she moved; and then noticed how old-fashioned her clothes were. The Major followed the lady upstairs and saw her enter one of the bedrooms; but when he knocked and entered, the room was empty. The white lady was also seen in Major Black's quarters by the little daughter of a soldier. Black's friend, Dr Craig, related these sightings in his book, *Real Pictures of Clerical Life in Ireland*.

These manifestations caused no fear or injury, but later in the 19th century, more violent events were reported. An army doctor, returning to his rooms from an afternoon's snipe-shooting, was stooping to pick up his key when he felt himself being dragged along the hall by an unseen force and pitched bodily down a flight of steps. He was knocked out, but remembered that as he fell, he had caught sight of a figure in white, which reminded him of a woman in a wedding dress.

Another officer, Captain Jarvis, had a similar experience a little later. He too had a glimpse of a white figure vanishing away as he approached his door. He could not get it to open, and when he tried to force it, he felt a powerful cold gust, and he too was thrown down the flight of stairs.

The white lady is still said to walk, especially on calm summer evenings, like the one on which her life came to its sudden and tragic end.

Ghost: Elizabeth Knight
Place: *West Clangdon, Surrey*
Date: *c.*1896

Lord Onslow was the owner of the Clangdon Park estate and along with about twenty others was witness to a strange occurrence in the grounds of the main house one morning. In the early hours, a seemingly mad woman was seen charging across the lawn towards the house waving a large knife in a most threatening manner. The keepers tried to dissuade her by firing their guns in her direction, and seem to have been successful for she disappeared straight through the nearest wall. There were other sightings of the woman and also a man with a long beard.

In 1896, Ada Goodrich-Freer wrote an article about the hauntings at the house and recounted the above story, along with an account of how a previous owner of the estate had been so distressed by the ghosts that seemed to frequent the house and its environs, that he had been forced to leave. In the article she could not hide her scepticism, and evidently was invited to stay at the house as a result of that article.

Her stay in the house was apparently enough to change her mind for, on 29 January 1897, at Westminster Town Hall, she gave a talk about her experiences at West Clangdon. She told a story about her encounter with a beautifully attired woman on the staircase of the house, who was obviously dressed for dinner. As Miss Freer approached the figure, it faded away until it was quite gone. She went on to say that the strange vision was that of Elizabeth Knight, the wife of a former baron and owner of the house. Their marriage had been so cheerless that the sad, unfortunate lady drowned herself in the lake within the grounds. Maybe the vision of the lady brandishing the knife had been a re-enactment of a previous, vicious quarrel, and the bearded man was her husband, the baron.

Ghost: Mrs Leaky
Place: *Minehead, Somerset, England*
Date: Various

Mrs Leaky lived in Minehead in 1636 with her son, a shipowner, his wife and young daughter. She was much liked in the area and had many friends who would sometimes tell her that they dreaded the day that she would die and they could no longer enjoy her company. Mrs Leaky pointed out to them that she too enjoyed their meetings, but that if they should see her after her death they might not relish the experience.

Eventually she did die and was buried, but shortly afterwards, stories began to circulate that she had been seen in the town and near the house of her son. A doctor, returning to town after a visit in the countryside, met an old woman and started to help her to climb across a stile. Her hand was so cold that he looked at her in surprise and noticed that although she spoke her lips did not move and her eyes were fixed and gazed straight ahead. He was so preoccupied by her appearance that he neglected to help her over the next stile on which she sat and barred his passage. When he turned aside to try to go through an adjacent gate she did the same again. After some time he managed to reach the edge of the town at which point Mrs Leaky's ghost kicked him, and told him to show more manners to old women in future.

Before long she was appearing night and day in her son's house and haunting his ships, scaring the crews to the extent that the vessels sometimes ran aground as they neared port. She often appeared at the top of the mast and whistled in an eerie, shrill, manner, raising such bad weather that the ship would founder. She became known as the whistling ghost and carried on in this way for so long that her son was ruined.

At night, her son's wife would often awake and see the ghost in her bedroom although it always vanished before she could alert anyone else in the house. One night the five-year-old Leaky child screamed from her bedroom. Her parents heard her cry out, 'Help! Help! Father! Father! Grandmother is choking me!' On reaching the child's room they found that she was dead having been strangled. When the day for the child's funeral came, her mother was brushing her hair when she saw, reflected in her mirror, her mother-in-law looking over her shoulder. The ghost told her that the family would be terrorised until the Lord Bishop of Waterford repented of a sin which she knew of and that if he did not he would be hanged.

Once, when staying at Barnstaple the Bishop, who was married to the ghost's sister, had a child by her daughter. After baptising the baby, he strangled it and dried its corpse over charcoal to prevent it from decaying and smelling. He then buried it in a room in the house. When confronted with this, the Bishop attempted to atone for his sin, and the ghost of Mrs Leaky was never seen again. One wonders why Mrs Leaky, so well liked in life, should have become so malevolent in death that she strangled her own granddaughter, particularly since another grandchild had already suffered a similar murderous fate.

Ghost: John Leith
Place: *Leith Hall, Kennethmount, Scotland*
Date: 1965–1971

During the late 1960s Leith Hall was the home of an American, Barrie Gaunt, and his wife, the authoress Elizabeth Byrd. While they lived there they encountered many strange things. They heard noises that, although they were recognisable, could not be rationalised. These included footsteps and doors slamming in empty parts of the house, and the sound of chanting and eerie pipe playing. Sometimes, strange smells of incense were encountered in various parts of the house.

Many inexplicable occurrences took place at particular locations in the house. On one occasion, in the room known as the Leith Room, Gaunt saw a woman acting in a furtive manner, dressed in clothes of the Victorian era.

Elizabeth found that she could not get a sound night's sleep in the master bedroom, which was on the second floor and contained a four-poster bed. One morning she awoke to find a heavily bandaged stranger standing close to the bed, but, after a few seconds, he slowly disappeared. There was a portrait in the house and Elizabeth thought that the bandaged man looked very similar to the person depicted. The portrait was of one John Leith, who had been shot by his wife in 1763, and died as a result of those wounds.

Ghost: Abraham Lincoln
Place: *Washington DC, USA*
Date: Several Times after Lincoln's Assassination in 1865

As most people know, the death of President Lincoln was a highly traumatic event; indeed it could be said to be highly dramatic as well since he was murdered by a dissolute fanatic, John Wilkes Booth, in full view of a theatre audience. As has been mentioned before, the existence of a traumatic death is often accompanied by different phenomena and in Lincoln's case, there have been several sightings of the president since his death. The first one recorded was made by the wife of Calvin Coolidge, the 30th President (1923–28) and a Republican. She is said to have seen Lincoln staring out of a window in the Oval Office. Since then, and possibly even before, apparently there were several sightings, mainly in Lincoln's old bedroom, known as the Lincoln Room or Rose Room, but also around the house.

John Kenney, a bodyguard of President Harrison who was in office between 1889 and 1893, was said to have been so disturbed by the ghostly footsteps of Lincoln that he made a public appeal for him to stop! The story goes that at a séance in Baltimore he pleaded for the president to leave him alone as it was interfering with his ability to guard the present incumbent. Apparently Kenney never heard the noises again.

Lincoln had not given up altogether however, because during the presidency of Roosevelt, in 1934, one of the White House Staff, Mary Eben entered Lincoln's bedroom only to find a man dressed in an old-style frock coat sitting on a bed pulling on his boots. She is recorded as staring at the figure for several seconds before the man disappeared.

One of the more distinguished observers was Queen Wilhelmina of the Netherlands who visited the White House and stayed in the Lincoln Room. She reported to Roosevelt, the president at that time, that she had had a strange visitor the night before. He was dressed in the fashion of the last century and wearing a stovepipe hat. Roosevelt remarked to her that the apparition was President Lincoln and that there had been many previous sightings of him in that room. He might have told her before!

Although it is not recorded whether Winston Churchill ever saw the ghost in one of his many stays at the White House, it is known that he did not like to sleep in Lincoln's room and often moved across the hall during the night to another chamber.

There is also an interesting, if rather suspect story, surrounding the transportation of Lincoln's body from Washington to his resting place in Illinois. The body was loaded onto a train in such a way that it could be displayed to the many mourners that lined the track at various suitable vantage points along the way. It stopped for eight minutes at each station. The story goes that a ghost of the train passes the same way each year. The original story, if true, has suffered from apparent over-embellishment in that it was reported that the train was manned by skeletal musicians and blue-coated men with coffins on their backs, and the clocks stopped for eight minutes.

Ghost: A MacDonald Piper
Place: *Duntrune Castle, Argyll and Bute, Scotland*
Date: Since 1615

Duntrune Castle is situated in an area of outstanding historic interest, north of a line between Lochgilphead and Crinan. Any visitors to the area are rewarded by numerous historical sites and prehistoric mounds and dwelling places going back to the Stone Age – all set in one of the most scenic parts of Scotland.

At the time of this story, Duntrune Castle was occupied by one of the many branches of the Campbell family. Both the Campbell and the MacDonald families had long periods of hegemony in Argyll and the west of Scotland. The MacDonalds are the oldest of the Scottish clans and Somhairle (Somerled) became Thane of Argyle in the 12th century. Duncan Campbell of Lochow, who became Lord Campbell in 1445, was the ancestor of the Dukes of Argyll. When neither family had predominance they were usually fighting each other in order to gain it. So, it is against this background of bitter friction between the two families, going back centuries, that this story is told.

In 1615, the MacDonalds decided to attack the Campbells at their seat in Duntrune Castle but before their venture they decided to reconnoitre the situation. In those times pipers had a special place in society and they were welcomed without question into any substantial household and given free board and hospitality in return for a little music. The MacDonalds attempted to use this custom to their advantage no doubt in defiance of the accepted code of conduct then current. They sent their best and most loyal piper to Duntrune Castle to survey its defences. All went well with this plan for a while, until the piper raised the suspicions of his hosts with too many detailed questions about clan numbers staying at the castle and the fortifications. The Campbells at last realised that the piper was not all that he seemed and imprisoned him in one of the towers.

The MacDonalds watched for the piper's return, but eventually became impatient with waiting and decided to go ahead and attack. From his cell window, overlooking the sea loch, the piper could see his clansmen approaching in their long boats. He realised, from his own treatment, that the Campbells had been forewarned of an impending attack and he bravely determined to warn his fellow clansmen. This he did by playing his pipes as loudly as he could. The tune that the piper played that day is known as 'The Piper's Warning to His Master'. As the MacDonalds came down the loch they heard their piper, recognised his playing, and realised that their plan of taking the castle by surprise had been thwarted. They decided that to continue the attack would be foolhardy and returned to their own firesides.

Their piper was not so lucky. He knew that the Campbells would not be pleased with him for issuing such a warning, but he did not count on the vicious way that they would go about seeking retribution. The Campbells, angry at both his audacity and ingenuity, dragged him from the tower and cut off all his fingers. Such was the violence of his treatment that the piper died from shock and loss of blood. The body was buried without ceremony, below a large slab of stone that formed part of the kitchen floor.

That was the end of the piper, at least in corporeal form. The castle itself was sold to the Malcolms in 1793 but the piper's ghost still lives on in the building. Strange sounds and knockings can be heard coming from various parts of the living quarters and occasionally the playing of a piper can be heard coming from the direction of one of the towers. The tune is always the same, 'The Piper's Warning to his Master'.

Ghosts: MacDonald Victims of the Massacre of Glencoe
Place: *Glencoe, Scotland*
Date: From 1692

Glencoe is not so much a battle site as the scene of a slaughter. The Massacre of Glencoe is one of the most famous events in Scottish history. In February 1692, a company of soldiers of the Clan Campbell took horrible and brutal action against the Clan MacDonald. They did this in the most cowardly manner, accepting the hospitality of the MacDonalds, then surprising them by night and slaughtering many of them as they slept. Forty or so MacDonalds lost their lives.

Glencoe is a popular haunt for climbers, who come to challenge themselves on the surrounding mountainsides. On a fine day, the glen is spectacular to behold, a place of outstanding beauty and grandeur, but the weather, fickle and dangerous as it is in these parts, can change in moments. Then the hills and the glen can take on another profile, just as impressive but awesomely so.

The MacDonalds still haunt the glen. Various people have seen ghostly appearances that bear witness to the dreadful atrocity that was committed against them all those years ago. The anniversary of the massacre, 13 February, is the time at which the phantoms are most likely to appear. The weather is at its bleakest at this time of year and the air can turn even chillier at the sight of the still, staring figures of the MacDonalds. It will turn coldest of all for those who go by the name of Campbell.

Ghost: Ewan Maclean
Place: *Glen More, Isle of Mull, Scotland*
Date: Various

The island of Mull, some forty minutes by ferry from Oban on the west coast of Scotland, is popular with visiting tourists from all over the world. Some visitors to the island may find more than they expect during their stay, for they might come across the headless ghost of Ewan (Eoghan) Maclean, astride his horse as it gallops through Glen More. The story of the ghost is rather gruesome.

On the eve of a battle with the Macleans of Duart, Ewan came across a woman crouched by a stream, washing some bloodstained clothes. Ewan must have realised that this woman was a banshee (*bean shi'th*), a supernatural creature whose appearance meant imminent death. The clothes that she washed were those belonging to men who were about to die. Having seen the banshee, Ewan probably knew that his chances of surviving the battle were not good. Nevertheless, he was committed to his cause and would not shrink from it.

The battle was fierce, and in the midst of the fighting Ewan was killed. It is said that he was beheaded by a blow so swift and sure that his headless body remained sitting upright in the saddle as his horse galloped away. Some say that the appearance of the ghostly headless rider in Glen More foretells a death in the Maclean family.

Ghost: The Sister of Irish Actor-manager, Michéal MacLiammoir
Place: *An Atlantic Liner*
Date: 1934

In October 1934 the Irish actor-manager, Michéal MacLiammoir, was returning from America on an Atlantic liner. Early one morning, as he was walking round the empty deck, he heard someone singing. First he recognised the song, an old French one, *Le Baiser* ('the kiss'), and then he recognised the voice of the singer. It was his sister. Gradually it seemed to him as though she were walking round the deck with him. He recalled: 'We walked around and around, and I began singing the song myself. I was extraordinarily happy, for I hadn't seen her for many years. She was a sister I loved very much.'

Five days later, when he got back to Ireland, he was met by his aunt, who said she had sad news to give him. His sister had died, just five days before.

Ghost: Rev Thomas Mackay
Place: *Lairg, Sutherland, Scotland*
Date: From the End of the 18th Century Onwards

At the end of the 18th century there lived in Lairg in Sutherland a mildly eccentric minister. In spite of being a humble clergyman, the Rev Thomas Mackay is said to have dressed in much grander ecclesiastical attire. He died early in the 1800s, and the manse was thereafter occupied by ministers with more sober habits of dress.

The minister who lived in the manse in 1826 had two daughters, and it was they who saw the ghost for the first time. They heard a knock at the front door and went to answer it. When they opened the door they saw an old man standing on the doorstep, dressed in a long black robe. He said nothing but peered into the house for a few moments before turning away from the girls and walking off. The girls thought that the visitor might be looking for their father, so they ran to find him. When their father came to greet the visitor, there was no sign of the old man, either at the door or in the surrounding area. It seemed as if he had vanished completely.

When the family told some other older parishioners about their strange old visitor and described his appearance and attire, the parishioners were able to enlighten them as to their visitor's identity. It was none other than the Rev Thomas Mackay, paying a visit to his former home.

The manse is no longer there; it fell into disrepair and became a ruin. However, the Rev Thomas Mackay is said to pop back from time to time to visit the site where it once stood. It is said that one night his appearance stopped the activities of two poachers in the neighbourhood. When they heard strange noises coming from the vicinity of the former manse they abandoned all ideas of a profitable night's work and fled.

Ghost: Mr McCartney
Place: *Ballycarry, Co Antrim, Northern Ireland*
Date: 1971

This story was related by Sheena Woodiwis. In May of 1971 Sheena was waiting for her husband to return from work at the nearby Ballylumford Power Station where he was engaged in the construction of an extension to the existing plant. They had rented a semi-detached house on the outskirts of the village and she was sweeping out the kitchen after having placed their dinner in the oven, when she felt someone standing behind her. She remained bent over but glanced behind her towards the door where she felt the person to be standing. She saw a man from the waist down standing in the doorway. He was wearing work boots and had string tied around his trousers just below the knee. Although the figure was not threatening in any way, Sheena was alarmed enough to run from the house without waiting to see any more and that is where her husband found her waiting for him.

Later on, she rather bashfully related the story to their landlord and his wife, Mary. After she had listened to the story, Mary told Sheena that the house used to belong to her family, the McCartneys. She said that her father used to tie his trousers in the manner described by Sheena, and often stood in the doorway chatting to her mother while she prepared his dinner.

Ghost: Dan McIlhenny or McIlvicken
Place: *Cookstown, County Tyrone, Northern Ireland*
Date: 1930s

The countryside west of Cookstown, County Tyrone, was a prime area for the manufacture of illicit whiskey well into the 1930s, if not later. 'Wee still' is the local name for *poitín*, and there are many local stories about its makers and their escapades. But only one still, or its site, is haunted. Out on the peat moss, or in secret places on the hillsides, is where they were set up in those days. One well-known maker (his name is given as Dan McIlhenny or McIlvicken) had an exceptionally good location, in a deep, dry hollow in the moss. He had covered this with branches and cut twigs of heather, so that it looked just like a flat patch of dead, dry heather. But in the middle, he had set an iron grid, so that the smoke from his fire could escape. Like some other *poitín*-makers, he had had the clever idea of getting his lookout men to make a peat fire on top of this iron grating. If any busybody or member of the Royal Ulster Constabulary (RUC) came along, they would see a young fellow sitting harmlessly by a smoking fire, passing the time with his mates. Most of the time, of course, the fire was kept low, and part of the grid open, to let the smoke from the still come out.

Unfortunately, one day, the lookouts neglected their task and left the grating completely covered up. The atmosphere below became gradually thicker and thicker, until Dan, intent on minding his brew, first became unconscious and then died of asphyxiation. The discovery of his body caused terrible consternation. It was brought home and cleaned up of soot, and a co-operative doctor found to ascribe the fatality to heart failure. Dan was duly 'waked' and buried.

But despite his fate, his distilling site was too good to abandon, especially with all its equipment, so, after a decent interval, some of his cronies began to use it again. But, inevitably, rumours of the true cause of Dan's death had spread around, and reached the ears of the RUC.

A discreet watch was kept on the place, and when the smoke was seen rising, a little troop of police rose out of the heather. Seeing them come, the lookouts immediately built peat up over their fireplace. But to the surprise of the lookouts, when the policemen were still some distance away, they hesitated, and stopped. For a moment they looked at one another, then they turned and ran. Soon they were out of sight over the hill. Greatly relieved, the *poitín*-makers cleared their incriminating evidence away on peat sledges as fast as they could.

It was only later that they learned what had caused the policemen to turn tail. While they themselves had seen nothing untowards, in front of the posse of police had appeared a terrifying figure, the form of Dan McIlhenny, his face a ghastly pale beneath streaks of soot, his eyes red and glaring. In the crook of one arm, he held an earthenware crock of familiar form; in the other he held a stout blackthorn stick. Seeing this apparition of a well-known man whom they knew to be dead and buried, the policemen were struck with fear. As he glided towards them, seeming to loom larger and larger, their terror got the better of them, and they bolted.

The news of this event was celebrated by the *poitín*-makers, with many toasts to his memory, at a second and even finer wake for their dead companion. By the end of it, Dan's last jar was well and truly empty.

Ghost: Mrs Molloy
Place: *Perth, Scotland*
Date: Early 19th Century

In the early years of the 19th century, Father McKay, a priest living in Perth, was approached by a woman who had been troubled for some time by a conscience-stricken ghost. The problem was solved without the need for exorcism or dramatic intervention of any kind.

Anne Simpson, the woman who sought Father McKay's assistance, was not of the Catholic faith, but she had good reason for asking the help of a Catholic priest. It turned out that the ghost that had been appearing to her night after night was that of a woman whom she had known as a familiar figure around the army barracks nearby. The woman's name was Molloy, and she had worked in the barracks' laundry. Mrs Molloy's ghost, when it appeared to Anne Simpson, was most persistent. Mrs Molloy owed money – three shillings and ten pence. She wanted Anne Simpson to tell a priest and ask him to set matters right.

So here was Anne Simpson, tired of constantly interrupted sleep, doing the bidding of a ghost! Lesser men might have sent the poor woman away and told her to stop talking such nonsense, but Father McKay listened to her story patiently and assured her that he would see what he could do.

He made inquiries at the barracks first of all. Sure enough, there had been a woman called Molloy working there, but she had died some time before. The priest wanted to know if she had owed any money to anybody in the barracks. But the answer was no, she had not owed any money there. The priest had to take his search a little farther afield. Visiting local traders, he found himself in the grocer's shop. When he asked about Mrs Molloy, he discovered that when she had died she was in debt to the grocer. And the amount of the debt – three shillings and ten pence exactly!

The kindly priest settled the outstanding amount and left the shop. When he saw Anne Simpson some days later, he asked whether

Mrs Molloy's ghost had appeared to her recently. He was quite relieved to hear that the ghost seemed to have gone. Obviously the spirit of Mrs Molloy felt at peace now that she had got all her affairs in order!

Ghost: A Murdered Old Woman
Place: *A House near Dublin*
Date: Late 19th Century

The family who took over a large, rambling house on the south side of Dublin had no notion that there was anything strange about it. It felt a friendly, comfortable, sunny sort of place. The period was the late 19th century. The two little girls of the family had a big bedroom at the rear of the house, as the younger child was an invalid and liked to have her sister share the room. But about a week after they had moved in, and when everyone was in bed, the elder girl came running up to her parents' bedroom, in great distress, crying that there was something rushing about in the girls' bedroom, which they couldn't see. The mother ran down, and even as she approached the open door, she heard the thuds of something apparently bounding about inside the room. But just before she went in, the noise stopped.

She spent the night with her two girls, and eventually they went to sleep. She remained awake and heard arise in one corner of the room what she described as 'a soft, sighing, whispering sound, which seemed to come out of the wall, and gradually crept all round the room till it reached where our beds were. Nearer it came, till it touched the bed, as if a winged beetle were fluttering against the quilt. All at once something heavy seemed to fall, and immediately the footfalls I had heard before sounded with a peculiar hollow thud, as if some animal (cat or dog) were jumping up and down; it lasted about ten minutes, and suddenly died away at the door. Next morning, both girls exactly described the first part of the noise as I had heard it, and it always came in the same way – an indescribable whisper in the beginning, and the conclusion a heavy thud.' The children named the invisible thing 'Pronc'.

Next day, the family were visited by an acquaintance to whom all of them were averse; especially the younger child, who always became feverish and unwell when this individual was in the house. The mother observed that before this unwelcome and unwanted visitor came, there was always a manifestation from Pronc – as if the unseen thing was sensitive to other malevolent beings – and she always made a point of remaining at home on the day following any nocturnal noises.

One evening, she was sitting with her younger daughter by the fire, telling her a story, when the child gripped her hand and motioned towards the fire. There on the rug, its back to them, was a large cat, staring into the flickering firelight. Thinking it was her daughter's pet cat, the mother called out to it, 'Well, Peter-puss! Are you come in for your supper?' Later, she related, 'The creature turned, and looked full at us for a moment with eyes that were human, and a face, which though black, was still the face of an ugly woman! The mouth snarled at us for an instant, and a sad, angry howl came from it. And as we stared in horror, the thing vanished. We never saw it again.' Nevertheless, they left the house as soon as they could. Later, they discovered that fifty years before a woman had been robbed and murdered in the house, by her own son, and her body had been buried by him under the hearth-stone. Twenty years afterwards, her skeleton had been uncovered by tenants living in the house. They too had been troubled by the ghost, and though they gave the remains a proper burial, it seems that its presence could not be dislodged so easily.

Ghost: A Mysterious Disappearance
Place: ***Eilean Mor Lighthouse, Outer Hebrides***
Date: 15 December 1900

Thomas Marshall was the head lighthouse-keeper of the Eilean Mor Lighthouse off the west coast of Scotland at the turn of the 20th century. He had a crew of two men, James Ducat and Donald McArthur. They lived a lonely existence, isolated as they were on the rocky outcrop for a couple of months at a time, sometimes longer, if the weather was particularly inclement. On 15 December 1900 the light ceased to function for several days so the local seafaring community decided to send out a party to investigate. On 26 December a group set out for the rock.

The crew of the rescue boat managed to get alongside the quay at the lighthouse but there was no welcoming party as usual. In fact, there was no sign of life whatsoever. They searched the small outcrop and throughout the lighthouse but could find no sign of the crew. Everything seemed to be in place and the only strange thing that they could find was a piece of unusual seaweed that none of the rescue crew had ever seen before.

They took the lighthouse log and made their way back to the mainland. At the inquiry into the disappearance of the three lighthouse-keepers, the last few entries of the log were read out to the court. They read:

> *12 December*: 'Gale north by northwest. Sea lashed to fury. Never seen such a storm. Waves very high. Tearing at lighthouse. Everything shipshape. James Ducat irritable.'
>
> *Later*: 'Storm still raging, wind steady. Stormbound. Cannot go out. Ship passing sounding foghorn. Could see lights of cabins. Ducat quiet. Donald McArthur crying.'
>
> *13 December*: 'Storm continued through night. Wind shifted west by north. Ducat quiet. McArthur praying.'
>
> *Later*: 'Noon, grey daylight. Me, Ducat and McArthur prayed.'
>
> *14 December*: No entry in log.
>
> *15 December*: 'Storm ended, sea calm. God is over all.'

What had the men been so frightened of? It seems that their experience had been so distressing that at the very first opportunity they had abandoned their post and set off in the lighthouse's boat. The storm must have been very exceptional because they were all used to rough seas. There was, however, something very unusual about this storm. It seems to have been extremely local. On the nearby island of Lewis, less than 20 miles away, there had been no such storm. Then there is the last entry – 'God is over all.' What did that mean?

The mystery is deepened by a further piece of evidence that was submitted to the inquiry. On the night of 15 December, two sailors on a ship passing near to the lighthouse had been discussing why it was in darkness, when they spotted a boat being rowed by three men dressed in their heavy weather gear. By the moonlight shining through a break in the clouds they watched as the boat cut under their bow. They called out to the men, believing them to be in difficulty, but there came no reply. The only sound was from their rowlocks as the men set about their task in urgent fashion.

Ghost: A Mysterious Stranger
Place: *Selkirk, Scotland*
Date: 19th Century

This story, which comes from the Border town of Selkirk, tells of the strange disappearance of a cobbler. The secret of what exactly happened to him is known only to the dead.

The cobbler was called Rabbie Heckspeckle, and he was, by all accounts, a skilled and industrious craftsman, quick and nimble with his fingers, who shod many a fine gentleman around the town of Selkirk.

One particular morning, the cobbler was up before dawn, as was his habit, working on a pair of shoes, when a stranger came into the shop. It was unusual for anyone to come looking for service at such an early hour, but Rabbie Heckspeckle was a shrewd businessman and did not like to turn down any opportunity to make a little money. Accordingly, he greeted the stranger with his usual courtesy and asked how he could be of assistance. The man was looking for a new pair of shoes.

The stranger was well dressed, but he had a certain air of decay about him, and there was something in his manner that the cobbler did not particularly take to. Nevertheless, Rabbie Heckspeckle politely obliged him by showing him a few samples of his work.

The stranger pointed to one particular pair of shoes that were to his liking, and although the cobbler did not have any in the right size, he measured the stranger's feet and assured him that he would be able to make some in time for collection the next day. The stranger said that he would be picking up the shoes early, well before dawn, and the cobbler, although a little surprised, said that such an arrangement would be quite convenient. The sun had still not come up when the mysterious stranger left the cobbler's shop.

Rabbie Heckspeckle worked all day and long into the night, completing the shoes for the stranger. When he had finally finished, the shoes were as fine as any he had made. Congratulating himself on a fine job, he turned in for the night, hoping to catch a few hours of sleep before his customer returned.

It was still dark when the cobbler heard a knock on the door, waking him from his slumber. Rubbing his eyes, he pulled on some clothes and went to let his customer in. The stranger tried on the shoes with hardly a word. They fitted him beautifully, but he was far from fulsome in his praise for the good cobbler's efforts. He merely tossed a handful of silver coins at Rabbie Heckspeckle, turned round and made for the door.

The cobbler was intrigued by this eerie man. He wanted to see where he lived. The man was certainly not a familiar figure around the streets of the town. Unable to contain his curiosity, Rabbie Heckspeckle set off to follow the stranger, keeping at a safe distance. He followed the stranger all the way to the kirk yard and watched as the sombre figure made its way through the serried ranks of gravestones to the far side of the cemetery. There, before the stupefied gaze of Rabbie Heckspeckle, the stranger lay down on one of the graves and disappeared.

The cobbler rushed over to the gravesite where he had seen the stranger vanish. There was no sign of digging or of disturbance of any kind. Where had the stranger gone? Hurriedly, the cobbler left a pile of stones on top of the grave as a marker and rushed off to tell everybody about what he had just seen.

At first, nobody would believe him. The cobbler must have imagined it. The stranger probably walked out the other side of the graveyard unnoticed. The idea that he had vanished into a grave was quite preposterous, after all. But in spite of all the ridicule, the cobbler persisted with his story, and after a great debate it was agreed that the grave should be opened.

The gravediggers were summoned and the coffin was disinterred. The coffin was then opened in full view of several witnesses. Inside the coffin they found the body of a man dressed just like the stranger had been and wearing a pair of brand-new shoes. The shoes were so beautifully crafted that they could only have been made by Rabbie Heckspeckle. The townspeople had to believe his story now.

Nobody really knew what to do next. After some debate it was decided that the best thing to do was to seal the coffin again and put it back in the grave. Time would tell whether the ghostly stranger was likely to put in another appearance in the future. But before the coffin was re-interred, the cobbler reclaimed the shoes that he had made. They were a fine pair, after all, and what use could they be to a dead person?

He had made a big mistake. Next morning, before dawn, the neighbours had a rude awakening. Sounds of a terrible struggle were heard coming from Rabbie Heckspeckle's cobbler's shop. Several people, who had all been disturbed by the thumping and screaming, ran to the shop to investigate. They could find nothing except a set of footprints leading from the shop to the graveyard. The footprints led right up to the grave that had been dug up the day before.

There was nothing else for it – the grave had to be dug up once again. When the coffin was lifted out and opened, the townspeople shuddered when they saw what lay inside. The corpse, it seemed, had got his new shoes back. There they were, on his feet, just as before. Of Rabbie Heckspeckle, however, there was no sign, apart from a piece of his shirt, which the corpse held in its pallid, decaying fingers.

Rabbie Heckspeckle was never seen again. The people of Selkirk were left to wonder, with fear in their hearts, what had happened to the cobbler at the hands of the ghostly stranger.

Ghost: Natalie
Place: *The White Dove Hotel, Aberdeen*
Date: Various

The White Dove Hotel in Aberdeen has been demolished, but the story of its haunting is well known.

One of the guests at the hotel had fallen sick. The woman was an actress, apparently, and her name was Miss Vining. She had become quite ill shortly after her arrival at the hotel. When a doctor was called to examine her, he decided that she was suffering from a rare disease, thought to be tropical in origin. The patient's condition grew worse and was causing concern. The doctor pronounced that she required constant care, so a nurse was called in to attend to her.

The nurse noticed a strange, eerie atmosphere in the room when she arrived, but put it down to the condition of her patient and the stormy weather raging outside. Miss Vining was too ill to speak, so the nurse spent some time attending to practicalities, monitoring her patient's condition and assuring her comfort, and then settled in a chair beside the bed to wait quietly beside her, reading.

After a while something made the nurse look up. Her eyes passed over her sleeping patient and came to rest on another chair at the opposite side of the bed. There, seated quietly, was the figure of a small girl. It was hard to make out the child's features, for she was wearing a large hat. The first reaction of the nurse was to protest with the child: how and why had she come into the sickroom without permission? But as the nurse rose from her seat, the child raised a hand to motion her back. The child seemed to be possessed of some strange power, for the nurse found that she could not move any farther. The nurse then tried to turn to her patient, who was showing some signs of distress. Once again, she found she was unable to move. It was a very strange feeling. She sat back in her chair, and although she had not been feeling tired at all, she could not prevent herself from falling asleep.

When the nurse woke up, the child had gone, but Miss Vining was delirious with a raging fever and needed attention. The nurse, thankfully, was now able to rise and care for her. When morning came, the nurse told the doctor about the child who had been in the room. He gave strict instructions that Miss Vining was too ill to be visited by anyone. The following night, he said, the nurse was to lock the door behind her when she took up her post by her patient's bedside.

The nurse did as she was told. The next night she made absolutely sure that she was alone in the room with Miss Vining. Then she locked the door firmly behind her, ready to start her shift.

Miss Vining was comfortable and peaceful, so the nurse sat by her bed for a while. She nodded off for a few moments, and when she stirred she saw the little girl in the room, just as before. Once again, when she tried to shoo the child away, the little girl raised her hand and the nurse was unable to do a thing. She was virtually paralysed.

Miss Vining's condition grew markedly worse, and the nurse was distressed to see this, but the child still held her under some sort of spell. There was nothing she could do to help her patient. At length, after what seemed to be an interminable time, watching helplessly as Miss Vining tossed and moaned in her delirium, the nurse saw the child rise from her seat and make for the window.

Finding that she was free to move, the nurse made a grab for the little girl, knocking her hat from her head. To her horror, she saw that the girl's face was that of a corpse. She was an Indian child and had obviously been very beautiful, but it was clear that her throat had been cut and now her face was twisted in death. The nurse fainted.

When the nurse came round, the child had gone and Miss Vining was dead. Afterwards, when hotel staff were packing up the belongings of the deceased, it is said that they found a photograph of a child, which the nurse identified as being the same child she had seen in ghostly form. On the back of the photograph were written these words: 'Natalie. May God forgive us.' Nobody could find out any more, for after the death of Miss Vining, the little girl was never seen again.

Ghosts: Battle of Nechtanesmere Survivors
Place: *Nechtanesmere, by Dunnichen Hill, Angus, Scotland*
Date: From the Late 7th Century Onwards

The ghosts of Nechtanesmere date from very early Scottish history. The Battle of Nechtanesmere, by Dunnichen Hill in Angus, was fought in the late 7th century between the Northumbrians and the Picts. The Picts, led by Brude mac Bile, were victorious over the Northumbrian men of King Ecgfrith. The battle put an end to the Northumbrians' progress northwards. King Ecgfrith and most of his men were killed.

One report of haunting close to the site of the Battle of Nechtanesmere dates from 1950, when a middle-aged woman, Miss E. F. Smith, had a strange experience while driving home from Brechin to Letham one night. It was January, and snow had fallen. Miss Smith's car skidded on the newly fallen snow and went off the road into a ditch. Unable to get her car back on the road without assistance, Miss Smith had no alternative but to walk the remaining 7 miles of her journey.

She was nearly at Letham when she caught sight of flaming torchlights in the distance. As she drew near to Dunnichen Hill, she saw men in ancient garb – brown tunics and leggings – wandering around in a field nearby. They kept their eyes to the ground, where the bodies of other men lay. The figures were oblivious of Miss Smith as they moved silently around. It would appear that Miss Smith was witness to the ghostly figures of survivors of the Battle of Nechtanesmere searching the battlefield for their dead and dying comrades.

Ghost: A Newlywed Bride, Name Not Known
Place: ***Braemar Castle***
Date: 1987

The castle at Braemar is still used as a residence by the Farquharson family who have lived there since it was built in 1628. During 1987 one pair of guests saw the ghost that haunts the castle. The ghost takes the form of a young blonde woman and is said to be that of a newlywed bride who spent her wedding night in the castle during the 19th century.

It is said that the young woman took her life when she awoke on the morning after her wedding to find that her spouse was not in their chamber or anywhere else in the castle. She assumed that her new husband had been so dissatisfied with the marriage that he had abandoned her. So distraught was the young wife that she threw herself from the window of their bridal chamber. But her husband did not leave her; he had joined his friends in the early morning to hunt game. Not long afterwards he returned to find a great commotion in the courtyard of the castle and learned the awful truth.

The poor woman's ghost is said to return to visit, or maybe to warn, any honeymooning couple who stay at the castle.

Ghost: Christian Nimmo, the 'White Lady'
Place: *Corstorphine, Edinburgh*
Date: From the 17th Century Onwards

Nothing remains of Corstorphine Castle apart from the ancient dovecot that stands near the east end of Dovecot Road in Corstorphine, a suburb on the northwest side of Edinburgh. The castle was destroyed in the 18th century. Beside the dovecot once stood an old, gnarled sycamore tree, the last of an avenue of trees that led westwards towards the castle. The tree, diseased and fragile, was carefully preserved as a well-loved historical landmark by the Corstorphine Trust until it finally gave way during a storm on the night of 26 December 1998. The trunk snapped in two leaving nothing standing but a jagged stump.

The story of the Corstorphine sycamore and the 'White Lady' who haunts it, is familiar to all in the district, young and old alike.

In the 17th century, when Corstorphine Castle was still standing, it was inhabited by the Forrester family, who owned most of the land in the surrounding area. The laird at the time, one James Forrester, was a charismatic man, whose overindulgence in alcohol and whose liking for a pretty face and curving figure were well known but, on the whole, forgiven on account of his great charm.

Laird James became embroiled in a passionate affair with a married woman, Christian Nimmo. The lovers were forced to meet in secret, which must have added both a great deal of excitement and a certain amount of tension to the liaison. One such meeting, in the shadows of the dovecot beside the sycamore tree, was destined to be their final. It began with a passionate embrace and ended in a murder.

When Christian Nimmo arrived at their appointed meeting place, Sir James was not there, but Christian knew his habits all too well and sent one of her servants to the Black Bull Inn nearby to seek him out. The laird was found in the inn, as anticipated, and he finally came to meet her by the sycamore tree. He had been drinking heavily, and Christian Nimmo, angered by his inconsiderate and objectionable behaviour, began to quarrel with him. The dispute swiftly took on frightening proportions until suddenly, seized by a fit of uncontrollable rage, the lady pulled her lover's sword from its scabbard by his side and plunged it into him. She escaped from justice initially but was eventually hunted down and taken to meet her end at the hands of the executioner. Her ghost, dressed all in white, haunts the area around the dovecot still, the bloody sword in her hand giving evidence of the dreadful consequences of her temper.

Ghost: A Nun, Possibly Marie Larre
Place: *Borley Rectory, Essex*
Date: 1900 and Since

Borley Rectory was described in the title of the book by Harry Price as *The Most Haunted House in England*. Other notable observers are rather more reticent. For example, John and Anne Spencer describe the house as the most 'investigated and publicised haunted house in England' and Sarah Hapgood describes it as the 'world's most written about haunted house.' Eddie Burks and Gillian Cribbs suggest that the title is likely to be given to a different house every year.

Despite these obvious reservations as to the house's pre-eminence in the field, there seems to be little dispute that there have been several mysterious happenings in and around both it and the neighbouring church. Mentioned here are just some of them.

On 28 July 1900, Ethel Bull, the granddaughter of the rector who had built the house and daughter of the current rector, was walking in the rectory garden with three of her sisters when she saw the figure of a female dressed in a nun's habit. Over the years there were several similar sightings by the sisters and other people who lived in the house. The figure had a distinctly ghostly appearance: it moved in a strange manner, seeming to float over the ground; no clear features could be seen, and it disappeared when approached. The Reverend Henry Bull became so interested in the ghost that he built a summerhouse near to the path where she was usually seen. The path became known as the Nun's Walk. There are several explanations. Some say that the rectory was built on the site of a 13th-century (sometimes 14th-century) monastery and that one of the monks had fallen in love with a nun from a nearby convent. Before they could run away together, however, their liaison was discovered and the nun was killed by her colleagues. The ghost is said to be that of the murdered nun. Another story is that, in 1667, a nun was forced to abandon her vows and marry one of the Waldegrave sons who lived at Borley Manor, and that she was strangled on the site of the rectory. Others say that she was a French nun called Marie Larre who had run away from France with her lover but soon after they arrived at Borley, they had

had a violent argument. Such was the intensity of their dispute that the nun's lover killed her, either by accident or intention. He is said to have buried her body in the cellar of the house that stood on the site at that time. This particular story was lent credence when the jawbone and skull of a woman were found on the site along with some religious artefacts.

Over the years the nun (sometimes called the Grey Nun) was seen by many other people. Mr and Mrs Cooper, who were in the employ of the Bulls between 1916 and 1920, claim to have seen a nun-like figure entering the house. During their time there they also witnessed other strange phenomena. On one occasion Mr Cooper saw a horse-drawn carriage drive swiftly into the courtyard, only to disappear into thin air just as rapidly as it had appeared.

In the early 1950s, the nun was also seen by a Mr Williams, the father-in-law of the owner, Mr Bacon, and on a different occasion by the owner's son, Terry. Significantly, he reported that the ghostly figure seemed to be moving along some distance above the ground. Maybe the ground had sunk since the nun originally walked that way. The nun was also seen by a young girl in 1949 and a man in 1951. Both sightings were in the vicinity of the Nun's Walk.

After the Bulls left the rectory, the post was taken up by the Reverend Lionel Foyster and his wife Marianne. This was in 1930. At about the same time Harry Price, a famous psychic investigator, became their acquaintance and carried out a series of investigations into the phenomena. This was the start of a long association that Price had with the building, lasting until his death in 1948. Marianne seemed to be particularly susceptible to psychic phenomena because soon after they arrived she started getting messages calling for help, written on scraps of paper and even scrawled on the walls. She also heard voices calling for help. It was only when she was violently assaulted by an invisible assailant that the couple decided enough was enough and quit the house.

The Reverend Alfred Henning was the next incumbent of the post. In July 1937, during an investigation conducted by one of Price's associates, Mark Kerr-Pearse, the Reverend and his wife Eva, gathered in a room adjacent to the garden. The house had been secured so that entry was only possible from the garden into the room in which they waited. As they waited in silence, they all heard someone elsewhere within the house although only the three of them were known to be present at the time. They clearly heard a door being opened and footsteps moving down the passage towards the room in which they sat transfixed. As the sounds approached the door of their room, one of the group pulled it open suddenly to reveal absolutely nothing!

Many other phenomena are reported in Price's book, *The Most Haunted House In England*; voices, writing on walls of mysterious provenance, unusual smells, objects being hurled across rooms and lamps being overturned. One of these incidents is said to have caused the fire that destroyed the rectory in 1939. At the time the house was owned by Captain H. Gregson and on 27th February, less than a year after he had moved into the house, an oil lamp is said to have fallen over of its own accord and started the fire that gutted the house. As the locals looked on helplessly it is reported that they noticed the figure of a nun in an upstairs bedroom window.

The destruction of the rectory did not bring the haunting to an end, however. As noted above, the nun herself was seen at least twice after that but other strange events have been witnessed. During the Second World War, because of the blackout regulations, no lights could be left burning at night. The church lamp, that in normal times was left burning overnight, was extinguished and the church door was locked. On several occasions, those opening up the church in the morning found that the wick of the lamp had been removed. Thinking it to be the work of mice or birds a heavy plate was placed over the lamp but the next day the plate was found smashed on the stone floor. Price reports that he was standing, along with several others, when they each heard the sound of approaching footsteps, but when they looked for the person no one was to be found. On other occasions the organ was heard playing but on investigation, the lid of the instrument was found to be locked. During the war, a local man, Herbert Mayes heard the sound of hooves as he drove past the site of the old rectory and ARP wardens were constantly being called to extinguish lights in the gutted building

There have been those who have downplayed the importance of Borley Rectory over the years, especially the role played by Harry Price in reporting the strange events. In *The Haunting of Borley Rectory* written by Eric Dingwall, Kathleen Goldney and Trevor Hall they practically accuse him of fraud. Despite these reservations there is no doubt that there are too many sightings by him and others to dismiss them all as being fabricated.

Ghost: James Ogilvie, 3rd Earl of Seafield
Place: *Cullen, Banffshire, Scotland*
Date: 18th Century Onwards

Cullen House is situated close to the fishing village of Cullen in Banffshire, on the northeast coast of Scotland. The house and its lands have been the property of the Earls of Seafield for more than 200 years. The ghost that haunts Cullen House is thought to be that of James Ogilvie, 3rd Earl of Seafield. James was known to suffer from a severely disabling form of mental illness and was often seized by fits of an uncontrollable nature, during which he was said to be a danger both to himself and to others. When one of these fits was imminent, his staff, who could recognise the signs, would do their best to secure him and keep him from harm.

On one occasion, however, they were unsuccessful. The 'Mad Earl', as he was known, had a particularly violent attack, in the course of which there was a struggle between him and a very close friend. The friend was killed. When the Earl regained his wits and realised what he had done, he was completely overcome with despair and anguish. So distressed was he that he took his own life. His ghost is said to wander the site even now.

Ghost: (Possibly) Max Perutz
Place: *Peterhouse College, Cambridge, England*
Date: Between April and November 1997

This is a story of events that happened recently and were reported in *The Independent* newspaper by their reporter Kathy Marks and on the radio. The ghost was seen in the combination room or refectory (where the students and dons gather for meals) of the famous Peterhouse College, Cambridge. This is the college that is said to be featured in Tom Sharpe's novel, *Porterhouse Blue*.

When Matthew Speller and his colleague, Paul Davies, reported that they had seen a spirit inhabiting the 600-year-old, oak-panelled, combination room they were treated to a certain amount of light-hearted ragging from fellow butlers, and scepticism from the rest of the college community. That scepticism was moderated, however, when the senior bursar, Andrew Murrison, who was formerly a sceptic himself, also witnessed the phantom. This witness was not so easy to dismiss. He was described by Dr James Carleton Paget, a divinity don at the college, as a 'hard-headed financier, who is a creature of the Enlightenment rather than the pulpit.'

The two butlers described what they saw as 'a cigar-shaped, person-sized apparition' that moved slowly above the ground towards the bay window. 'When we told the fellows about it they treated it as bit of fun,' Mr Speller complained.

Mr Murrison described the event that he witnessed when he went into the dimly lit combination room like this: 'I became aware of a presence in a corner of the room. At first I thought it was Max Perutz, one of the Nobel Prize winners, because it was smallish, slightly built and balding. It was wearing a wide collar, like a pilgrim, and seemed to be holding a large hat. I moved closer to get a better look. I wasn't frightened in the slightest; I was more concerned about frightening it away. It was very benign. After a few seconds, it quietly disappeared. The room was very cold, although a fire was still burning in the grate. It was a quite extraordinary experience. I didn't mention it to the other fellows for a while. I'm supposed to be a financial administrator, not some nutcase who goes around seeing ghosts.'

The dean of the college, the Rev Graham Ward, was said to be considering an exorcism of the combination room by holding a requiem mass, but such a response was thought by some to be 'over the top.' Andrew Murrison was in the forefront of those pooh-poohing the ceremony. He thought it to be 'a load of mumbo-jumbo'. He went on, 'Anyway, he's not causing anyone any harm. It's not as if women undergraduates are throwing themselves out of windows.'

Much talk at the college these days is centred on just whose spirit it is. In a place with such an august history, going back to its foundation in 1284, and populated over the years by formidably intellectual men (women were only admitted in 1985), there is no shortage of candidates. One of the favourite choices of the historians that inhabit the college is Francis Dawes. He was a former bursar who strung himself up following the election of an extremely unpopular master of the college. No doubt he could not stand the thought of working with the odious man. Anyway, he went out with a bang (or at least a clang) because he tied himself to a bell rope in 1789. Other candidates include James Mason, the actor, Kingsley Amis, the author and even James Clark Maxwell, the 19th-century scientist. This last is said to be keen to demonstrate the latest of his many discoveries in his chosen field, electromagnetism. Clearly the fellows of Peterhouse are treating the ghost with more than a touch of cynicism.

Lord Dacre, the historian, a former master of the college, comments, 'I was aware of some poltergeists in human form, but I never heard of any less substantial apparitions. Some people, even fellows of Peterhouse, will believe anything.'

Ghosts: The Pluckley Village Ghosts
Place: *Pluckley, Kent*
Date: Various

Pluckley is regarded as the most haunted village in England. A gypsy's ghost, wrapped in a shawl and smoking a pipe, is often seen near a bridge. Nearby are the shattered remnants of an old oak tree where a highwayman, run through and pinned to the tree by a sword, manifests himself. The whole bloody episode is enacted in silence.

Various buildings in the village are haunted. In one of them, the Church of Saint Nicholas, the ghost of Lady Dering appears. She died some hundreds of years ago and her husband had buried her in a beautiful dress with a red rose on her breast. Her coffin, lead-lined and airtight, was placed in a second one and both of these in a third, all lead lined. The three coffins were finally placed in one of oak and she was buried in the family vault. She walks in the churchyard some evenings with the red rose, unwithered, on her breast. Strange lights have been seen in the windows of the Dering Chapel and a woman's voice has been heard in the churchyard. A monk's ghost haunts a house named Greystones and the voice of a former owner of another house, Rose Court, is often heard there as she calls her dogs. Even the old mill is haunted by the ghost of a miller searching for his lost love by the light of the moon.

Ghost: Dunty Porteous
Place: *Spedlins Tower, Dumfries and Galloway, Scotland*
Date: From the End of the 17th Century

Spedlins Tower in Dumfries and Galloway was, once upon a time, haunted by a particularly hungry ghost. At the end of the 17th century, Spedlins was the property of Sir Alexander Jardine, brother-in-law of the 1st Duke of Queensberry, William Douglas.

One of the laird's tenants, a miller by the name of Dunty Porteous, fell out of favour with his master. The laird, having right of pit and gallows, apprehended Porteous and took him to Spedlins. Porteous was locked in the dungeon of the tower to await judgment and suitable punishment for his misdemeanours. It was a grim place to sit and ponder one's fate – an underground pit with no light source. The only access to the dungeon was through a trapdoor. No sooner had Dunty Porteous been put away than Sir Alexander had to leave Spedlins to attend to some business in the capital city. He would have to deal with Dunty on his return.

Unfortunately, when the laird set off for Edinburgh, he took the key of the dungeon with him. In his absence, it would appear that either Dunty was forgotten about or nobody thought to break down the door of the dungeon and come to his aid. Whatever was the case, Dunty was abandoned, with tragic consequences.

Some time later, when Sir Alexander finally returned to Spedlins and the dungeon was unlocked, Dunty was found to have died of starvation. It is said that in the agonies of his dreadful hunger, the poor prisoner had chewed at his own hands. Any regret that Sir Alexander felt for what had happened was clearly not great enough, for as soon as the spirit of Dunty Porteous was released from the confines of the dreadful dungeon it started to run riot at Spedlins.

Dunty's ghost was persistent and troublesome, running through Spedlins Tower screaming out in pain and hunger, crying for mercy and food. The spirit would give no peace to the Jardine family. Eventually, a chaplain was summoned to try to exorcise the ghost. His efforts were not entirely successful, for the ghost would not go away.

Nevertheless, after a concerted effort, the minister and the family were able to confine Dunty's raging spirit to the dungeon with the help of a Bible that was left at the site.

In time, the binding of the Bible became worn and in need of repair, so it was sent to Edinburgh to be rebound. No sooner had the Bible left the premises than Dunty's ghost was on the loose again, tormenting the laird and his family as before. The Bible had to be repaired and returned with all possible haste in order to confine the ghost once again.

The Jardine family eventually moved from Spedlins. The ghost of Dunty followed them, but the Bible was moved too and Dunty remained subdued.

Ghost: Laird Pringle
Place: *Buckholme Tower, near Galashiels, Scotland*
Date: Since the 17th Century

Buckholme Tower, now in ruins, stands close to the Border town of Galashiels. Three centuries ago, it was the home of a terrible and tyrannical man, Laird Pringle. He had a violent temper and a sadistic nature. So abusive was he to his wife and son that they were forced to flee from Buckholme, leaving the laird to live alone, apart from the long-suffering servants on whom he vented his spleen with startling regularity.

As well as indulging in his fondness for large quantities of drink, Laird Pringle is said to have spent much of his time hunting. It would seem that blood sports were one way he used to express the cruel side of his nature. One night, however, he was offered the chance to hunt not animals, but humans.

The 1680s were years of much bloodshed in Scotland. It was the time of the Covenanters, strong Presbyterians who wanted to worship as they pleased, contrary to the laws passed by the parliament in England. Forced to meet in secret, they were constantly being hounded by the English Redcoat forces, driven out of their hiding places and punished most cruelly.

Pringle hated the Covenanters, and when he was called upon to assist a band of Redcoats intent on raiding a secret Covenanters' meeting on the moor near his home, he was delighted to help. He called his ferocious hunting hounds to heel and set off on horseback.

The Redcoats were too late. Someone must have warned the Covenanters, for their meeting had broken up and they had fled. The 'hunting' expedition was not entirely fruitless, however, for in the course of their search, the troops came upon one old man and his son, hiding nearby. The old man had fallen and injured his back and had been unable to escape, so his son had stayed by his side. The pair could not deny that they were Covenanters, for to do so was to deny God.

Pringle would have killed the two of them then and there, but the officer in charge of the Redcoat troops prevented him from doing so. The captives were to face a proper trial, he insisted. Besides, they were of more use alive than dead, since with a little 'persuasion' they might be induced to share some useful information with their captors. Pringle was to take them back to Buckholme Tower and hold them there to await further questioning and subsequent trial.

Pringle dragged the two men back to Buckholme and threw them into the cellar. The laird's sadism and thirst for blood were, however, stronger than any respect he might have had for the law. Later that night, his servants heard him lurching drunkenly down to the cellar. They listened with great apprehension.

Sounds of a scuffle could be heard, then crashes and thumps, roars and screams of agony. Too terrified of their master to take any action, the servants could only listen outside the door and wait. The screaming stopped. The laird stumbled out of the cellar, covered in blood and triumphant.

'Swine should be treated as swine!' he raged, shoving his men aside as he made his way unsteadily upstairs again. When he reached the entrance hall, he was met by a local woman standing at the door. She was the old man's wife and had come to beg for the release of her husband and son. Laird Pringle dragged her down to the cellar and threw open the door to reveal what was inside. There, suspended on the wall, iron hooks through their jaws just like two slaughtered pigs, were the man and the boy.

Pringle watched with obvious relish as the woman subsided into hysterical sobbing. Then, after a few moments, she composed herself and turned to face the laird. She cursed him for what he had done. Just as his hounds had hunted down the Covenanters, his awful deeds would come back like the Hounds of Hell and hunt him down for eternity.

For the first time in a long time, Pringle was really frightened. For the remainder of his life he was tormented by visions of ghostly hounds, their teeth bared, saliva dripping from their jaws as they moved in for the attack. After his death, people began to hear the strangest sounds at night – the baying of hounds on the hunt and the agonised screams of a man in fear for his life.

Although the rest of Buckholme Tower lies in ruins, the cellar remains. Sometimes at night, it is said, you can still hear the noise of dogs and of Laird Pringle's tormented screams.

Ghost: Rev C. Pritchard
Place: *London, England*
Date: *c.*1850

In his last year at school, Spencer Nairne was strolling through Clapham, London, with his friend Henry Stone when they saw the headmaster of their school walking briskly towards them. As he drew near the two boys raised their hats in the manner of the day and the Rev Pritchard returned their salute. He seemed to be distracted and did not speak.

A few minutes later they were surprised to see the headmaster approaching again. The boys again greeted the headmaster who acted as if nothing strange had happened. They discussed the event but could find no rational explanation. He could only have been there by doubling back at speed in order to get in front of them again, not a very likely occurrence.

Ghost: The 'Radiant Boy'
Place: *Somewhere in the North of Ireland*
Date: Late 18th Century

Robert Stewart, Viscount Castlereagh, was the son of the Marquis of Londonderry. Educated at Armagh and, briefly, Cambridge, he entered politics and became Chief Secretary for Ireland, then later Minister of War in the Westminster government. In 1822, he committed suicide. As a politician, he had made himself greatly disliked and it was said there was a 'shout of exultation' as his funeral procession made its way to Westminster Abbey.

This story is taken from John H. Ingram's *The Haunted Homes and Family Legends of Great Britain*, published in the 1880s; Ingram himself got it from an earlier compilation, the *Ghost Stories* of Mrs Crowe, published earlier in the 19th century. The story is said to originate with Castlereagh's own family, describing an early stage of his career, when he was Captain Robert Stewart, a member of the Dublin parliament, and was out hunting, somewhere in the north of Ireland.

He was fond of sport, and one day the pursuit of game carried him so far that he lost his way. The weather, too, had become very rough, and in this strait he presented himself at the door of a gentleman's house, and, sending in his card, requested shelter for the night. The hospitality of the Irish country gentry is proverbial. The master of the house received him warmly and said he feared he could not make him as comfortable as he would have wished, his house being full of visitors already. Added to which, some strangers, driven by the inclemency of the night, had sought shelter before him; but that to such accommodation as he could give he was heartily welcome. Whereupon the master of the house called his butler, and, committing his guest to his good offices, told the butler he must put Captain Stewart up somewhere, and do the best he could for him. There was no lady, the gentleman being a widower.

Captain Stewart found the house crammed. And a very good party it was. His host invited him to stay, and promised him good shooting if he would prolong his visit a few days. The Captain thought himself extremely fortunate to have fallen into such pleasant quarters.

At length, after an agreeable evening, they all retired to bed, and the butler conducted him to a large room almost divested of furniture, but with a blazing peat fire in the grate, and a shakedown bed on the floor, which was composed of cloaks and other heterogeneous materials. Nevertheless, to the tired limbs of Captain Stewart, who had had a hard day's shooting, it looked very inviting. However, before he lay down, he thought it advisable to take off some of the fire, which was blazing up the chimney in an alarming manner. Having done this, he stretched himself upon his makeshift bed, and soon fell asleep.

He believed he had slept about a couple of hours when he awoke suddenly, and was startled by such a vivid light in the room that he thought it was on fire; but on turning to look at the grate saw that the fire was out, though it was from the chimney that the light proceeded.

He sat up in bed, trying to discover what it was, when he perceived, gradually disclosing itself, the form of a beautiful naked boy, surrounded by a dazzling radiance. The boy looked at him earnestly, and then the vision faded, and all was dark.

Captain Stewart, so far from supposing what he had seen to be of a spiritual nature, had no doubt that the host, or the visitors, had been amusing themselves at his expense, and trying to frighten him. Accordingly, he felt indignant at the liberty; and on the following morning, when he appeared at breakfast, he took care to evince his displeasure by the reserve of his demeanour, and by announcing his intention to depart immediately. The host expostulated, reminding him of his promise to stay and shoot. Captain Stewart coldly excused himself, and at length, the gentleman, seeing something was wrong, took him aside and pressed for an explanation; whereupon Captain Stewart, without entering into any particulars, said he had been made the victim of a sort of practical joking that he thought quite unwarrantable with a stranger. The gentleman considered this not impossible amongst a parcel of thoughtless young men, and appealed to them to make an apology; but one and all, on their honour, denied the impeachment.

Suddenly a thought seemed to strike him: he clapped his hand to his forehead, uttered an exclamation, and rang the bell.

'Hamilton,' said he to the butler, 'where did Captain Stewart sleep last night?'

'Well, sir,' replied the man, in an apologetic tone, 'you know every place was full – the gentlemen were lying on the floor three or four in a room – so I gave him *the boy's room*; but I lit a blazing fire to keep *him* from coming out.'

'You were very wrong,' said the host. 'You know I have positively forbidden you to put anyone there, and have taken the furniture out of the room to ensure it's not being occupied.'

Then retiring with Captain Stewart, he informed him very gravely of the nature of the phenomenon he had seen; and at length, being pressed for further information, he confessed that there existed a tradition in his family that whoever the 'radiant boy' appeared to would rise to the summit of power, and when he reached the climax, would die a violent death.

'And I must say,' he added, 'the records that I have kept of his appearance go to confirm this persuasion.'

In the years after this experience, Stewart's career indeed took him to the summit of political life – almost – for he never became prime minister. Nevertheless, it was while still in office that, believing himself to be blackmailed for his homosexuality, he committed suicide at his house in England.

The vision of the 'radiant boy' seems to have been an unusual one in Ireland, though it has been recorded from places in England and Germany. It is not always seen as a portent. Sometimes it is related to the murder of a child in the house. Clearly it is a phenomenon of great power.

Ghost: Sir Walter Raleigh
Place: *Byward Tower, Tower of London, England*
Date: Many Times Since 1618

Raleigh epitomised the spirit of the Elizabethan era. As a courtier, soldier, sailor, poet, historian and chemist he was at the forefront of pioneering the nascent British Empire, founding many of the American plantations. He was also an MP for several constituencies in the West Country, which was his home. Raleigh was a great favourite of Elizabeth I, and mounted several successful expeditions to the West Indies that conferred great honour and wealth on the Queen's court. Along with all his other accomplishments, he is credited with the arrival of tobacco and the potato on England's shores.

The court, however, was a hotbed of intrigue and Raleigh was replaced in the Queen's favour by Essex. This was probably the result of Raleigh's marriage to one of the Queen's Maids of Honour, Elizabeth Throgmorton. Queen Elizabeth was notoriously jealous, and Raleigh was ostracised from the court and eventually thrown into the Tower in July 1592. He was too useful to the Queen, however to remain incarcerated and in 1596, having been returned to her favour, he took a leading part, with Essex, in the Cadiz expedition.

Shortly after the accession of James I, in 1603, Raleigh was to renew his acquaintance with the Tower when he was charged with plotting to place Arabella Stuart on the throne. He was sentenced to death but had a last-minute reprieve, and lived on with his wife and son in the Bloody Tower until 1616, when he was released in order to lead another expedition.

On that expedition he became embroiled in a conflict with England's old enemies, the Spanish. However, by this time, relations with the Spanish had returned to near normality and when he returned, the Spanish Ambassador demanded recompense. The Lord Chancellor, Bacon, laid against him the old charge of treason, and he was taken from the Tower to the Old Palace Yard, Westminster, where he was executed.

By the time he eventually met his death, Raleigh had spent many years in the Tower. During this period he would have been quite well treated by the standards of the time. He would have had his family around him and even been allowed servants. He would have had free access to the grounds of the Tower and was probably on good terms with his gaolers, chatting with them as they went about their duties.

The ghost of Sir Walter has been reported many times over the years. In 1983, one of the Beefeaters was sitting in the guardroom when he heard the handle of the door being rattled. He put it down to the wind that was blowing strongly that February night, but looked up anyway and was astonished to see a figure dressed in Elizabethan garb looking into the room. What is more, the figure was dressed exactly like Sir Walter Raleigh in the portrait hanging in the Bloody Tower. The figure, which looked quite substantial, remained for a few moments before disappearing. The ghost was again seen, this time by another yeoman some months later.

Ghost: The Rat of Howth
Place: *Howth Castle, Ireland*
Date: From the 17th Century Onwards

The rat of Howth, sometimes said to be a white rat, was reputed to appear when evil threatened the House of St Laurence. Its first appearance was in the 17th century, to a Lord of Howth.

On a stormy winter evening, a ship was seen in difficulties in Howth Bay. Thrown on the rocks by an easterly gale, she broke up while the watchers on shore could do nothing to reach her. Every soul on board was presumed to have drowned, but, in the morning, a woman was found clinging to some wreckage that had been washed up on to the beach. More dead than alive, she was brought to Howth Castle, and cared for.

When the Earl of Howth came to see her, he was struck by her pallor and her beauty. Once she had recovered from the ordeal, he pressed her to stay on in the castle, and she did. Soon he was madly in love with her, but although he pressed her often to marry him, she always refused, and begged him to look for some other bride.

At last, driven by vexation and frustration, he did so, and found a bride from a nearby family. The lady from the sea gave him a ribbon, its material interwoven with strange words and signs, and asked him to wear it always on his wrist, in memory of her. Soon afterwards she left Howth Castle, and nobody knew where she had gone.

The Earl's new bride was intrigued by the ribbon, which he wore night and day. One night, soon after they were married, she undid it from his wrist as he lay sleeping in their chamber, and took it over to the fire, to look at it more closely. By ill luck she dropped it; it was sucked into the flames and immediately burned. When Lord Howth discovered its loss, he was very distressed.

'Ill fortune will come of this,' he said.

Not long after that, while a feast was going on in the castle hall, the dogs of the place chased a rat into the room. The hunted beast sprang up on the table, right in front of the Lord of Howth. Its posture and expression seemed so pleading that he saved it from the dogs. From then on, much to the distaste of his wife and family, the rat became his pet. Wherever he went, even if he did not bring it, the rat seemed to follow him. Even to France, where he went with his brother on a tour. The rat had been left behind, but as they sat by the fire in a Marseilles hotel, it appeared, soaked and limping, as if it had travelled a great way. Exasperated, his brother took a heavy poker and, before he could be stopped, killed the animal.

'You have murdered me!' cried the Earl.

That same night, he died. But the rat still haunts the castle.

Ghost: The Ringcroft Ghost
Place: *Ringcroft of Stocking, Dumfries and Galloway, Scotland*
Date: 1695

These paranormal disturbances are documented and attested in a 19-page report, prepared at the time by the ministers of five adjacent parishes, by the lairds of Colline and Millhouse, and other responsible witnesses.

The dwelling at Ringcroft had long had a reputation for strange happenings. The mysterious occurrences related here began in February 1695, and although there were numerous children in the house, they were all under observation at the time and could not have been responsible for any of the events that took place. Initial disturbances were at night and outside the house. The occupier of the house, Andrew Mackie, found one evening that all his cows had been led from their sheds and that their ropes had been cut. The following night the same thing happened and, even worse, one of the cows had been tied to a roof beam, feet barely in contact with the floor. A stool and blanket were found to have been made into a shape which roughly resembled a human, stones were thrown, although mainly at night and never on Sundays, and various pot hooks vanished from the house only to be found, days later, in places which had already been searched. One day, a large quantity of peat was mysteriously brought into the house and set alight. The stone throwing now took place even on Sundays and was at it worst when the household was at prayer.

Peace briefly returned after a month when the disturbances stopped. However, the lull lasted for only seven days and then the family had its life disrupted more violently than before. There were strange knocking noises throughout the house, stone throwing and, this time, various members of the family were struck. Children had the bedclothes ripped off their beds and people were struck and badly beaten by some unidentifiable presence. While the family prayed, a voice was often heard to say, at the end of each sentence, 'Hush. Hush.' The dog, hearing the strange voice, ran to the door barking. In addition fires were started, pieces of burning peat were thrown about while the family prayed, balls of fire fell in and about the house and strange groans and whistling noises were heard.

The house had been built 28 years before and every person who had lived there was questioned by a local magistrate. These inquiries led to the discovery of human remains buried just outside the house and it was assumed that they were those of the victim of an unknown murder. As it was suspected that the disturbances were caused by the unquiet spirit of the corpse, five local ministers held a service of exorcism but they had hardly begun when stones were thrown, seemingly from nowhere, at the ministers and around the house. For the next few days the disturbances continued and then a cloud-like black mist was seen in a corner of a room. This gradually increased in size until it filled the house. The next day, 1 May 1695, the disturbances stopped for good.

Ghost: Charles B. Rosma
Place: *Hydesville, New York State, USA*
Date: 1848

In 1843, Charles B. Rosma was murdered in a house in Hydesville. He was an itinerant pedlar who had spent a night in the house and had been killed for the sum of 500 dollars that he had with him. Lucretia Pulver, who was a servant of the tenant, Mr Bell, said later that she had left the house when Mr Rosma was there but there was no sign of him on her return shortly afterwards. She suspected from Mr Bell's demeanour that he had murdered him.

The same house was occupied in 1848 by a family named Fox: James, a farmer, his wife Margaret and their daughters Margareta and Kate. They had moved in during December 1847 and it came to their notice that the previous tenant, Michael Weekman, had heard loud knocking noises which he could not explain. Soon they heard them too.

As March drew to a close, bangings began to keep the Foxes awake, but since the weather was stormy they thought nothing of them. Then, on 31 March, the family went to bed earlier than usual to try to make up for their lost sleep. Mr Fox tried the shutters to make sure that they were firmly closed and his daughters observed that as he shook them, the noise was responded to as though by an echo. Kate clicked her fingers and said 'Mr Splitfoot, do as I do' and rapping sounds imitated her, but since the next day was 1 April the children thought that their parents were playing a joke on them. Mrs Fox was so disturbed by the mysterious noises that she decided to test her children, suspecting them of mischief. She later wrote, 'I then thought that I could put a test that no one in the place could answer. I asked the noise to rap my different children's ages, successively. Instantly, each one of my children's ages was given correctly, pausing between them sufficiently long to individualise them until the seventh child, at which a longer pause was made, and then three more emphatic little raps were given corresponding to the age of the little one that died . . . ' She then asked 'Is it a spirit? If it is, make two raps.' Two bangs loud enough to shake the whole house answered this question and on being asked if the ghost was an 'injured spirit' the noises were repeated. Subsequent questions led to the information that the spirit was that of a man murdered in the house who had left behind a wife and five children.

As witnesses, the Foxes asked in about 14 neighbours who included William Duesler. He, unlike the others, had the courage to go into the bedroom from which the noises emanated and took over the interrogation of the spirit, uncovering the tale of the murder five years before. The spirit foretold that the murderer would never be brought to justice. Then, on 2 April, the murdered man told Duesler that his corpse could be found buried in the cellar and the neighbours and Mr Fox went down there and dug up the floor. They reached a depth of about a metre then stopped as water started to fill the hole. Later that year, in July, the water level dropped and they tried again until, at a depth of a metre and a half, they found some human bones and some hair, decayed in quicklime. Mr Bell was accused but, as predicted by the spirit, never stood trial.

A committee was formed to investigate the strange noises but not all of its members believed that the sounds were the result of a supernatural force. It was never implied that the Fox family was responsible, but it soon became evident that the noises were only heard with the children in the house, in particular, Kate. Three investigations came to the conclusion that Margaret was not responsible for the spirit manifesting itself, and the two children were separated.

The spirit followed them both, Margaret to Auburn and Kate to Rochester, where she stayed with an older sister, Leah. People felt themselves pulled by invisible hands and the rapping noises resumed. Leah had a boarder named Calvin Brown, who scoffed at the notion of spirits until, with no one in evidence, objects were thrown at him. The cap was pulled from Mrs Fox's head and when the family prayed they were jabbed with pins.

The whole family eventually moved to Rochester in the hope that finally leaving the haunted house would bring them some relief from the torment but to no avail. The haunting continued with the noises now so loud that they could be heard miles away. Mrs Fox's hair turned white with stress and shock.

One day, a visitor asked the ghost a few questions and the reply was a thunderous barrage of knocks and bangs. Then, by means of an alphabet code, the spirit passed a message in which it said, 'Dear friends, you must proclaim this truth to the world. This is the dawning of a new era; you must not try to conceal it any longer. God will protect you and good spirits will watch over you.'

Believing that this was a sign from the spirit world, Spiritualists held their first organised meeting in the Corinthian Hall, in Rochester, on 14 November 1849.

Ghost: Lord Rossmore's Banshee
Place: *Mount Kennedy (the Home of Lord Rossmore) in the Republic of Ireland*
Date: 18th Century

A remarkable account of the banshee is given in Sir Jonah Barrington's *Personal Sketches of His Own Times*. Barrington, an Anglo-Irishman, was a lawyer and a member of the 18th-century Irish parliament. The aged Lord Rossmore became a friend of his and invited Barrington and his wife as guests to his home, Mount Kennedy. Whilst they were there, their host was summoned away to Dublin Castle. Barrington's story goes as follows:

> Towards two in the morning, I was awakened by a sound of a very extraordinary nature. I listened: it occurred first at short intervals; it resembled neither a voice nor an instrument; it was softer than any voice and wilder than any music, and seemed to float in the air. I don't know wherefore, but my heart beat forcibly; the sound became still more plaintive, till it almost died in the air; when a sudden change, as if excited by a pang, changed its tone; it seemed descending. I felt every nerve tremble; it was not a natural sound, nor could I make out the point from whence it came.

At length, I awakened Lady Barrington, who heard it as well as myself. She suggested it might be an Eolian harp, but to that instrument it bore no similitude; it was altogether a different character of sound. My wife at first appeared less affected than I, but subsequently she was more so.

We now went to a large window in our bedroom, which looked directly upon a small garden underneath. The sound seemed then obviously to ascent from a grass plot immediately below our window. It continued; Lady Barrington requested I would call up her maid, which I did, and she was evidently more affected than either of us. The sounds lasted for more than half an hour. At last, a deep, heavy, throbbing sigh seemed to come from the spot, and was shortly succeeded by a sharp, lone cry, and by the distinct exclamation thrice repeated of 'Rossmore, Rossmore, Rossmore!'

The terrified maidservant fled from the window; Barrington and his wife were hardly less alarmed. With great difficulty, he persuaded Lady Barrington to return to bed. She asked him not to mention the experience to anyone, for she was sure they would be laughed at.

But at seven in the morning, there came a knock at their bedroom door. It was Lawler, Sir Jonah's servant. All he could say was, 'Oh, sir!'

'What is the matter?' asked Barrington, but Lawler only said, 'Oh, sir! Oh, sir!' Then Lord Rossmore's footman appeared. He announced to Sir Jonah that Lord Rossmore, having returned late in the night from Dublin Castle, had gone straight to bed, apparently in good health. Then at half past two, the valet who slept in the adjoining room, heard him make a strange noise, and hurried into the room. He found Lord Rossmore dying, and before he could summon any aid, the peer was dead.

Sir Jonah Barrington's testimony is of special interest as, among the members of the 'Ascendancy', the belief in banshees, ghosts and fairies was usually somewhat derided. Priding themselves on their robust common sense, they left such beliefs to the 'native Irish'.

Ghost: Angus Roy
Place: *Victoria Terrace, Edinburgh, Scotland*
Date: Beginning of the 19th Century

The story of Angus Roy is not one of dreadful deeds or sinister happenings. It is merely sad – the story of a man tormented and bullied to despair. Angus Roy was a sailor who lived at the beginning of the 19th century, serving on a ship that sailed out of the port of Leith. His sailing career was cruelly cut short by an accident from which he was lucky to have escaped with his life. He fell from the top of the ship's mast, and, although he miraculously survived, he was terribly badly injured. One leg was left virtually useless after the accident, dragging behind him as he limped along.

Angus came to live in Edinburgh's Victoria Terrace after his discharge from the merchant navy, but far from being able to live out what remained of his life in peace, he suffered continual torment at the hands of the local children. They teased and bullied him because of his disability, following him along the street, taunting him and calling him names. It was only after his death that Angus was able to exact some sort of revenge upon his tormentors. His ghost returned to haunt the area, a harmless spectre but frightening enough to have the effect of making those who had mistreated him regret their behaviour.

It is said that the sound of Angus Roy's damaged leg scraping along the ground behind him as he makes his way along the street is still heard from time to time around the area where he lived.

Ghost: Wing Commander Roy
Place: *Egypt*
Date: Early 1940s

Egypt was the foothold in North Africa, from which the British fought the North African Campaign during the Second World War. An important part of that campaign was the bombing of the Mediterranean shipping routes used to reinforce the German troops. The convoys were heavily defended and losses were heavy.

One evening two British officers, Commander George Potter and Flight Officer Reg Lamb were enjoying a drink in the Officers' Mess. Not unusually for those times, the bar was noisy and at a nearby table there was a particularly jovial group. Potter happened to glance in the group's direction only to be confronted by a horrifying sight.

He suddenly had a vision of the death of a member of the group, that of a Wing Commander Roy. That he was dead was not in doubt, but what was strange was that only the head and shoulders were visible and he was surrounded by what appeared to be a surreal darkness. As he stared at the vision his companion tugged him back to reality. Lamb asked if he was all right and Potter described what he had seen. The two had a good idea what the vision might mean but they also realised that they had no real evidence. To describe it to Roy would merely alarm him unnecessarily.

Roy took off the next night for a mission over the Mediterranean and soon reports came back to base that his 'plane had been shot down but that the crew had managed to scramble into a life raft.' Potter was vastly relieved to hear this but later he learned that Roy had, indeed, been lost. Potter then realised that the vision he had seen was of Roy floating in the sea, supported by his lifebelt.

Ghost: Royalist Supporter
Place: *Galdenoch Tower, Galloway, Scotland*
Date: 17th Century

Galdenoch Tower dates from the 16th century. It was originally owned by nobility but after one hundred years or so it changed hands and became part of a farm.

The farmer's family at Galdenoch found themselves in the midst of the struggles of the Covenanters. The farmer was a staunch Presbyterian and proud to have a son who took up the cause against the Royalists.

However, the Covenanter forces were losing the struggle, and the son found himself on the run, hounded by Royalist troops. Taking a chance that he would find an ally therein, he knocked at the door of an isolated farm one night and asked for shelter. The owner was initially hospitable, but after some time his attitude became more menacing. When the young Covenanter decided that it would be prudent to try to leave, his host attempted to prevent his departure by force. Terrified at the prospect of being handed over to the Royalist troops, the young man fought with his captor and killed him. He then fled for his life, back to Galdenoch. No one had seen him arriving or leaving the farmhouse, so he hoped that the dreadful secret of what he had done would never be discovered.

The young man's crime did go unpunished by law, but he had not seen the end of the man whom he had killed. At Galdenoch a few nights later, the young man was roused from sleep by the ghost of his victim. The ghost made further sleep impossible for the young man by throwing objects and furniture around the room, and laughing and shrieking maniacally. The ghost then set about tormenting the rest of the family, and soon all the inhabitants of the farm spent their days in dread and their nights in fear. For weeks on end the activities of the murdered man's spirit continued relentlessly. A minister was summoned to help, and he tried to exorcise the ghost, but the ghost was having none of it. The torment went on, night after night, week after week, until, driven to distraction, the family fled.

The ghost remained at Galdenoch, and when a new family moved in it started a campaign of mischief of another sort. For most of the time it was quiet, but then, unexpectedly, it would play sudden and dangerous tricks.

The family, sitting by the fire one night, were startled into frantic activity when a peat from the fire suddenly flew out of the hearth. Within moments, one of the outbuildings in the farm was ablaze.

On another occasion the malicious ghost lifted the grandmother of the family from her chair, carried her to a nearby stream, ducked her in the freezing water, lifted her out again and left her on a nearby wall, wet, shivering and frightened half to death.

Many attempts were made with the help of various members of the clergy to rid the tower of its unwanted inhabitant, but the ghost seemed to have the measure of anyone who came. It would taunt people with its demonic voice and laugh at their feeble attempts to banish it.

Finally, one particularly determined minister came to the house. Summoning a band of followers with good, strong voices, he took on the full force of the ghost. The minister and his helpers opened their psalm books and began to sing with gusto.

The ghost was stirred into activity by the sound of the singing and, rising to the challenge, began to sing its own songs in response, louder than the minister's choir. So the minister urged his people to sing louder as well. The louder the choir sang, the louder the ghost sang, until both parties were singing at top volume.

All night the minister urged his choir on as they worked their way through psalm after psalm. When all the psalms that they knew had been sung, they started with the first one again. The people in the choir were very tired and their voices were croaking, but still the minister urged them on, his voice rising above the others as he sought to outdo the ghost. As the first light of dawn glimmered in the distance, the ghost had to admit defeat. Finally, it had found a force stronger than it was. Its creaky voice was heard for the last time as it told the assembled crowd that it had given up.

The minister and his victorious forces, exhausted, made their way home. The ghost of Galdenoch was never seen again.

Ghost: Amelie Saegee's Double
Place: *Livonia, Latvia*
Date: *c.*1846

Amelie Saegee was a teacher who was seen by her pupils to have been in two places at the same time. This happened several times and on each occasion she was in reality in close proximity to the vision of herself. Several pupils gave witness to the fact that the two were either very close together or separated by less than a metre. On one occasion when she was seen to be sitting in a chair in the garden of the school, she simultaneously seemed to be writing on the blackboard at the front of the class. It was reported that the vision standing in the classroom was rather insubstantial. She was apparently unaware of what was happening to her but she did remark that as she sat in the garden, she became worried that the class would be unattended and thought that she should be teaching them.

On another occasion there were two Amelie Saegee's standing before the class. Eventually she was asked to leave the school because these events were becoming so frequent – even though they were beyond her control. She could not have been totally surprised at this because she told them such happenings had occurred to her many times before!

Ghost: The Samlesbury Hall 'White Lady'
Place: ***A677 Road near Samlesbury Hall, Lancashire***
Date: 1987

Mr Dunderdale and his wife were driving along the A677 near Samlesbury Hall in Lancashire when a woman dressed in a white cloak suddenly appeared in front of them. Alex Dunderdale, who was driving at the time, swerved and braked as hard as he could but was unable to avoid running right over her. When eventually the car came to a halt Dunderdale rushed back down the road to offer what assistance and first aid that he could, but the lady was nowhere to be seen. Although he looked for some time he could not find her and eventually had to give up his search.

Other people have reported similar sightings of the white lady in different circumstances. Sometimes they have stopped to give her a lift only to find she has disappeared. Sometimes they have seen her on the road ahead but as they walked towards her she has, again, disappeared.

Ghost: Alexandrina Samona
Place: *Palermo, Sicily, Italy*
Date: 1910

Alexandrina Samona died at the age of 12 in Palermo. Three days after her death, her mother, Adela, told her husband, Carmelo Samona, that she had had a dream in which Alexandrina told her not to mourn for her as she was going to come back some day. In the dream she showed an embryo to her mother, but Adela ignored the symbol as she knew that she could not have any more children. Some time later, as Adela and her husband were talking about their dead child, they were startled by three loud bangs. They enlisted the help of a medium and were spoken to by two voices, one of which claimed to be Alexandrina and the other an aunt who had been dead for many years.

Alexandrina's voice said that she would be reborn, before Christmas, as one of a pair of twins. On 22 November 1922, two girls were born to Adela. The twins had completely different characters and personalities and one of them had two birthmarks in the same places as Alexandrina and was also left-handed as she had been. This twin was named Alexandrina.

The parents were sceptical about the possibility of their child being brought back to them – until one day when the twins were ten. The children were to be taken on a trip to another town, Monreale, and Alexandrina said that she had already been there with her mother and with a lady with horns, and was able to describe the church and some 'red priests' she had seen. The first Alexandrina had, in fact, been to the town with her mother just before she died, and with them had gone a woman with prominent warts on her forehead which could have looked, to a child, like horns. They had all gone to the church where they had seen some Greek priests who wore red robes.

Carmelo was now convinced that his daughter had been brought back from the dead.

Ghosts: The Sandford Orcas Ghosts
Place: ***Sandford Orcas, Sherborne, Dorset***
Date: Various

Sandford Orcas was built in Tudor times and has been the home of the Medlycott family since the middle of the 18th century. The house is said to be haunted by several ghosts but most of the stories relate to two in particular.

One ghost is said to be that of a former house servant who was said to have been particularly interested in very young women. Today, he would stand accused of sexual harassment, maybe even of child molestation. Anyway, a most unsavoury character! He is blamed for unusual noises heard around the Nursery Wing of the house. One witness, said to be a Mrs Gates of Taunton, while staying in the Nursery Wing one night, saw the ghost of a man whom she described as being in evening dress. This was most likely to have been the footman whose formal attire Mrs Gates mistook for evening dress.

The second ghost, said to have been witnessed by several people, is thought to be that of an 18th century local farmer who had committed suicide in the house. Why he did not do it in one of his own buildings is not recorded! He is usually to be seen in the vicinity of the kitchen and is identified by his white smock, typically worn by agricultural workers at that time. The same ghost has reportedly been observed by a Colonel and Mrs Claridge when they were staying at the house. Rumour has it that they have captured an image of the farmer on film.

Other phenomena that have been reported are an old lady seen on the stairs, a priest who apparently dealt in black magic, and a young boy who, reputedly as punishment for killing another, or possibly to hide himself from justice, was locked in a back room of the house for the rest of his days. His screams can still be heard on occasion. Voices have also been heard in the inner courtyard and unexplained footsteps and smells are also reported.

Sir Mervyn Medlycott is the present owner and personally shows people around the house when it is open to the public. It is reported that the only strange phenomenon that he believes to be true is the disembodied footsteps that have been heard in the cellar on occasion.

So what are we to make of the other stories if the one person who knows most about the house discounts them? Certainly the house is extremely atmospheric, some would say forbidding. In such a building, it would not be surprising for visitors, especially if they come from humbler dwellings, to feel a little uneasy in its surroundings. Any large house in the 18th century was occupied by many people – family, servants, guests. It was really like a small community operating on several levels. With so many people spread over many generations, such a community would be bound to have its own small tragedies and scandals that passed into local folklore. In those circumstances, any unusual noise or trick of the light might take on a more sinister construction. We cannot say for sure!

Ghost: Michael Scott
Place: *Melrose Abbey, Scottish Borders, Scotland*
Date: Since the Late 13th Century

The ruins of Melrose Abbey are believed to be the haunt of a rather more sinister ghost than some. Several people have reported noticing a strange chill in the atmosphere near the place where a man called Michael Scott was buried in the late 13th century.

Michael Scott was a very intelligent man of great learning, interested in philosophy and science. During his lifetime he acquired a reputation as a practitioner of the black arts, and he was said to possess strange supernatural powers. It may have been the case that he was simply rather a scary intellectual, whose brain and knowledge seemed threatening to other less educated or intelligent people. Nonetheless, he was a man who inspired fear among many people, both in life and after death. The site of his grave in the abbey is believed to be haunted by his spirit. The sensations that are felt by those who are sensitive to such things are not pleasant ones. Many people reportedly have felt an ominous chill in the air when they have stood in the vicinity of his grave.

Ghost: An Elderly Seaman
Place: *Waterford Coast near Helvick Head, Republic of Ireland*
Date: Not Known

As a young man, still a student, Arthur Frewen, the playwright and schoolmaster, was walking on the Waterford coast near Helvick Head. The day turned misty and dark, and he began to look ahead anxiously for the lights of a village where he might find a bed for the night. As he came to the expected village and walked among the houses, he found the place oddly deserted and dark.

The first light he saw came from the little pier, and walking along it, he found himself looking down on the deck of a fishing boat. The hatchway was open and as he stood there, the grizzled face of an elderly seaman appeared in it. Frewen asked if he could have the use of a bunk for the night, and the man gruffly agreed. He showed the young man through to the fo'c'sle where a bunk was built into each side. Frewen took off a red scarf of his sister's that he was wearing, and hung it on the door between the fo'c'sle and the cabin, where the old man sat mending a net. Presently, the old man called him through and gave him a meal of potato soup.

Frewen then went to lie down in his bunk, but almost as soon as he lay down, instead of dropping off to sleep, a growing feeling possessed him that something was wrong, that something terrible was going to happen. Eventually his terror grew to such a pitch that he got up, and slid the bolt in the door to bar it. Immediately after that he felt the door being tried. It rattled, and shook.

Then there was a hard pounding on it and a furious voice cried, 'Open up!' Frewen was certainly not going to do that. As the battering on the door increased, he heaved himself up on the bunk, smashed through the thick glass of the little window fitted in the deck, hoisted himself out, sprang from the boat to the pier, and ran for his life.

He stayed out the rest of the night, but when morning came, he walked into the village and found it a normal little hamlet, with people going about their morning business. Someone commented on his scratched and haggard appearance, and he blurted out the story of his night's experience.

'It was that boat, tied up just there,' he said.

The man to whom he was speaking looked at him strangely then walked with him to the pier. There was no fishing boat. Canted against the side of the pier was the derelict remnant of a boat, its timbers warped and slimy, with great cracks in the side and the deck – at first sight nothing like the trim vessel of the night before with its bunks and stove. But yet, as he looked at it incredulously, he saw it was the same sort of boat, with an open hatchway down to a central cabin, and a square hole in the foredeck, where the skylight window of the fo'c'sle would have been, its glass long since vanished.

'This boat has been mouldering here for nearly 50 years,' said the local. 'There is a bad story about it.'

He explained that, 50 years before, a young student on a walking holiday had been murdered on board this boat. The fisherman had been arrested, convicted of the crime, and hanged at Dungarvan. Ever since then the vessel had lain there.

Emboldened by the daylight and the presence of the interested villagers, young Frewen scrambled down into the decayed vessel. There was nothing in its hull but sand and seaweed. But when he pushed open, with great difficulty, the door between cabin and fo'c'sle, there, on a nail in the door, was hanging his red scarf.

Ghost: Mr Sellis
Place: *St James's Palace, London, England*
Date: Since 1810

Sellis was the valet of Ernest Augustus, the Duke of Cumberland and Teviotdale, and also the King of Hanover. There are several accounts of Sellis's ghost haunting the rooms of St James's Palace. The ghost is seen with blood pouring from a fatal wound to the throat and there have also been reports of shouting and the sounds of struggle.

That Sellis had his throat cut is not in dispute; however, the events leading up to his demise are less clear. The official inquest found that Sellis had committed suicide but there was much circumstantial evidence to point to him having been murdered by the Duke. Firstly, the razor with which he was said to have performed the act was found some distance from the bed in which he was found. The Duke was also said to have seduced Sellis's wife or perhaps even his daughter.

The Duke told the inquest that he was attacked as he lay asleep by an unknown assailant using a sabre. Furthermore he had the wounds to prove this assertion. He said that he had called for help and that his other valet, Neale, had come to his assistance, at which point his attacker ran off. Neale called to Sellis for help and when he did not appear Neale discovered him lying in his bed with his throat cut. There are several questions that come to mind. If the Duke had been asleep, surely an attack with a sabre would be fatal? Why did the inquest not find that the unknown attacker had also killed Sellis? What happened to the attacker? How did he escape from a palace full of people without anyone seeing anything?

A more rational explanation is that the Duke, probably awake, had been attacked by an outraged Sellis for seducing his daughter (maybe even raping her) and later, in an act of vengeance, he had cut Sellis's throat while he lay asleep. Despite the evidence to the contrary, the official inquest returned a verdict which would reflect best on the Duke. Maybe this had something to do with the fact that he was the son of King George III! The Duke was not a popular man, being known for his viciousness and arrogance, but after this outrage he was never able to go out in public without receiving people's scorn.

Ghost: Isabella Shiel
Place: *Tibbie Shiel's Inn, Peebles, Scotland*
Date: Since the Early 1900s

In the early 1820s, a young woman from the Scottish Borders by the name of Isabella Shiel found herself widowed. She was an enterprising person, and in order to feed herself and pay the rent, she opened her cottage to passing travellers, offering food and drink and letting out one of the rooms. The cottage, situated between Moffat and Selkirk, soon became a very popular stopping-off point, for Tibbie Shiel's hospitality and cooking were fine indeed. Her visitors were not only travellers. Many famous literary figures of the time, scholars and religious men took to gathering at the inn, taking advantage of the chance to meet in convivial surroundings and enjoy good food, fine ale and stimulating conversation. Amongst the well-known visitors to the inn were James Hogg ('the Ettrick Shepherd'), Robert Louis Stevenson and Sir Walter Scott.

Tibbie Shiel died in 1878, but the original inn, greatly extended over the years, still exists. The inn holds on to the ghost of its original landlady with a certain amount of pride, and visitors have claimed that Tibbie's presence can still be felt as she pushes through the crowd of customers on her way to warm herself at her favourite spot by the fire.

Ghost: Alexander Skene
Place: *Loch Skene, Scotland*
Date: Hogmanay (Since the 17th Century)

Hogmanay by Loch Skene sees the return of the phantom coach and horses of Alexander Skene, who lived in those parts around the end of the 16th and beginning of the 17th century.

Alexander Skene was renowned as a practitioner of the black arts; he is said to have spent some years on the continent studying black magic. His gruesome activities while at home by Loch Skene were rumoured to include digging up the corpses of unbaptised babies from the nearby churchyard and feeding them to the crow that is said to have accompanied him wherever he went, perched on his shoulder. People were fearful of Alexander Skene and claimed that his imposing figure cast no shadow, even when the sun was at its brightest.

The appearances started after his death. The story tells that he tried to cross the loch on his coach and horses using his magical powers and that as he neared the other side he came across the Devil. The coach then sank into the icy waters and Skene was drowned.

Ghosts: The Skryne Castle Ghosts
Place: *Skryne Castle, near the River Boyne, Republic of Ireland*
Date: *c.*1740

In *More Ghosts in Irish Houses*, Michael Reynolds tells the story of events at Skryne Castle not far from the River Boyne, for long the home of the Palmerston family. In 1740, the house was lived in by Sir Bromley Casway, and his ward, Lilith Palmerston, a girl of great beauty but shy and retiring by nature. Not far from Skryne lived another country landowner, Phelim Sellers. Sellers was a widower, but there were stories that his wife had died as a result of his ill treatment. He was a hard-riding, hard-drinking, foul-mouthed character, who came to Skryne to play cards with Sir Bromley, but who was clearly interested in the girl. On one occasion, in the grounds, he made an approach to her, which was rejected; and only the intervention of one of the castle gardeners prevented him from attacking her.

Lilith Palmerston wanted to leave Skryne for Dublin, where her guardian had a town house, to get away from Sellers, and Sir Bromley agreed. But on the eve of their departure, Sellers broke into Skryne Castle, entered Lilith's room, and killed her by thrusting foxglove fronds down her throat. He then fled, but was ultimately caught, and hanged for the crime.

Visitors and residents of Skryne have heard screams in the night from no obvious source; and some have seen the figure of a woman in white, clutching at her throat, running from the house. Others have told of a big man, with a hard hat and a stick and a dog beside him.

Ghost: Charles Smyth
Place: *Giant's Causeway, Northern Ireland*
Date: 1910 Onwards

In a typical outing for a well-to-do household in Edwardian Belfast, the Smyth family set off early one day in July 1910 on a train and tramway excursion to the Giant's Causeway. The party consisted of Mr Smyth, a linen-works manager, his wife, two teenage daughters, his son Charles, aged nine, and their maid, Kate Kennedy. They reached the Causeway shortly before lunch on a fine, sunny day. It was a city holiday, and there were numerous other groups.

The Smyths walked some way along, below the cliffs, to a quieter area, and settled down on their rugs to enjoy a picnic lunch from the baskets they had brought with them. After the lunch, Mr and Mrs Smyth decided to take a little nap, leaving Kate to supervise the children. Charles, an adventurous boy, was especially warned to be careful, in jumping about on the many levels of the rock formations. The girls did not go far away, and Kate kept a lookout for the boy, but among the pillars of varying height, it was very hard to keep him in view. The last time she saw him, he seemed to be making his way down to the water's edge, and she called to him to take care; he waved back jauntily.

Suddenly, Mrs Smyth sat up.

'Charles!' she said, 'Something's happened!'

'No, he's fine,' said Kate. 'I saw him just a moment ago.'

But when they both stood up and looked around, they could not see the boy. Alarmed, they woke Mr Smyth, who hurried down towards the sea. Although it was a calm day, there was a smooth swell on the sea, which rose and fell almost silently among the rocks, with hardly any breaking or spray. It was a deep, dark blue, almost ultramarine in colour. There was something sinister in the heavy, noiseless movement which struck a deep chord of unease in him. Distraught by now, the whole family combed the area, and Kate rushed up to the tramway terminal to get further help. But the boy had disappeared. A few days later, his body was found about 3 miles along the coast. It was assumed he had lost his footing and slipped into a deep channel, and been carried away by the current of the outgoing tide.

Soon after that sad event, reports began to be heard, of people who had seen a small boy in a sailor suit, down by the water's edge. One young couple almost stumbled on him as they negotiated the rock pillars. They thought that he seemed to be looking for someone. 'Are you lost?' the man asked. Then they noticed that his face was deadly pale, and his clothes seemed to be soaking wet. And then . . . he vanished. Since then, the boy from the sea has been seen on a few rare occasions.

Ghost: The St Rule's Tower Ghost
Place: *St Andrews Cathedral, St Andrews, Fife*
Date: Various

St Andrews Cathedral, dating from the 12th century, lies in ruins now but was once the largest cathedral in Scotland and a powerful and influential religious centre. In all, building work took almost two hundred years. The royal burgh of St Andrews, in which the cathedral stands, is a very old and beautiful university town, of great interest both to the historian and the ghost-hunter. The cathedral has a male ghost that is particularly well known.

In the grounds of the cathedral at St Andrews is St Rule's Tower, a remnant of St Rule's Church, which was built before the cathedral and used to hold the relics of St Andrew. It is here that the male ghost has been seen. The tower is quite high, and the view from the top, looking over the town, is well worth seeing, so it is quite a popular visiting place.

One visitor to the tower several years ago was startled by a figure in a cassock who appeared as he was climbing to the top. The tourist missed his footing on one of the steps and stumbled. Far from wishing to frighten the tourist, the cowled figure had genuinely intended to be helpful, for the tourist heard him offer to give him his arm on the way up the stairs. The tourist, swiftly recovering his balance, refused politely, and the figure stepped to one side to allow him to pass and then vanished without trace.

When the tourist came out of the tower at the end of his visit, he asked the man at the door whether anyone else had been in the tower at the same time as himself. The man at the door said that there had been no one else there, but he knew who, or what, the tourist had seen. The tourist discovered that the figure that he had seen was well known to those who knew the tower. He was a monk who would appear from time to time at St Rule's Tower – not a malevolent spirit at all, it would seem, but a kindly ghost who liked to make sure that visitors made their way safely to the top of the spiral staircase.

Ghost: Lt James Sutton
Place: ***Portland, Oregon, USA***
Date: 1907

Lt James Sutton was an officer in the American Navy who, according to official investigations, got into a drunken fight on his way back to his base from a navy dance in the naval town of Annapolis. When he arrived back at base, it was reported that there was an attempt to arrest him but before that could be accomplished Sutton, after recklessly letting loose several rounds of ammunition, placed one of the two pistols that he was carrying up to his head and committed suicide.

Lt Sutton's mother, who lived on the other side of the continent in Portland, Oregon was a well-known psychic and before she could have been told by conventional means, was already well aware of the circumstances of his death. Mrs Sutton knew this because she had been told the details by her son in a vision. Not only did she know the details of his death and his wounds, but also that the official version, when she eventually heard it, was incorrect and that, in fact, her son had been killed by others and the event dressed up to look like suicide. Mrs Sutton took her information to the American Society for Psychical Research who, after investigation, were so impressed by her story that they backed her demand for an inquiry.

The pressure was such that the body of Lt Sutton was exhumed two years after his death and the subsequent examination found several wounds described by Sutton's mother but not mentioned in the official report. Despite the fact that no reason for the fight or Sutton's suicide were ever put forward in the official report, and that witness testimony was inconsistent, the Navy took no further action. Lt Sutton, however, had shown that he had not committed suicide and after the investigation his ghost was laid to rest.

Ghost: Mr Swan
Place: *Ann Street, Edinburgh, Scotland*
Date: The End of the 19th Century Onwards

Ann Street is a particularly beautiful and desirable place to live in the heart of Georgian Edinburgh. At the end of the 19th century, one of the houses in the street was home to the Swan family. An uncle of the family was a great traveller, and the family was used to receiving letters from far-flung places describing his latest exploits. The traveller would take off for months at a time but would always keep in touch by mail and would appear from time to time, sometimes without warning, to draw breath between his adventures.

One evening the family was particularly surprised to see Mr Swan appear in their midst. They had expected him to be far away at sea, but they were delighted all the same. They rose to greet him as he strolled in through the front door, but before they had time to make him welcome, Mr Swan merely smiled at them, waved and disappeared. It was the oddest thing. The family was left to ponder the strange occurrence for some weeks until news finally reached them that Mr Swan had drowned when the ship in which he had been travelling to some distant place had sunk. The time of his death coincided with his mysterious appearance in the family home. His 'visit' had apparently been a wish to keep in touch with his nearest and dearest in death just as he had in life.

Mr Swan still returns to his old family home in Ann Street. Far from being a malevolent figure, it is said that he is very much a friendly ghost, popping in to say hello.

Ghost: Richard Tarwell
Place: *Devon Estate of George Harris*
Date: *c.* 1735

Richard Tarwell was a kitchen boy in the household of George Harris where the butler was Richard Morris.

When George Harris returned from a trip to London he was confronted by an agitated Morris who told him that the previous night the house had been burgled of all its silver. He told Harris that he had been awoken by loud noises coming from the area where the silver was kept. He said that he was surprised that the robbers had got in because he had carefully secured the house as usual and the thieves would surely have made some noise while breaking in. When he opened the door of the silver room he was confronted by two burly roughnecks and Richard Tarwell, who had been appointed to the household only weeks earlier. Morris was overpowered and spent an uncomfortable night trussed up, until discovered by the household's early risers.

Neither the two men nor Tarwell were seen again and it was assumed that the boy was in league with the robbers and had let them into the house. That would have been that, but for a remarkable encounter experienced by George Harris. Some time after the robbery, he was awoken suddenly by a figure standing by his bed. He immediately recognised it as Richard Tarwell but, instead of being frightened, there was something about the figure's demeanour that reassured him. Tarwell indicated that Harris should follow him, which he did. Tarwell led Harris down the stairs, through an unlocked door and out into the garden grounds. After some little distance, Tarwell indicated a spot under a tree and then moved slowly away and eventually disappeared. The next morning, Harris ordered his gardeners to investigate the place under the tree. They reported that they had discovered the remains of a young man who was later identified as Richard Tarwell.

Pondering on this and the unlocked door, Harris remembered that Morris had always been conscientious to the point of obsession about locking all doors at night and he was the only one who had access to the keys. He concluded that Tarwell had been murdered at the time of the robbery and further that he could not have let the burglars in, since only Morris had the keys. Harris contacted the police and after interrogation, Morris admitted to stealing the silver and being an accomplice to Tarwell's murder, which had taken place during a violent struggle when the robbers were disturbed by the unfortunate boy.

Ghost: William Terris
Place: *Covent Garden, London, England*
Date: Since the 1950s

William Terris was a well-known actor of the 19th century. In 1897, he was brutally murdered by a fellow actor – stabbed in the street outside the Adelphi Theatre, where he was appearing.

Many years later his ghost was identified by Jack Hayden and a fellow worker. During most of the 1950s, Jack worked in the nearby Covent Garden tube station. One night, after the last train had gone, Jack was locking up when he saw a tall man still inside. He shouted after him but when Jack reached the spot where he had been seen, there was no sign of anyone. Some days later, Jack had another similar experience. He was having his supper in the staff canteen before making his way home when the same figure appeared in the doorway. He was slightly annoyed that he had missed the stranger when he had locked up, and asked him roughly what he was doing in the station, pointing out that the next train was not due until morning. This time, Jack noticed as the man walked off, that he was strangely dressed in the style of the previous century. Jack put the man down as an eccentric, but when he went after him to make sure that he had left the station he could not find him, even though he was only a few paces behind. The stranger had disappeared.

Jack might have put the incident down to his tiredness or imagination, or maybe it was one of his colleagues from a different part of the railway or a cleaner who had left something at the station. However, the next day such possibilities were ruled out buy another colleague. Jack was working in his office when he suddenly heard a loud scream. He ran outside only to find his workmate in a terrible state. Apparently he had seen a tall man, smartly dressed in the style of a Victorian gentleman. As his workmate had walked towards the man, the apparition had disappeared before his eyes. Jack, of course, recognised the description as that of the man he had seen himself. However, Jack's associate was so taken aback by his experience that he resigned his job immediately.

By chance, about a week later, Jack went to see a performance at the nearby Adelphi Theatre. The foyer was decorated with portraits of famous actors from the past and one of them, William Terris, looked remarkably similar to the gentleman that he had seen in the station. He contacted his former colleague and together they agreed that the portrait was indeed that of the man they both had seen; he was even wearing the same clothes!

Several people have seen the ghost at Covent Garden underground station since he was first spotted by Jack Hayden. He is mostly seen when the station is empty, apart from its employees, and often in the vicinity of the canteen. Some have even heard ghostly footsteps on the track. They are always heard going in the same direction – towards the actor's home!

Ghost: Juliet Tewley, Tewsley or Tousley
Place: *Ferry Boat Inn, Holywell, Cambridgeshire, England*
Date: Several Centuries Old

The Ferry Boat Inn is many centuries old, perhaps over 1,000 years, and stands beside the River Ouse at Holywell. It is one of several that lay claim to being the oldest in England.

The story goes that centuries ago Juliet Tewsley was so distraught when her relationship with a local man broke up that she hanged herself. Not surprisingly, details after more than 1,000 years are sketchy but it is said that she was buried beside the river and her grave marked by a stone. When, some time later, the inn was built, the stone is said to have been incorporated into the bar room floor. She is said to have killed herself on 17 March and makes her presence known on this date. However, no positive siting has been made for several decades. At other times, unexplained noises can be heard from different places around the inn and these are put down to her ghost.

It is quite possible that this ghost story is the result of a marketing ploy by successive landlords of the Ferry Boat Inn! Old gravestones are often used as building materials and this might have given rise to stories told late at night by revellers to amuse each other. The management certainly do not keep Juliet a secret, and there are several framed press clippings referring to her on the pub's walls! One of the restaurants is even named after her! There have been investigations held on the anniversary of her suicide but she has not shown herself on these occasions. On one such occasion, in 1954, so many people turned up that the police had to be called to keep order! Beer sales were probably quite good that night!

Ghost: The Theatre Royal (London) Ghost
Place: *Theatre Royal, Drury Lane, London*
Date: Since Mid-19th Century

There is a ghost which haunts the Theatre Royal in Drury Lane, London. It has been seen on numerous occasions by many different people. The ghost has the appearance of a man dressed in the style of the 18th century. He always arrives at roughly the same time of day, between breakfast and teatime, and always at the same place, sitting in a seat in the upper circle. Sometimes, after several minutes he gets up and saunters across the theatre and through a wall.

The ghost was reported by the actor Morgan Davies who was on stage in the musical *Carousel* at that time. He watched the strangely dressed man for some minutes before the ghost rose and stretched out his arm. Davies could see straight through it! On another occasion during the rehearsal of a play that required many actors on the stage together, over 50 of those present claimed to have seen the ghost.

The ghost is thought to belong to a man whose remains were discovered in 1848. The remains were found evidently some time after his death, by workmen in a secret room at the back of the upper circle that had subsequently been walled up. The man had met with a violent death for the body was found with a knife firmly embedded between its ribs.

Maybe he was a fan of the theatre. Certainly, the actors seem to think he is friendly and he also seems to have good taste in drama, for he is said to appear only at successful productions!

Ghost: A Time Slip in Dieppe
Place: *Puys near Dieppe, Northern France*
Date: 1951

Dieppe is a town on the coast of northern France; ferries travel there from Newhaven in East Sussex. During the early 1950s air travel was still in its infancy, and even cars were not that common. It was fairly unusual for British holidaymakers to travel abroad and if they did venture across the Channel, it was usually not very far. So it was probably quite adventurous of Mrs Naughton and her sister, in August 1951, to rent a house at Puys a few miles down the coast from Dieppe.

On the night of 19 August Mrs Naughton was woken by her sister, who told her to come quickly. She told her to come outside as there were extraordinary noises coming from the direction of Dieppe. The town seemed to be under attack from the air; they could hear gunfire, anti-aircraft fire and dive-bombers. The two women knew exactly what they were hearing because their own experiences of such attacks were all too recent, this being only six years after the end of the Second World War. Despite the noise, which continued for almost three hours, they knew this was not a real attack; there were no visible signs either from fires or explosions. Only the perfectly ordinary streetlights were visible. The two women eventually retired to bed and the next day asked their French neighbours what the commotion had been all about.

Their neighbours reported that they had heard nothing but did remark on an extraordinary coincidence; during the war, Dieppe had indeed been the target of several Allied bombing raids. The largest and most destructive of these had taken place exactly nine years previously, on 19 August.

Ghost: A Time Slip in Norway
Place: *Oslo Fjord, Norway*
Date: 1950

This story concerns a party of eight adults who had driven into the countryside near Oslo to take advantage of a clear, sunny, winter day that offered excellent skiing conditions. The group consisted of friends who were officials from the British and American Embassies and their wives. One of the group was a brigadier and they were a sophisticated and worldly-wise group not given to flights of fancy.

They parked their cars on a long, straight road in open countryside, in clear conditions nearly 200 metres from a small farm. The field they chose to ski in was obviously part of the farm, but in Norway it was traditional to allow free access for skiing since the snow would protect even the most fragile flora.

At the end of a successful day, the party made their way slowly back to the cars. The brigadier and his wife, along with one of the American group reached the cars first a little way in front of the rest of the party. As they were removing their gear, they were suddenly and aggressively confronted by a woman of about 60 years of age. The three were further surprised that she spoke to them in perfect English, although with a decidedly Scottish accent. She was rather oddly dressed in an old-fashioned tweed suit, with a matching long skirt over laced boots, all topped off by a flat cap. Her concern seemed to be that they had been skiing on her land and she said that they had no right to trespass on it. Their apologies fell on deaf ears and eventually she stormed off. It must have been quite a sight to see these sophisticates getting such a telling off from an old peasant woman, and the encounter left the three quite unsettled.

As the other members of the party approached the cars they realised something was not quite right and asked what had happened. The brigadier explained about the old lady who, although only a few moments had passed, was now nowhere to be seen. She could not have gone anywhere because they had a clear view of the surrounding countryside and, becoming slightly concerned for her safety, the group searched for her. They searched in vain, however, and eventually, risking further opprobrium, they decided to inquire at the farmhouse. At the farm they found a young family consisting of a couple and their two children. The farmer said that they were quite welcome to ski on the field, which was part of their farm.

When the brigadier described the old lady to the farmer he said that no one of that description lived at the farm or, indeed, thereabouts. He did however mention a strange coincidence. The farm had been handed down from generation to generation in his family, since his great grandfather's time and he had been married to a woman from Scotland.

Ghost: A Time Slip at the Tower of London
Place: *Byward Tower, Tower of London, England*
Date: *c.*1950

This story relates to a yeoman who was in the guardroom at the Tower of London when he suddenly realised that something was different about the room. Although it was the same room, the furniture and other contents were quite different. There was a log fire that he had not noticed before around which sat several other guards whose presence he did not recall. They seemed quite at home and he was surprised to see that they were dressed in the uniforms of a long-past administration, and were smoking clay pipes.

He went outside for a moment to find someone to whom he could report this occurrence, but when he went back he found that everything had returned to normal.

Ghost: A Time Slip in Wallington
Location: ***Wallington, Surrey, England***
Date: 1968

While working in Wallington, Surrey in 1968, Mr Chase was waiting for a bus when he noticed, for the first time, two old thatched cottages with thatches and charming gardens. One of them had a date on the gable, which showed that they had been built in 1837. He thought no more of it until he casually mentioned to a colleague of his who lived locally, that he had not noticed the cottages before. His colleague told Mr Chase that he had been mistaken and that there were two quite modern brick houses at the place described.

Mr Chase was so sure that he had seen two old cottages that he went back to the spot to investigate, only to find that his workmate had indeed been correct. So intrigued was he that he investigated further to find that the older locals remembered two old thatched cottages on that spot, but which had been demolished some years ago to make way for the two more modern houses.

Ghost: Anne Trebble
Place: *Abbots Langley, Hertfordshire, England*
Date: Various

The housekeeper at the vicarage of Abbots Langley, Anne Trebble, was treated very badly by the wife of the former rector shortly after the First World War. Anne is buried in the churchyard but her ghost has been reported as having been seen in three places: between the church and the vicarage, in her old bedroom, where she appears to be gazing from the window toward the church, and in the village streets. From cottages facing the rectory, Anne's face has been seen at the bedroom window at the same time as she is reported to have been seen by someone inside the house.

A former rector, who found the ghost quite active when he moved into the vicarage, said that while deciding on alterations to the house he was told by a local builder that there was no point in doing any work to an old fireplace which stood in the haunted room because 'It will be out again within six months'. The builder explained that Anne had died a horrible death in the room and that the rectory would never be free of her. In spite of this, the fireplace was repaired and, as prophesied, within six months it fell out of the wall. Bad workmanship was blamed and the fireplace repaired, but within a few months it fell out again.

The same rector, soon after moving into the vicarage, met a parish priest who had been in Abbots Langley and who told him that ten years before, on All Saints' Day, he had seen the manifestation of a woman during Mass. The woman disappeared when the Invitation was given, and was seen by nobody else at the service. When the priest and his wife returned to the vicarage after the service, the haunted fireplace was cracked from top to bottom.

A year later another priest saw the same woman in his congregation, and reported the matter to his bishop. This led to the church being exorcised in accordance with the medieval service of exorcism. After this, except for a broken grate, the church and vicarage were at peace – apart from strange noises from the haunted room.

Late one night on another occasion, footsteps approached a curate, alone in the church, and he felt clothes brush against his face as he kneeled at prayer.

The ghost has not been seen for many years and the once haunted room is now used regularly.

Ghost: Admiral George Tryon
Place: *Eaton Place, London, England*
Date: 1893

On 22 June 1893, the British fleet was sailing through the Mediterranean in two columns. One column was led by Admiral Tryon on the *Victoria* and the other by Admiral Markham on the *Camperdown*. For some reason Admiral Tryon ordered the columns to turn in towards each other making a collision almost inevitable. Both his officers and those on the *Camperdown* were shocked and tried to have the order rescinded, but to no avail. As the *Camperdown* headed for the *Victoria* Admiral Tryon seemed to realise his mistake and ordered the ships to reverse their engines, but it was too late and the ships collided. The *Victoria* started to sink and as it went down, an officer who survived heard the admiral cry out that it was all his fault. Staying with his ship until it went down, Admiral Tryon drowned.

At that very moment Lady Tryon was giving a party in London. The London season was in full swing and her house in Eaton Place was filled with guests when there was a hush in the conversation as a figure in full naval uniform walked, unannounced, into and across the room and vanished. He was recognised as Admiral Tryon.

Ghosts: Dick Turpin and Others
Place: *'Woodfield', Apsley Guise, Bedfordshire, England*
Date: Various

A few years ago at 'Woodfield' in Woodcock Lane, the sound of a horse's hooves was heard and a phantom man was seen to enter the grounds. A pair of lovers is said to haunt the house.

The site of the house was once occupied by an inn and there is a local legend which accounts for the sightings. The legend involves local lovers who were thwarted in their designs for each other. Some 200 years ago, a house on the site was occupied by a girl who had a secret lover who would visit her whenever her father was away from home. One night, when the lovers were together, the father returned unexpectedly and saw them through a window, as they tried to hide themselves in a large cupboard in the pantry. In his anger, the girl's father pushed a heavy table, and other heavy items of furniture, against the cupboard door to trap them and left them there to die.

The bodies were discovered later when the highwayman, Dick Turpin, broke into the house and, by accident, found the remains. Realising the value of his discovery, he woke up the girl's father and, on hearing the story, blackmailed him into using the house as a hide-away in return for his silence. Having the father's assurance that he could do this, the bodies were buried in the cellar.

There is some evidence, from an owner of the house now on the site of the inn, that the area was visited by Dick Turpin on more than one occasion. The sound of a horse's hooves, heard over the years, were said to be those of Turpin's horse, Black Bess. At the site of an old entry to the property, now covered by a thick hedge, there have been reports of a ghostly figure on horseback who proceeds to dismount and enter the grounds. During a séance, a girl giving the name of Bessie was contacted and she gave an account that agreed quite closely with the legend.

People still report seeing, on occasion, a horseman disappear through the hedge, hearing the sound of hooves and seeing a phantom white lady.

Ghost: An Unknown Man
Place: *Pontefract, Lancashire*
Date: 1966

In 1966 Joe and Jean Pritchard, their son Phillip and daughter Diane, became the unwilling objects of a haunting. It started with the appearance of pools of water on the kitchen floor when Phillip was alone in the house (Diane being away on holiday). The pools appeared for two days and then the manifestation stopped. It was assumed that it was Phillip who was attracting the attentions of the spirit but, when they restarted in 1968, Diane had become the focus. At night a noise began and objects moved across the rooms. Lights switched on and then off again and on one occasion, all the family china kept in a display cabinet, fell out on to the floor but, remarkably nothing was broken or even cracked. Diane was frightened but not unduly so, as she always seemed to know when something was about to happen. She was thrown from her bed under her mattress, but was not injured; she was trapped under the hallstand when it moved through the air and landed, pinning her to the floor but avoided injury. When the family's grandfather clock hurtled down the stairs and broke into pieces, she once again escaped unharmed.

Then the ghost started to show itself, as a tall figure dressed as a monk with its head covered by a cowl. It first appeared to Mr and Mrs Pritchard when they saw a figure standing in the doorway of their bedroom, and then to a neighbour who found it so solid and real that she was not in the least frightened. The climax was near. The family were at home one night when the lights went out and Diane screamed in terror. By the time the family reached the front hall, the ghost was dragging Diane up the stairs with one hand pulling on her cardigan, and the other on her throat. Her parents seized her and pulled her free, her throat bearing red finger marks. The figure was seen once more and for the last time as it walked into the kitchen and vanished into the floor. The family were never troubled again.

Ghost: An Unknown Man and Woman
Place: *Langenhoe, Essex*
Date: 1937–59

The Rev E. A. Merryweather went to Langenhoe in 1937 having spent most of his life, until then, in the north of England. His church stood near the manor house overlooking the marshes. He was in the church on 20 September 1937, a quiet autumn day, with the west door lying open, when it crashed closed with such force that the whole building shook. Then, on two occasions in November, the rector's case, in which he carried his vestments and books, was found to be locked while he was in the vestry. All attempts to open it failed while in the vicinity of the church and it was only when he reached the lane outside that he managed to open the lock.

The next strange occurrences were in 1945. On Easter Sunday a Mrs Gertrude Barnes and her daughter Irene were helping Mr Merryweather to decorate the church before the service, and had left some flowers in a vase on a pew. On returning to collect them Mrs Barnes found the flowers tipped from the vase and scattered over the pew. Subsequently, flowers were moved or appeared and disappeared inexplicably.

In 1947, Mr Merryweather called at the manor house and was shown around by a Mrs Cutting. When they entered a front bedroom, Mrs Cutting said that it was never used as there was something strange about it. She preferred sleeping in another room although that one faced north and had a far less attractive view. She stayed in the room for only a few moments, then left Mr Merryweather, saying as she went 'I don't like this room.' The rector admired the sweeping views from the window and, on turning to leave the room found himself 'in the unmistakable embrace of a naked young woman'. Although this lasted for only a few seconds, the rector was quite sure that it had occurred even though the experience was purely tactile and no sound or smell had accompanied it.

Next year, 1948, members of the congregation heard thuds from the direction of the vestry door but, when the noises were investigated, neither cause nor explanation for them could be found. The thuds continued for about a month and, in November that year, the rector, while raking coal beside the church with an iron rod, felt that something or someone was near him in the churchyard. He stuck the rod into the heap of coal and hung his hat from it to be amazed to see the hat revolve, slowly, in front of his eyes. Only five minutes later he heard a voice from the supposedly empty church and, thinking that it might be vandals from the village, armed himself with a dagger, a gift from his son in Cyprus. He entered the church and when he reached the altar felt the dagger pulled from his belt, to be flung to the floor. A voice, coming from behind him from the tower of the church, said 'You are a cruel man' and the west door, which he had left ajar, slammed shut.

Later that year, a series of strange noises were heard from a blocked-up door, previously used as a private entrance for the manor house occupants. The credence bell rang, a loud report was heard and a pile of broken stained glass was found in the church. Then, on 21 August 1949, the rector saw the apparition of a young woman in the church. She looked about 1.6 metres tall and was wearing a white or grey dress and a flowing head covering which fell down over her shoulders. She walked from the north side of the church to the southwest corner, where the wall seemed to open to let her pass through, and then close again. Another apparition was seen in the church on Christmas Eve 1950 when the rector saw a vague form walk up the nave. The figure had appeared from nowhere and resembled a man wearing a suit. It moved toward the chancel and, on climbing into the pulpit, disappeared. A month later, one quarter of an hour after the rector arrived at the church, he found the imprint of a woman's hand on the vestry door. It gradually faded over the next ten days.

The haunting has been reported since the early 1900s.

Ghost: An Unknown Nurse
Place: ***St Thomas's Hospital, London***
Date: 1943

This is a story that was told to Nick McIver and which he recorded in his *Great British Ghosts*.

Charles Bide was a workman at St Thomas's during the war. One day he was asked by his boss to go and retrieve some furniture from a part of the hospital that had been damaged in the previous night's air raid. He recalled that it was a very cold day but that inside the empty building it was even colder than outside. This, however, is quite normal. The thermal mass of a building is such that it takes some time for it to warm up after a particularly cold snap, even if the external temperature is by now raised.

However, the events that followed were anything but normal. Charles was searching around for the furniture that he was supposed to secure; he was on his own and would have heard anyone else in the building because his footsteps rang out loudly on the bare floors. Suddenly, as he searched the top floor, he became aware that the temperature had suddenly dropped even further. At the same time he glanced in a mirror that was still miraculously intact and hanging in its place on the wall. In the mirror he saw, standing quite close behind him, a nurse. She was no ordinary nurse. For a start she was wearing the uniform that they used to wear in Victorian times and she looked completely distraught, as if she had no reason to go on living. Charles stood transfixed without turning to look at the vision, until he at last managed to break away and run out of the building.

Charles reported the ghost to a doctor but such were the pressures on the hospital at that time that he was told to keep the sighting to himself as they had enough to worry about without concerning themselves with spirits as well. Over the years, other people have reported seeing the ghost but none have had the misfortune to come across her alone, and in a building that was cold, empty and in such a disorderly state.

Ghost: An Unknown Nurse or Nun
Place: *Southfleet, Kent*
Date: Various

The former rectory at Southfleet has a history of hauntings going back for hundreds of years. An apparition appears, often and most frequently, in the 'Monk's Room' which has in it a stained glass commemorating the fact that, in 1874, the Bishop of Rochester tried to exorcise the ghost.

Between 1891 and 1898 the ghost was frequently seen. Three visitors apologised over breakfast one morning for having been so inconsiderate as to stay in the house when there was someone seriously ill. They were told, to their amazement, that nobody was sick and that the nurse, who they said had visited them during the previous night, was not a mortal person. The figure was thought to be that of a nurse as it had some white at the cuffs of its sleeves. The same figure has been seen many times by various occupants, sometimes only partly visible and also as a complete outline. Footsteps have been heard in a corridor and rustling papers, the swish of a starched uniform, and the noise of opening and closing doors.

The figure was seen one night by a servant. It was 7.30 and the servant was going upstairs to prepare the housekeeper's bed. She was working in the housekeeper's room and heard the sound of rustling paper, opened the door and found nothing. She closed the door and the noise restarted. This time she went out into the corridor with a lamp and later said, 'I stood at the top of a small stair just outside the room, and to my surprise saw a nurse dressed in a clean staff uniform, standing at the end of the passage. Feeling a little nervous at seeing her there, I very timidly walked down the three stairs and along the passage towards her. As I did so, she began to walk forward as if to meet me, then she seemed to drift gently backwards, facing me all the time, until she reached the door of a small room at the end of the passage. There, to my surprise, she vanished backwards through the door.'

In 1920 four friends stayed at the rectory. They waited on an upstairs landing while keys were found to unlock the doors of their rooms and they saw a woman's figure leave the Monk's Room, walk down the corridor to where they stood, turn the corner and go to a door at the end of the landing, entering the chamber behind. When the keys arrived, they tried the door and found it locked. On another occasion, a rector and his wife saw a 'shadowy shape' in the corridor outside the Monk's Room and it was later seen in the dining room during the daytime. It was described as looking like a nurse with a flowing veil and having a smile on her face, but perhaps the nurse was, in fact, a nun.

The rectory is built on the site of a former friary where it is said that a nun was once found in the company of one of the monks and that she was bricked up into a cellar while still alive, only to die there. The west door of the church was once blocked by rubble and when this was eventually cleared away by the churchwardens, a lid of a tomb was found in the pathway. The lid is engraved with an inscription saying that the tomb is the burial place of an excommunicated monk.

Ghost: An Unknown Old Woman
Place: *Near Tomintoul, Scotland*
Date: 1953

In the summer of 1953, David Campbell was a civil engineer working for a firm of Edinburgh consultants who had won a contract to carry out some investigations into possible sites for new hydroelectric schemes for the Scottish Hydro-Electric Board. All the potential sites were in the Grampian Highlands, a particularly scenic part of the country. David was not long wed and as he would be away for a few days, he decided to take his wife, Margaret, along for the trip. It would turn a business trip into a more pleasurable experience.

On the evening of their first day they were making their way along the Cock Bridge to Tomintoul road and their hotel in Grantown-on-Spey. The road had recently been remade with loose chippings, which was possibly the cause of a puncture that they suffered a few miles after they had left Cock Bridge. They were unconcerned since at that time of year, there were still many hours of daylight left and the sun was still very warm. David set about changing the Standard Eight's wheel while Margaret sat at the side of the road enjoying the scenery.

While David worked on the wheel, an old lady dressed in a long plaid skirt and a headscarf came slowly up the road in the direction from which they had come. She seemed to be carrying something wrapped in a shawl and was accompanied by a small black dog. As she passed, she asked them if there was anything she could do to help. David thanked her but assured her that he could manage and in any case he was nearly finished. When she had gone a little further on, David and Margaret remarked on the traditional friendliness of Highland folk and joked about what help she could have been in changing the wheel. Margaret then casually mentioned that she had not seen her on the road. David said he had not seen her either and had not noticed any track or building for at least 3 miles. In the next minute or so, they were on their way again and decided that they should offer the old lady a lift; maybe she was making for Tomintoul also.

They drove for about 400 yards but could see no sign of her. The light was still good, it being only about 6 o'clock. The countryside was open on all sides, there were no buildings, small tracks or even a ditch but of the old lady there was no trace; she had vanished! They stopped the car some way ahead and got out to get a better view, but without success. Eventually, they continued on their way. Over the years, David travelled down that road many times and always kept a look out for some small building or track that he had missed on that first day, but he never saw anything that could explain what had happened, or where the old woman could have disappeared, or even hidden, if she had been so inclined.

Ghost: An Unknown Sea Captain
Place: *Buckingham Terrace, Edinburgh*
Date: 19th Century

Shortly after the Gordon family took a large apartment in Buckingham Terrace, Edinburgh, Mrs Gordon complained to the night porter about noises coming from the flat upstairs. She knew that the flat was usually empty and only used as a furniture store but she could not understand why they had to use it in the middle of the night. The night porter told Mrs Gordon that she must be mistaken. The room was seldom used during the day and never late at night. He suggested that it might be someone next door as it was often difficult to locate the source of a noise, especially late at night when one had just woken. He reminded her that they were the only occupants of the building because, apart from the furniture store, the ground and first floors were given over to offices and only occupied during working hours. Mrs Gordon was unconvinced by the night porter's explanation. The noises were directly over her bedroom and whoever it was seemed to take a real pleasure in making a din. She said she would take it up with the landlord.

That night she awoke abruptly from a sound sleep with feelings of extreme dread that she could not readily explain. She was not given to fantasy and was extremely sceptical about the existence of ghosts, but the feelings would not go away. She became aware of an unseen presence. As she lay petrified in the darkness she decided to use the bell at her bedside in an effort to rouse her daughters, who lay sleeping in their bedrooms nearby. Her desperate lunge for the bell only resulted in her breaking one of her nails and increasing her alarm. After a few minutes she realised that the unseen presence had passed through the door and was ascending the stairs. Where before it had been silent, it now became anything but, and when it reached the upstairs room it seemed to get even louder. It actually seemed to be jumping about the room. This continued for as long as 30 minutes before ceasing. Once the noise had stopped she quickly recovered her equilibrium and decided to wait until morning before discussing the strange happenings with her daughters. They had heard absolutely nothing and Mrs Gordon was starting to think that it had been her imagination or some kind of waking dream.

No more of the unseen presence, for that is what Mrs Gordon had started to call it herself, was heard for almost a month. However, one night when Mrs Gordon was staying away with friends and her daughter Diana was using her room for some reason it emerged again. Diana had just entered the room when something indistinct brushed past her and noisily ran up the stairs in the direction of the furniture store. Curiosity overcame her considerable fear, and Diana chased after the shape. She knew it had entered the furniture store because she could hear it on the other side of the door rummaging noisily about. Diana flung wide the door to discover that the thing making all the noise was no more than a faint but tangible shape doing something inside an old grandfather clock; winding it, perhaps. The sight of such a strange thing, for it could not be called human, struck Diana to the core and she became rooted to the spot, incapable of any movement. What if the thing should turn around and notice her? What if it had friends up here? As it turned towards Diana, she thought she would be crushed by the terror and die right there, but just then the voice of her sister broke through the atmosphere and she was free to run as fast as she could down the stairs. Not unreasonably, she stayed that night in her sister's room.

The next day Mrs Gordon returned and peace resumed in the household until one evening the figure of a man appeared in the doorway of her room as she lay resting. Despite the fact that this figure was more substantial than the one Diana had seen, she was nevertheless considerably alarmed at the appearance of a stranger in their home. His appearance was rather rough and he carried an aura of malevolence with him. Rather oddly, in his hands he carried a bundle of rags and a lump of lard. In an instant the figure turned and raced upstairs where it disappeared. Mrs Gordon had by then had enough and the next day, even though they had to pay a penalty for leaving before the end of their lease, the family departed.

Mrs Gordon subsequently carried out some research into the history of the house. She found out that it was well known locally to be haunted and the subject of many stories. One story seemed to fit her personal experience better than the others. A retired Merchant Navy captain had previously lived in the apartments and was an alcoholic, a worldwide occupational hazard for seafarers, and had rather a short fuse. He became particularly annoyed by the cries of a small baby that often disturbed his fitful sleep. One night, while the baby's mother was out, the yells so enraged him that he stormed upstairs and cut off the baby's head. In his drunken judgement he thought that a rational way to hide his crime would be to stuff the remains into a grandfather clock in the corner of the room. He was soon arrested but was found to be insane and sentenced to spend the rest of his life in an asylum for criminal lunatics. Either because of his insanity, or out of remorse for his wicked deed, he committed suicide some years later.

Ghost: An Unknown Servant Girl
Place: *Bristol*
Date: Early 1900s

A 'horrible and pale-faced' servant, a girl, is reputed to have haunted a house in Bristol during the early years of the 20th century. Half-witted and hunch-backed, always wearing a pink dress and living a life of misery the girl was beaten and half-starved until she drowned herself in a garden pool. She was the natural daughter of the man who owned the property 50 years before her death.

A colonel's wife and her three daughters leased the house but could not find a housemaid for some weeks. However, soon after they took possession of the property, a young woman was seen, on the stairs, cleaning with a brush and pan. The daughter who saw the girl assumed her mother had found a temporary maid and gave her only a fleeting glance, seeing an untidy, sluttish person wearing a pink dress and very soiled cap. The girl, white-faced and almost hump-backed, glided down the stairs while smiling horribly over her shoulder at the daughter, and vanished through a red baize door which closed behind her.

A little later, one of the daughters, alone in the house, went to the basement for hot water and, on pushing open the kitchen door, was surprised to see the girl, still wearing the pink dress, with her back to the door, busy at the kitchen range. On being challenged by the daughter the figure turned and, leering impudently, ran into an adjacent room from which there was no way out. The daughter followed, sure of catching the girl at last, but on entering the scullery found it empty with no sign whatsoever of the mysterious figure. She was terrified and ran from the kitchen and saw, through the landing window which was about 9 metres above the ground, the face of the ghostly maid. She fainted and was so ill afterwards that she was sent to a spa to recover. Soon afterwards, her mother and sisters left the house.

The next family to move in stayed for only a month and the next even less time than that – until the house was left empty, apart from the ghostly maid.

Ghost: An Unknown Spanish Lady
Place: *Blythswood Square, Glasgow, Scotland*
Date: 19th Century

Blythswood Square in the centre of Glasgow is a square of fine Georgian buildings with a mixed history. Now the site of offices of lawyers and accountants, it once had a reputation as being something of a red-light district. In years before that, it was more of a residential area and considered to be a very desirable place to live.

One particular gentleman, house-hunting in the area, came upon a house in Blythswood Square that was for sale. Upon inspecting the property, he was very impressed with it all, with the exception of the bathroom. There was something about the bathroom that gave the house a very unpleasant air, and the gentleman could not quite put his finger on what it was. The room had a cold and dreary atmosphere, but there was something else, something foreboding. The room made him shudder. Nevertheless, the thought of having a prestigious address such as this was too tempting for both the gentleman and his wife. The bathroom would surely take on a brighter atmosphere with a few coats of fresh paint and new fittings. They bought the house and moved in.

The gentleman still felt very uneasy about using the bathroom, in spite of its bright new appearance and in spite of his family's reassurances that all was normal. He did not like to close the door when he was having a bath. His wife, however, protested at such immodest behaviour. Reluctantly, the gentleman had to respect her wishes. The next time he went to take a bath, he summoned up the courage to close the door behind him.

The gentleman could see that there was no one else in the bathroom, but in spite of this he still had the distinct feeling that there was someone else there. It was uncanny. Trying to ignore his feelings of misgiving, he placed his candle at the edge of the bath, undressed and stepped into the water.

Hardly had the gentleman got into the bath, however, than he heard strange sounds coming from the fire grate. He tried to ignore them but they persisted. He got up to investigate, his heart hammering. Cautiously he stepped out of the bath. Suddenly the candle went out, and as the room was plunged into darkness, the gentleman tripped and fell to the floor. Frozen with terror, he then heard the sounds of loud splashing coming from the bath. Someone was in the bath, washing! But that was impossible – there was nobody there!

The gentleman hardly had time to ponder upon this, for after only a few seconds he heard the cupboard door behind him opening. A figure stepped out of the cupboard. The gentleman could hear the rustling of skirts and smell the cloying scent of perfume. The gentleman had no time to get out of the ghostly figure's way. A chilly foot in a high-heeled shoe stepped on his back quite carelessly as the spectre of a woman, apparently oblivious of the gentleman's presence, made her way towards the bath.

The gentleman gasped and listened. Sounds of a struggle came from the bath, a violent struggle. There was much splashing and thrashing about. Then, all of a sudden, the noises stopped. The woman turned to face the gentleman, and through the darkness he saw a ghostly white face quite startling in its luminosity. The face was obviously that of a beautiful woman, but it was contorted with an expression of pure hatred.

The gentleman had seen and heard enough. He fumbled his way to the bathroom door, unlocked it and fled to the safety of his bedroom. When he told his wife what had happened, he was met with ridicule and told not to be so foolish. His fear was dismissed as mere hysteria.

Then one morning the gentleman's son went to use the bathroom and was greeted with the sight of a dead man floating in the bath water. His screams alerted the rest of the family, who came running. When they went into the bathroom they could see nothing. But when they were coming out, they were all witness to the sight of a beautiful dark-haired woman, a look of unmistakable hatred on her face, sweeping past them into the bathroom cupboard.

The family left the house – no matter how desirable the address, the spectral inhabitants made life there unbearable. Once they had found themselves a suitable, less sinister place to live, they made inquiries about the history of the house in Blythswood Square.

Their investigations were quite enlightening. Apparently the house had once been the property of a wealthy man married to a Spanish woman with a violent temper. The man had been found drowned in his bath one morning. The circumstances had been suspicious, but no foul play could be proved, and his beautiful widow left the country.

The gentleman and his family knew the terrible truth about what had happened, and the gentleman now realised that what he had experienced was the ghostly re-enactment of the whole sordid affair.

Ghost: An Unknown Stonemason's Apprentice
Place: *Rosslyn Chapel near Edinburgh*
Date: Various

Rosslyn Chapel lies quite close to Edinburgh, to the south of the city. Founded in 1446 by William Sinclair, Earl of Orkney, it is a popular visitor site and a place of historical, religious and architectural interest.

Historically, the chapel is the subject of much controversy. Some historians believe that the chapel had strong links in the past with the Knights Templar. Many theories have been proposed as to the supposed existence of religious relics – some believe this includes the Holy Grail – hidden within an underground vault beneath the floor of the chapel. The most recent theory at the time of writing is the most astonishing – that the chapel has buried beneath it the mummified head of Christ, which was worshipped by the Knights Templar hundreds of years ago. The trustees of the chapel are under constant pressure to carry out excavations to find out whether there is any truth in any of the many theories about its mysterious past.

Architecturally, Rosslyn is interesting for several different reasons. The interior of the chapel is unusually ornate for a Scottish church and is unique amongst its contemporaries. Scottish religious buildings of the time were characteristically very plain in design, and although Rosslyn is essentially a Gothic building, its fanciful decoration and exotic – some would say eccentric – ornament make it stand apart from all others. There is evidence to suggest that many foreign craftsmen were employed in its construction, which would account in part for some of the decorative elements that are in evidence in the building. One piece of particular merit within the chapel is a very ornate and beautifully carved pillar known as the Apprentice or Prentice Pillar.

The Apprentice Pillar has a story of its own to tell. The story goes that when the chapel was being constructed a stonemason was requested to carve this pillar in the style of a particular column in Rome. The mason was finding it difficult to reproduce the desired effect using the picture he had of the column as his only source of inspiration. To prepare himself adequately for the task, he decided to travel to Rome to see the original column for himself. A journey of this sort was quite an undertaking in those days, and the mason was away for some weeks. In the absence of his master, the stonemason's apprentice, who had been left behind, decided to try to carve a pillar himself. He studied the picture that his master had been given and set to work.

When the stonemason returned from Italy, he found that the work that his apprentice had done was far superior to anything he might have been able to carve himself. In a fit of rage and jealousy, he killed his apprentice on the spot. The story of the murder is given credence by the fact that there had to be a delay between the construction of the chapel and its eventual consecration, which took place only after an Act of Reconciliation had been sought from the Archbishop of St Andrews.

The ghostly apprentice returned to haunt the chapel and the work of which he was so proud. His mournful figure has been seen standing beside his pillar and the sound of his weeping has been heard by many people who have visited the chapel over the years.

Ghost: An Unknown Young Farmer
Place: ***Preston, Lancashire***
Date: 20th Century

This story comes from a book by Professor Colin Gardner called *Ghost Watch*. It recounts a series of episodes that came to light when the Institute of Psychical Research, of which he was a member, was called in to investigate a number of sightings that always took place in and around the month of October.

A young couple had recently moved into a semi-detached bungalow near the wife's parents' house. The bungalow bordered onto a nearby farm and had been built on ground that used to be one of its former fields. Although quite new, the bungalow had been inhabited by several couples who only seemed to stay for a short period.

Not long after moving in, the wife had an unnerving experience. As she worked at the kitchen sink she became aware that something was moving about outside in the back garden. She looked up to see a young man dressed like any local farm worker, walking about in the garden and then marching straight through a hawthorn hedge into the adjacent field. Containing her initial alarm, she rushed outside to find out what he was doing in her garden but before she could confront him he had disappeared.

Over the next few weeks she became used to the stranger. He always seemed to be distracted, walking with his head down and always along the same path. She often saw him walk through the thick hedge and he always seemed to disappear at the same spot in the field. At times he appeared more solid than at others. She was convinced that she had been in the presence of a ghost and although she often saw the young man herself, her husband never did. He was rather dubious about the ghost's existence, that is, until a Sunday some time later. His wife's parents had come on a visit and as they got out of their car they saw a man walking around the side of the house. They did not want to intrude if the family had guests so they thought that they would just say hello and depart. They followed the man around the house and entered through the back door which was wide open. They went through to the dining room where they found the family having their lunch. They said that they would not stay if the family were entertaining, only to be informed that they were alone. The parents described the man who matched the description of the person their daughter had often seen.

That was the last time that anyone saw him for many months until about a year later when he appeared again on several occasions over a period of a few days. On one occasion, the parents were sitting with their daughter when the ghost appeared quite clearly before them, quite oblivious to their presence. He did not even react when they shouted at him. By this time they had had quite enough and contacted the Institute for Psychical Research.

After some work, the investigator found out that where the house stood there once ran a path. It seemed that the ghost, who never wavered from his course, was walking on that path. Further investigation revealed that the farmer had once had a son for whom his parents were very ambitious, wanting him to get a university degree. The son, however, wanted to stay on the farm but he did not wish to upset his parents and spent many troubled days tramping the fields trying to resolve his feelings. October, the month of the hauntings, is also the time when many universities start their academic year and this may be why he was so troubled at that time. The investigator also learned that sadly, the lad never resolved his dilemma. Instead he drowned himself in one of the farm's ponds.

Ghost: An Unknown Young Girl
Place: *Blue Bell Hill, near Maidstone, Kent*
Date: 13 July 1974

This well-researched story is taken from *The Evidence for Phantom Hitchhikers*. In the early hours of 13 July 1974, Maurice Goodenough was driving home to Chatham when a figure suddenly appeared in front of his car. She appeared to be a young girl, about ten years old, wearing a white blouse, skirt and white ankle socks. Mr Goodenough stamped on the brakes but he could not avoid hitting her, and the car struck her with sickening force. Mr Goodenough brought the car to a skidding halt and rushed back to the small girl. He found her battered and bleeding at the side of the road. She looked a lot better than he had feared, but aware that in such a state it might be dangerous to move her, he grabbed a blanket from his car and tenderly wrapped her in it before going to get help.

He went to the police station in nearby Rochester, and police officers came back with him to the spot where he had left the girl. They found the spot, marked by a now empty blanket, but although they searched long and hard they could find no sign of her. A tracker dog was called in but could not get a scent. Maybe another motorist had picked her up, but if he did so, he did not take her to one of the local hospitals as there were no matching accident admissions that night. The police were obviously convinced of Mr Goodenough's sincerity but apparently got a little suspicious at that point because they inspected Mr Goodenough's car, only to find no sign of damage. Had the whole thing been the product of a tired mind playing tricks on a lonely road in the middle of the night?

One fact is not in dispute: Mr Goodenough is not the only one to have experienced strange appearances of young women on Blue Bell Hill, although his is the most well-documented case.

Ghost: An Unknown Young Guardsman
Place: *The Grenadier Pub, Wilton Row, Knightsbridge, London*
Date: Various

The building that is currently occupied by the Grenadier Pub in Wilton Row, Knightsbridge was once part of the barracks of the Duke of Wellington's regiment. At that time it was used as the officer's mess where the young men could let off steam, skylarking, gambling and no doubt drinking to excess. The bar of the mess used to be situated where the cellar is now and it is in the bar that the origins of the haunting are said to have taken place.

One night a group of young men were said to be drinking heavily and unwisely decided to play cards. It is not known whether one of them acted intentionally or if he made some drunken mistake, but the story goes that one of them was caught cheating. The others, driven by the absurdly strict moral codes of such regiments at that time, are said to have stripped the offender bare and flogged him without mercy. The poor unfortunate died of the injuries he received that night, and has been locked in his misery from that time forth. This story is corroborated by Gillian Cribbs, who wrote the book *Ghosthunter* in collaboration with Eddie Burks, a psychic. In the book she tells how Burks described a conversation with the poor guardsman in the cellar of the house. According to Burks, the guardsman claimed that he did not cheat intentionally and that his death was an accident; the result of over enthusiastic young men trying to teach one of their number a lesson. Burks went on to describe the man as being unable to forgive his erstwhile friends, and his torment in not being able to free himself from his purgatory. Burks claimed that he was able to help free the guardsman from his torment and asserts that in the future he will not be seen in the Grenadier Pub. Time will tell if he is correct.

Other, less dramatic but still interesting stories, are told of poltergeist activity in various places in the pub but mainly in the cellar and bathroom. Peter Martin the landlord, was having a quiet drink after closing time with his friend, Edward Weber, when they witnessed a bottle float off a shelf and explode in mid-air. Luckily, but perhaps strange in itself, it was not a bottle of spirits! On another occasion, keys went missing but were seconds later found in the place where they were always kept. This is a story that is repeated in more than one book, but I have to admit that it also seems to be quite a commonplace event, certainly in our household!

One final note about the activity at the Grenadier; it always happens at about the same time of year, in September. And by coincidence, the guardsman who suffered so terribly at the hands of his colleagues also died in September!

Ghost: An Unknown Young Woman
Place: *Quartecanaux Bridge, Palavas, Montpelier, France*
Date: 1981

About 11 o'clock at night on 20 May 1981, two couples were making their way back home from a trip to the seaside, when they came across a woman hitchhiking towards Montpelier. Since it was so late and the woman was alone, the driver stopped despite the fact that the car, being a Renault 5, was really only designed to take four people. The driver said they were going as far Montpelier and the hitchhiker nodded without saying anything. The front passenger and one of those occupying the back seat, got out to allow the hitchhiker to squeeze into the back of the car where she sat in between the two women.

All went quietly until the hitchhiker screamed out, 'Look out for the turns, look out for the turns. You're risking death!' The driver slowed down for the approaching bend only to be further alarmed by more screams from the rear; this time from his friends who had just sensed the sudden departure of the hitchhiker. The driver stopped the car and the two couples searched the area, though without success.

They reported what had happened at the local police station where Inspector Lopez warned them about time wasting. He listened to their story and although he was won over by their sincerity could offer neither an explanation nor help.

Ghost: Lady Blanche de Warenne
Place: *Rochester Castle, Kent*
Date: Since 1264

Rochester Castle was one of the castles built in the first few years after the defeat of the Saxon King Harold by William the Conqueror at the Battle of Hastings in 1066. Two hundred years later, the hegemony of the Normans still held sway and, in 1264, Rochester Castle was the subject of a dispute between the Earl of Leicester, Simon de Montfort, and the occupiers, Ralph de Capo and his fiancée Lady Blanche de Warenne. The occupiers seemed to be winning and the attackers in retreat, so de Capo lowered the drawbridge to pursue them. He was some distance from the castle when he chanced to look back only to be horrified at what he saw; he could make out a figure on the battlements that appeared to be his betrothed and she was being assaulted buy a man. Ralph immediately gave up the chase and headed back to the castle. As he got nearer he could see the two figures more clearly; the woman was indeed his fiancée and the man was an old rival for her hand in marriage, Sir Gilbert Clare, an ally of Simon de Montfort's. Their struggle was obviously violent and Ralph was concerned that she would be killed before he could reach them, so he took his bow and fired at Sir Gilbert. Unfortunately, the arrow struck Lady Blanche through her heart and she subsequently died.

On the anniversary of her death it is reported that her ghost, still with an arrow stuck in its chest, frequents the battlements. Others have heard her ghostly footsteps in the same area.

Ghost: Robert Webbe
Place: *Linton, Cambridgeshire*
Date: Since 1971

This story includes examples of events that could have been imagined, albeit in good faith, by the observer but also others that are very hard to explain.

The principal observer of the phenomena that appeared at Linton was a 16-year-old boy called Matthew Manning who lived with his parents in their 17th century house. Matthew first came across the ghost in 1971 when he saw the figure of a man standing on the stairs. So solid looking was this figure that at first Matthew took him for an intruder. But why would an intruder be clothed in a frock coat and breeches and wearing a wig? What is more, the man needed two sticks to help him to walk. Matthew realised that he was witnessing a haunting. Matthew showed a surprising degree of sang froid for one so young, for not only did he observe the apparition, he also had the presence of mind to sketch it and ask its name! What is more, the ghost responded; he said his name was Robert Webbe and that this was his house. He said he had been born there in 1678 and had been a successful trader in farmers' produce. He apologised to Matthew for giving him a fright and explained that he had to keep moving about because he had 'troublesome legs'. Matthew developed quite a rapport with the ghost, and learned that he was very proud of the house and had built a large extension to it, about three years before he had died in 1733. Maybe he was so proud of the house that he could not bear to be parted from it.

On one occasion, Matthew said that he offered the ghost his hand in friendship but although the ghost responded, the handshake was with thin air! Matthew then tried to offer it a gift, the wooden clog from one of his sister's dolls. Matthew said that the ghost took the gift and as it did so, he had an extraordinary feeling of being suspended in time. Shortly thereafter, Matthew watched as the ghost disappeared along with the wooden present.

In addition to seeing the long-ago owner of the house, Matthew later discovered that he had been endowed with the gift of automatic writing. This happens when the writer's hand is taken over by a spirit so that the latter is able to communicate with the living world. Matthew had many such sessions with Robert Webbe. During these occasions, he was able to find out things that he could subsequently check in local records. At the height of this period, Matthew began to write on his bedroom wall. He wrote the names of over 500 people from as far back as 1355 up until the latter part of the 20th century. To each name was appended a date.

The apparently psychic behaviour of Matthew seemed to infect his family as well, because it is reported that his father, Derek Manning, an architect, also experienced strange phenomena. He said that while lying in his bed he had the sensation that someone was lying next to him; sometimes he could hear the rasp of a man's beard on the sheet. At other times, he felt as though he were inside the entrance of a cave gazing out and, even more strangely, felt as if he was looking out of someone's mouth. He also experienced a tingling sensation in his legs as he lay in bed; could this be referred pain from the ghost?

Other events happened which included poltergeist-like activity. Things disappeared only to be found in an unexpected place later on. Pyjamas that had previously been folded tidily, but left unbuttoned, were later found untidy but buttoned up. The bed, although properly made in the morning, looked as if it had been slept in. Strange noises that were difficult to account for occurred, like the ringing of a hand bell and footsteps coming from empty rooms. Even more peculiar, unlikely smells were experienced by the family. These included pipe tobacco, although no one in the family was a smoker, and stale fish.

What are we to make of this story? Many of the events that are recorded could, conceivably, have been the subject of a hoax on the part of Matthew Manning. Most people who see a ghost for the first time are highly alarmed and would have called for others to see it, or, at least, if they had been transfixed during the actual episode, would rush off to tell them about it after wards. But Matthew drew a sketch. No one else *saw* the ghost and Matthew could have surreptitiously moved items around the house and made his parents' bed look as if it had been slept in. He could have carried out some research among the parish records to find out the names and dates of the residents of the village. Since no one saw him writing on the walls he could have copied the names and dates from a list. The automatic writing would be easy enough to fake.

But what about his father's experiences? If the thought of ghosts had been planted in his head these experiences may have been quite ordinary. He may have imagined that some noise he was in fact generating himself was being caused by some other entity, and he always seems to have had these experiences when he is lying in bed. Maybe he was half-asleep? The smells and noises are more difficult to explain. They were witnessed by others and would have been very difficult to fabricate.

On a final note, Robert Webbe's ghost is recorded as informing Matthew that he did not believe in ghosts! On the basis of this story it must be said that the jury is still out!

Ghost: Major Thomas Weir
Place: *The West Bow, Edinburgh*
Date: 17th Century

In the early part of the 17th century there lived in the West Bow of Edinburgh, along with his sister Grizel, one Major Thomas Weir. To all appearances, Major Weir was a worthy bachelor indeed – outwardly respectable, a veritable pillar of society. Deeply religious and knowledgeable about all things spiritual, he was a familiar figure at prayer meetings and gatherings, often playing a leading role. He was a large man of imposing appearance, and he was rarely seen without his 'trademark', a black staff. He seemed to be so reliant upon this black staff that people began to speculate that perhaps it possessed some sort of magical or spiritual power. The speculations were dismissed as foolish rumour, idle and fanciful gossip. It served no good to speak of a pious man like Thomas Weir in such a way.

In 1670, however, Major Weir, for no reason that anyone could fathom, did something that sent waves of shock through Edinburgh and eventually sealed his own death warrant. He made a confession, one that would give credence to any malicious rumours that might have circulated about him, and much more. Accustomed to addressing religious gatherings, he stood up at one particular meeting and prepared to speak. When he did speak, it was not the prayers they had been expecting that his audience heard. It was a catalogue of the most heinous and sinful deeds imaginable, especially offensive to those of religious leanings. Major Weir accused himself of having lived in an incestuous relationship with his sister for years. He told of sharing with his sister in the knowledge and practice of witchcraft, satanic rituals and necromancy. He claimed to have consorted with the devil himself.

The first reaction of his stunned audience was to assume that the Major had taken leave of his senses. These were the ravings of a madman, surely! Doctors were consulted, priests were sought out for their advice, but Weir persisted. His stories were consistent and detailed. He could not and would not be ignored. Doctors finally pronounced Major Weir to be sane. There was no option but to believe his stories.

Major Weir and his sister were both executed for crimes of witchcraft. Major Weir was strangled and then burnt, a standard means of execution for condemned witches at the time. His black staff was burnt with him. Onlookers at the time were to report that the staff took on a life of its own when subjected to the heat of the flames – it danced and squirmed in a most alarming fashion. Grizel was hanged. As an act of final defiance, she attempted to take all her clothes off on the scaffold, prompting the hangman to act more quickly than he might have preferred.

It was not long before people had signs that Major Weir had returned to his old haunts after his execution. His house remained unoccupied for the most part of the one hundred and fifty years following his death – it had unpleasant associations. For a while, it was inhabited by a family with the name of Patullo, but they soon left, alarmed by the strange apparitions that plagued them. Empty or not, however, the house often seemed full of life – sounds of raucous merrymaking and devilish laughter were heard coming from the building. Lights were seen in the house at night, giving it an eerie glow. The sound of Grizel's spinning wheel was reported to have been heard by several people.

The house was finally demolished in the first half of the 19th century, but Major Weir and his sister have never gone away. They continue to haunt the area around the West Bow, although the street as it once was, from Edinburgh Castle to Grassmarket, has long gone. The Major has been seen striding about the streets, swinging his staff as he walks. The sound of Grizel's spinning wheel can still be heard from time to time. Sometimes Major Weir is seen to ride out on a phantom black horse. And from time to time, it is said, the sound of galloping horses and clattering wheels can be heard as the devil himself comes riding in his coach for another assignation with Thomas and Grizel.

Ghost: Dr Aaron Westall
Place: *Portrush, Antrim, Northern Ireland*
Date: Late 19th Century

Dr Aaron Westall was a medical practitioner in County Antrim, who flourished in the late 19th century. An able doctor, he was a popular figure in his locality, with a large number of patients in the countryside. Dr Westall, like many other medical men, liked the good life, with plenty of food and drink. Despite the resultant stoutness, he was also a keen sportsman, with a particular enthusiasm for golf, a sport to which the sandy links of the coast are ideally suited.

One afternoon, he was enjoying a round of golf with two friends (the place is sometimes identified as Portrush); it was a competitive game, and they were playing with a half-sovereign stake on each hole. Westall was having an excellent game and by the 13th hole was £8 richer by having won eight holes. But then a lad came Zrunning on to the course, calling for the doctor. A patient of his, who lived a mile away, on the Bushmills road, had been taken seriously ill. At first the doctor was reluctant, but then professional ethics prevailed, and he agreed to come immediately.

'But,' he said to his fellow-players, 'I'll be back. I haven't had all my money's worth out of you yet.'

They agreed to wait for him, and he departed at full speed in his gig.

But the doctor never returned. Having treated his patient, he set off again for the golf links, as fast as he could make his horse gallop. But, almost in sight of his destination, and swerving to avoid some hens in the road, he drove into the ditch. The gig overturned, he was thrown out, and killed instantly. The match was never completed.

But when his friends, McGruer and Watson, next went to play golf together, they had a strange experience at the 14th hole. Both had played their first shots, and were walking on, when they heard a voice behind them call, 'Fore!' and the unmistakable thwack of an iron striking the ball. Stumbling aside in haste, they looked back, and were amazed to see nobody on the green. But both were utterly convinced that the voice they had heard was that of their recently dead fellow-player, Dr Westall. With some trepidation, they continued their game, but the doctor did not disturb them again.

Ghosts: The Willington Mill House Ghosts
Place: ***Willington Mill House***
Date: 1830 Onwards

The stories surrounding Willington Mill House are many. They mostly concern the family of Joseph Proctor who lived in the house, which was built beside a tidal stream, at Willington, near Newcastle. Proctor came from a family of Quakers and was a devout man, with a solid, down-to-earth reputation. This sensible attitude to life did not help him or his family in the trials that lay ahead when they moved into the Mill House.

The house had been built on the site of a cottage which itself was the site of a terrible murder some years previously. The story went that a woman who lived in the cottage had been refused the confessional by the local priest as a result of horrendous events that took place in her home. One can only imagine what sort of atmosphere must have existed in the cottage. It is highly unlikely that the violent occurrence that brought such calumny on the woman was an isolated event. It is much more likely that it was the culminating episode in a whole series of fights and arguments going back over the years.

Against this background, it is not totally unusual for disturbed spirits to be left behind, long after the events that caused the distress in the first place. So it was for the unfortunate Proctor family. The Proctors started to witness hauntings just after they moved into the house. At first there were peculiar sounds and knockings that could not be placed but then the sounds became more recognisable as a person moving around. The footsteps could be heard coming from empty rooms but whenever anyone went to investigate, the noises stopped and nothing was found.

The family tried to determine the nature of the thing making the noises and by now, even considered that they were witness to supernatural events. They tried to get a trace of the ghost by sprinkling flour on the floor but even though they heard it walking in the area covered, no tracc of footsteps was found.

Then, one morning they were left in no doubt as to the spectral nature of the visitor. They were gathered in the sitting room for morning prayers, when they each heard heavy footfalls coming down the stairs and approaching the chamber where they were kneeling. Transfixed with fear, they watched as the footsteps came to the door, and felt great relief when they passed along the corridor towards the front door. Nothing was seen. At the front door they heard the ghost throw back the two sturdy bolts and turn the heavy lock that secured it in place. Mr Proctor rushed after the sounds only to find the front door ajar but nothing visible; only the departing footsteps as they crossed the courtyard.

Later, the sounds became even more frequent. They included the noise of small feet, rustling sounds of a woman's dress, heavy breathing and furniture being moved. One Whit Sunday things became even more serious and frightening; the family and their retainers started to see the ghosts as well as hear them. One of the few servants that had remained loyal to the Proctors through their troubled stay at the Mill House, was a maid called Mary Young. While she was carrying out some kitchen duties she was disturbed by a noise outside in the passage. She glanced in the direction of the noise and saw a well-dressed lady disappearing in the direction of the stairs. Mary followed and saw her enter one of the bedrooms, but when she looked inside there was no sign of her. That night the activity was more intense than usual.

There were other witnesses apart from the members of the Proctor household. Two of Mrs Proctors's sisters came to stay for a while and their experiences all happened at night while they were in bed. They shared the same four-poster bed surrounded with curtains. On different occasions, their bed was lifted up while they lay rigid with fear and the curtains were shaken vigorously. The final straw was when a figure of a woman said to be of a bluish hue, drifted through a wall and stood over them before retiring back from where she came. After this, the sisters refused to stay in that room and one of them decided to take lodgings with a couple who lived close by.

By this time, the family had realised that some rooms were more susceptible than others to the visitations, so they set up a stratagem to find out more. A specialist in spiritual investigation, Edward Drury, was invited to the house in an attempt to obtain some relief from the intrusions. On an evening in early July 1840, Drury duly arrived with a friend and set up watch in the bedroom that the two sisters had occupied. Drury took the first watch while his friend dozed off in a chair. They were not to be disappointed because shortly before one o'clock a ghostly apparition, that of a woman, appeared as if through a closet standing in the room. Drury watched transfixed as the figure cautiously approached him. It appeared to be in some pain or distress as if it had a 'stitch' or something even worse. Just before it reached Drury, the ghost turned towards his friend and stretched out its arm towards him. Thinking that his friend was in some kind of danger, Drury leapt to his defence and rushed at the spirit. That was the last thing he remembered for the next three hours. Witnesses say that they heard a terrific commotion and found Drury in a state of extreme terror, and had to carry him bodily down the stairs.

This was the most dramatic occurrence but by no means the last that happened at the Mill House. As she walked past the house with her new landlord, Thomas Mann, and his family, the sister who had previously left saw a priest-like figure moving around inside. It seemed able to move with ease through walls and looked out of the window for some time.

Although the above account refers to the occurrences at Willington Mill House at the time the Proctors stayed there, other strange phenomena had been reported before they moved in. One Thomas Davidson is said to have been the boyfriend of a girl who lived at the Mill House in 1834. He was calling on the girl one day when, as he walked up the path, he came across a white cat. The animal wrapped itself around his ankles in the way that cats do. Cats have never caught on to the fact that there may be more urgent thoughts on the mind of the human to whom they have attached themselves! Thomas attempted to push the cat away with his foot but it went straight through the creature. Thereafter it disappeared. As if upset by this experience, the cat returned a short while later and as if to show it really meant to be noticed, it started to hop about like a rabbit! Again, it failed to invoke the desired response from Thomas. The story goes on to relate that the next time it appeared, it was the size of a sheep and was luminous! Such a story does not lend credibility to the study of the supernatural so we will not dwell on it here!

Ghost: The Younger Brother of One George Wilson
Place: *Cavnakirk, Clogher Valley, Ireland*
Date: Not Known

At Cavnakirk in the Clogher Valley, in a house that has since been razed to the ground, lived George Wilson and his sister. They kept cows and farmed some acres of mountain ground. They had a younger brother, but he had been on very bad terms with his family, especially his sister, and had emigrated to Canada some years before. They had heard nothing from him, and hoped that he would stay away.

One summer evening, George Wilson took his cows down to the byre, left them there for his sister to do the milking, and went in to the kitchen for his supper. From where he sat, he could see through the open door to the byre, where his sister sat milking a cow and singing as she did so. He could hear the hiss of milk going into the pail.

Then he looked away, and as he looked back, he thought he saw a shadowy figure flit across the yard. Then all at once his sister gave a cry, and he got up and rushed out to her. He could hear what sounded like a furious struggle in the byre, and when he went in, he found her half-collapsed against the wall, her face gone black, her eyes staring, as if she were being strangled, while her hands pulled and tugged at her own throat as if trying to dislodge some invisible grip. As her brother came in, the strangling force suddenly abated, and he carried her back to the house.

When she was able to talk, she described what she had seen. Her other brother, who had gone to Canada, appeared round the side of the house. She thought he had returned, but the figure turned dim and shadowy, and abruptly flew at her, seized her by the throat, and started to strangle her. She could feel his grip, and see a shadowy pair of arms and hands, but there was nothing that she herself could get a grip on. Yet she was convinced that if it had not been for George, she would now be lying dead in the byre. When he had come in, she felt the shadowy form loosen its grip, but she had caught a glimpse of an evil, malevolent face, and she recognised it as that of her younger brother.

That night they both went to sleep in the same room, but as soon as night had fallen, a terrible noise began in the kitchen. George Wilson lit a candle and went to investigate, but could see nothing. The noises continued through the night. Next day, the Wilsons told their neighbours what had happened, and two or three volunteered to stay the next night with them. As they sat in the kitchen, all was quiet. But as soon as the kitchen light was put out, and the company moved into the other room, the same crashing, clanging noise broke out in the kitchen. Again, when they went to look, there was nothing to see and no sign of any damage. They returned to the other room and immediately the crashes and thumps resumed, and so it went on all night, and on subsequent nights. George Wilson and his sister were forced to seek the hospitality of their neighbours in order to get a good night's sleep.

At last they enlisted the help of one Richard Robinson, a man who had dealt before with similar situations – he was deeply religious and possessed no fear of ghosts. He stayed in the bedroom with the brother and sister. They lay down on their beds, and he sat with a lighted candle. By and by there was a crash, and a moment later a chair was tipped over. The woman screamed as her bed began to heave up into the air. Robinson slashed beneath it with a sword, and the movement ceased, but another chair went over, and then the bed heaved again. Distracted by a crash from the kitchen, Robinson ran in there to look, but a scream from the sister brought him back. She had seen and felt a dim figure spring on to her bed and reach for her throat.

News came from Canada that the younger Wilson had died there, and when they checked the date, they found his death had occurred on the day of the attack in the byre. Not knowing what was the best thing to do, the two eventually sold their land and emigrated themselves, leaving the baleful spirit of their brother behind.

Ghosts: The Wilton Castle Ghosts
Place: *Wilton Castle, Republic of Ireland*
Date: 1836 Onwards

Wilton Castle, in southeastern Ireland, was destroyed by fire during the War of Independence. It had been the home of the Anglo-Irish Alcock family since the 17th century. It had a famous ghost in the form of Harry Alcock, head of the family, who died in 1840. On the anniversary of his death, it was said that he could be seen at sunset, driving slowly away from the castle gate in a ghostly carriage. Crowds would gather to watch out for the spectacle. A local blacksmith even claimed to have talked to the landlord's spectre.

Another unquiet spirit inhabited the same neighbourhood, that of Archibald Jacob, a friend of the Alcocks. In the uprising of 1798, Jacob was prominent among those who tortured anyone thought to have information about the rebellion. He died in 1836, by a fall from his horse, and his ghost haunted the roadside, liable to terrify late-night passers-by. On one occasion, when a priest was called to the castle to carry out an exorcism, the figure of Jacob was seen to appear in the fireplace, then vanish again in a cloud of smoke.

Ghost: A Woman Dressed in White
Place: *Blandford, Dorset*
Date: 1837

Polly Allen was three years old in July 1837 when, playing in the back garden of her home, she saw a figure coming down the hill opposite. She ran inside and asked her mother to come out and look at a 'woman dressed in white'. Her mother dismissed what she said, and when Polly and her sisters went outside the figure had vanished.

Probably no more would have been heard of this little story, but later on that day the local vicar arrived to tell Polly's mother that her husband had died. It turned out that he had been drowned along with two of his colleagues while they were cutting reeds in the nearby River Stour. The strange thing was that the time of his death coincided with the child's vision.

John Allen seems to have been particularly sensitive to the spirit world, because several months earlier he had apparently been warned of his impending demise. He came home one evening in a great deal of distress. He wept bitterly for over an hour, but the only explanation that his wife could extract from him was that he had seen 'that which told him he should not be long here'. She never learned what he had seen – whether, for example, it was a vision of his own death or his gravestone or whatever, and the story just emphasises the problems of trying to rationalise the inexplicable.

Ghost: A Woman in a White, Hooded Nun's Habit
Place: *Cheltenham, Gloucestershire, England*
Date: 1939

Miss Margot Smith was at one time in the 1930s a nurse at a private school in a large house in Cheltenham where a ghost appeared regularly at 6.15 p.m. One night in 1939, she was called by the headmaster to witness the apparition in the grounds. The figure was some distance from the house, perhaps 45 metres away, and at the far end of the school playground as seen from an upstairs window. As Miss Smith and the headmaster watched the figure, which seemed to be wearing a white, hooded nun's habit, it appeared to sit down although there was no seat in its vicinity. Miss Smith was asked to watch as the headmaster went to see if a clearer view could be had from a lower floor but the figure vanished.

When telling the story later, in 1951, Miss Smith said that she had seen the ghost on subsequent occasions. It had appeared on the New Year's Eve of 1940 but had, on that day, been seen at 7.15 p.m. as British Summer Time was then in force. It was seen at the same place as before and, this time, the headmaster and Miss Smith had gone to the edge of the playground. The figure had appeared as solid and distinct as when it had been seen the previous year. A torch was shone on the apparition but it instantly went out and could not be made to work. The pair were so disconcerted at this that they forgot their resolve to try to speak with the figure and retreated to the school buildings.

Fairies and Phantoms

Fairies

It is hard, perhaps impossible, to separate ghosts and fairies into distinct entities, for the stories and beliefs that relate to them are closely intertwined. For example, the fairy and the ghost were much the same according to certain traditions. Some fairies were not so much perceived as 'little people' but rather as spirits of people long dead, either imprisoned on earth or left on earth after having been denied entrance to either heaven or hell. Some fairies were believed to be evildoers and mischief-makers, abducting women and children; others were less malevolent, granting wishes and effecting changes for the better in the lives of the mortals who crossed their paths.

Human interaction with the fairy world was fraught with problems. There was always the danger that if you crossed a fairy the consequences could be unpleasant in the extreme. Thus, there are stories of people who have discovered a magic salve that, if rubbed on their eyes, helps them to see fairies. When this facility is discovered by someone in the fairy kingdom, the mortal concerned at the very least has the facility taken away, but more often will have the offending eye or eyes put out.

There are countless tales of people who have seen into the world, or kingdom, of the fairies, whether through gift, by chance, through the use of a magic salve or in a dream. Stories of people who have had such access to, or sight of, the world of the fairies often tell how a living person has looked into the fairy world and recognised relatives, friends or acquaintances who have died and are now living in the fairy realm. Tales such as these reinforce the idea of a link between the ghost or spirit of the dead and the fairy.

The fairy world, much like the world of the spirits, has its own time, which bears no relation to real time. This uniqueness of time, or perhaps timelessness, which is associated with fairyland, is illustrated by one particular story that comes from Inverness.

The Dance at Tomnahurich Hill near Inverness

The story tells how two fiddlers were visiting Inverness, looking for places to perform, when they met an old man who asked them if they would play at a dance for him. This they agreed to, and they followed the old man to a place called Tomnahurich. They reached Tomnahurich, a small hill outside Inverness, towards nightfall. They entered a opening in the side of the hill and found themselves in a richly decorated hall where scenes of great merriment were taking place. A party was well under way, with food and wine laid on in astonishing quality and abundance. The fiddlers found themselves in the company of many beautiful, but very small and fine-boned, women. The men were allowed to eat and drink their fill at the feast before the dancing began. When they took up their fiddles to play, the party got into full swing. The fiddlers played their hearts out but did so with great pleasure as the music was enlivening and uplifting and the dancing ladies were a joy to behold. Time passed, and they hardly seemed to notice it.

At last, when it seemed that morning had come, the dancing came to a halt and the fiddlers packed up, ready to leave. The old man who had hired them paid them generously with a bag of silver and the fiddlers departed from the hillock in fine spirits. It had been a great night and a most profitable one. They wandered back towards Inverness, and it was here that things seemed to take a strange turn. Everything was different. The town itself had changed so much that they hardly recognised it as the same place. New buildings had sprung up, as if from nowhere. The people had changed too. They all wore very different clothes and laughed when they saw what the fiddlers were wearing, calling their attire 'strange' and 'old-fashioned'.

The fiddlers could not work out what was wrong and decided to return to their own home town. Here they found that the situation was much the same. It was as if several tens of years had passed in the real world while the fiddlers had been away playing at the dance at Tomnahurich.

Finally, the two men tried to take refuge in religion and went to their local church. Their appearance caused quite a stir, but the congregation were silenced when the minister started to speak. Then, at the first mention of the name of God, the two fiddlers crumbled to dust in front of all those present.

The fact that the men were said to crumble to dust when the name of God was mentioned bears out another widespread belief about fairies – that their existence was somehow at odds with God and God's world; that they were, in fact, more associated with things demonic. Other stories about fairies often relate how the little creatures disappear at the mention of God.

Taken byFairies

The fairies, or wild spirits of the Irish countryside, were notorious for their snatching of human children. Boys especially were at risk. Many old photographs vouch for the fact that in the far West of Ireland, and well into the twentieth century, many boys even of ten or eleven were kept in dresses, to fool the fairies into supposing they were girls. One of W. B. Yeats's most haunting poems is the fairies' call to the mortal child:

Come away, O human child,
To the waters and the wild,
For the world's more full of weeping than you can understand.

Mary Scannell's Baby

Mary Scannell was a young wife who lived with her husband not far from Castle Martyr, on the road from Cork to Youghal. She had a baby in the spring, and when it came to harvest time, she took the baby with her out to the fields, wrapped up in her brown cloak, by the edge of the field. But when she came over to feed the child, she found a baby in the cloak that was not half the size of her own child, with a wizened little yellow face, that set up such a crying and screeching it was worse than a sick cat.

Guessing what had happened, Mary picked up the little creature in the cloak, pretending to talk fondly to it, as if it were her own baby, and took herself as fast as she could to a wise woman. The wise woman looked at the little yellow-faced thing, and told Mary Scannell not to feed it, and to pinch and slap it without mercy, no matter how loud it howled. This she did, and after a week of days and nights in which she got no rest and no sleep, with the screaming of the creature, at last a night came in which she fell asleep, and when she woke in the morning, her own child was by her side again.

Mrs Sheridan's Child

Old Mrs Sheridan 'was wrinkled and half-blind, and had gone barefoot through her lifetime', according to Lady Gregory (a friend and patron of W. B. Yeats whose *Kiltartan Notebooks* contain many first-hand accounts of the occult). But she was in contact with the invisible world. Among her stories of 'taken' children that were taken was one of her own:

There was a child I had, and he a year and a half old, and he got a quinsy and a choking in the throat and I was holding him in my arms beside the fire, and all in a minute he died. And the men were working down by the river, washing sheep, and they heard the crying of a child from over there in the air, and they said, 'That's Sheridan's child'. So I knew sure enough that he was taken

The Ballymacduff Drownings

Another of Mrs Sheridan's stories was both more circumstantial and more gruesome:

One time when I was living at Ballymacduff there was two little boys drowned in the river there, one was eight years old and the other eleven years. And I was out in the fields, and the people looking in the river for their bodies, and I saw a man coming away from it, and the two boys with him, he holding a hand of each and leading them away. And he saw me stop and look at them, and he said, 'Take care, would you bring them from me, she'll never come home to you again.' And one of the little chaps broke from his hand and ran to me, and the other cried out to him, 'Oh, Pat, would you leave me!'

So then he went back and the men led them away. And then I saw another man, very tall he was, and crooked, and watching me like this with his head down and he was leading two dogs the other way, and I knew well where he was going and what he was going to do with them.

And when I heard the bodies were laid out, I went to the house to have a look at them, and those were never the two boys that were lying there, but the two dogs that were put in their places. I knew this by the sort of stripes on the bodies such as you'd see in the covering of a mattress; and I knew the boys couldn't be in it, after me seeing them led away.

The 'Taken' Bride

In Galway in the nineteenth century, a man from Duras married a girl from Ardrahan. The wedding was at the bride's home, and at the end of it, the young couple left for the groom's house, she riding behind her uncle on his horse, as it was customary for the bride to be escorted to her new home by her nearest male relative.

As they were passing by the churchyard at Ardrahan, the uncle felt her break out into a fit of shivering so violent that she almost fell off the horse. When he asked her what ailed her, she said that passing the graveyard had caused her to think of her dead mother. He put his hand behind to help support her, but her body felt as limp as a piece of tow.

They arrived eventually at the groom's house, and she lived there for a year, and had a baby. But she died giving birth to the child. Everyone however believed that the night she was taken was that of her wedding.

Biddy Purcell

Carrigogunnell Castle, near Limerick, is famously described in Frank McCourt's memoir of his boyhood, *Angela's Ashes*. But long before that, its ruins had a reputation for spookiness. Biddy Purcell was a bright, cheerful young girl of eighteen or so, who went one Sunday with her sister and other girls to pick rushes from the boggy land between the castle and the River Shannon. Just as they were passing the castle gateway, a small child, or what seemed to be one, came out and gave Biddy a touch between the shoulder-blades with a switch of wood. She felt a strange pain pass through her, into her heart, and out again. But the other girls laughed, and on they went to gather rushes. Biddy was by herself and had gathered a good pile of rushes, when a strange little old woman came up to her and said, 'Biddy Purcell, give me some of your rushes.' Something about the old woman made Biddy afraid, but she still said, 'The bog is big enough for everyone; pluck your own.'

The little old woman flew into a rage, and gave the girl a slash across the knees and feet with a little whip she had. Now, with the pain at her heart, and the pain in her legs and feet, Biddy was in a bad way. She stumbled home crying, and lay sick in her bed for five days. She told her sister that she had seen a vision of fairy men riding out from underneath the castle, and all but one had a girl mounted behind him; that one was waiting for her.

The family sent for a man supposed to have skill in bringing people back, and he made a potion of herbs which he told them to boil. If it turned green, then Biddy might still be saved; if it turned yellow, then she was already too far gone. The potion turned yellow; and when they gave it to her to drink, she very soon after died. And though she was given Christian burial, there were those who believed that the company of riders under Carrigogunnell Castle was now at last complete.

Glaistigs

In Scotland, the glaistig was another supernatural being, a female who appeared in various forms and was sometimes associated with spirits of the dead. Some of the forms that this phenomenon was supposed to take on included half-woman, half-goat, a dog, a sheep, a woman in green and a monster. Whether or not the glaistig was a malevolent being is uncertain. Supernatural occurrences both catastrophic and benign have been attributed to glaistigs in different parts of Scotland at different times. Glaistigs have been commonly associated with water, said to live in places such as waterfalls, lochs and burns. Some were said to be particularly attached to, and protective of, animals, the young and the feeble, herding cows, playing games with children and caring for the sick and elderly. Some stories associate mischief with the concept of the glaistig, and activities similar to those of a poltergeist have been attributed to glaistigs in various folkloric tales. Other tales tell of much more sinister events, however, such as the waylaying and killing of travellers and the pronouncing of curses. Some people, accordingly, saw the glaistig as a manifestation of evil.

Where the glaistig came from or how she came into existence was also a matter of differing opinions, but the link with the dead was never far away. She was sometimes perceived as a human being who had fallen under fairy enchantment; sometimes she was seen as a spirit of a dead person, sometimes a devilish creature with malicious intent. Whatever she was, or wherever she came from, the glaistig was tied in with traditions that link the idea of an afterlife with that of some sort of realm coexistent with the world of the living but inhabited by supernatural beings.

Green Ladies

There are links between the concept of the glaistig and the many tales that are told of green-lady ghosts. Green ladies pop up here, there and everywhere in Scotland, and are often regular visitors and familiar sights to the people and the places that they haunt. Glaistigs, as has been already mentioned, were sometimes said to appear as ladies dressed in green.

Some green-lady ghosts have acquired a reputation for a certain amount of mischief. This links them with some traditional perceptions of the glaistig. In addition to this, certain green-lady ghosts have been said to be able to assume different forms, such as those of a dog or a horse, a feature held in common with glaistigs.

Glaistigs were anonymous creatures, but this is not always the case with green-lady ghosts. Their identities and the reasons for their presence are often known to those whom they haunt.

The Caoineag

The caoineag was another grim spirit who made her presence felt when death was close, but she was less accessible to humans than the banshee. Like the banshee, she was heard to mourn and lament at the edge of a river or stream, but the caoineag was not visible to the human eye. She could not be approached and no one could talk to her. Those who heard the sound of her mourning were said to be doomed to face death or great sorrow.

She was believed to be the spectre of a woman who had died in childbirth. It was widely believed that when a woman died in such a manner, all her clothes had to be washed at once. If this was not done, the woman, who had died before her time was due, would be condemned to wash and to wail in some sort of limbo until she reached her 'due time' on earth; that is, until a time was reached when it would have been more natural and appropriate for her to die.

Devilish Struggles

There was a certain fascination, verging on preoccupation, with the devil long ago in Scotland. If anything or anyone was particularly feared for any reason, the hand of the devil had to be in there somewhere. Thus it was that men like John Graham of Claverhouse, 'Bonnie Dundee', came to be associated with the black arts. He was greatly feared, and the actions he took against his enemies, in particular the Covenanters, earned him widespread hatred. Stories began to circulate that his work was more than human and that he was in some way devilishly inspired. The rumours grew wilder over time. He was said to have consorted with the devil, to have practised the black arts and to have struck a deal with the devil whereby he would become invincible in battle. As the fear and loathing of the man increased in intensity, so the stories about him became more fantastic. Sir Tam Dalyell, a contemporary and ally of Claverhouse, earned himself a similar reputation.

The devil could be a convenient excuse for getting rid of someone who was proving to be a particular nuisance. Many a woman met a terrible death in Scotland in the sixteenth century, condemned for witchcraft and satanic practices. Some of these women might have been guilty of certain unsavoury practices; some, undoubtedly, practised the black arts. Nevertheless, it cannot be denied that, as far as many of them were concerned, they had done nothing to deserve their fate. Sometimes it was the case that a woman simply knew too much for her own good – a superior intellect and an inquiring mind were often treated with suspicion and could be enough to inspire a witch-hunt. Some women were too gossipy, others kept themselves to themselves too much, and the remainder simply behaved in a way that somebody, somehow, found offensive.

Those who did practise the black arts, both women and men, were said to be well acquainted with the devil. Those who admitted to such knowledge, or were forced into admission of such knowledge, suffered greatly for it. Some survived the rumours, but their notoriety lived on after them. If the stories that are told about them are to be believed, the spirits of people like these almost always seem to return. So we hear of the ghost of Major Weir (see page 275), who consorted with the devil and still haunts the Old Town in Edinburgh, and the ghost of Alexander Skene, riding in his coach across the lake every year on Hogmanay to meet with Auld Nick (see page 226).

The devil made frequent visits to the land of the living, according to tradition. He prowled the world of mortals in various forms, haunting the virtuous, tormenting the indecisive and tempting away the impious. Whether he appeared as man, beast or monster, the devil could always be identified by his cloven feet.

The story of Earl Beardie of Glamis Castle. related on page 114, is another of the many legends that tells of a visit from the devil to mere mortals – with disastrous consequences for foolish Beardie.

The Devil and the Highlander

Another story, which comes from Galloway, tells of a meeting in Glenluce between a proud Highlander and the devil. Plague was rampaging the countryside, sent by the devil himself, and the Highlander and his family were among the fortunate few who had not caught it. The Highlander had jokingly boasted that he owed his own survival to two things – first, the fine Highland blood that coursed through his body; secondly, the fine malt whisky that also ran through his veins in large quantities.

The devil had been annoyed that someone should have the effrontery to speak of the plague in such a light-hearted manner. He appeared in front of the Highlander one night as the bold man was making his way home from the local hostelry. The devil challenged the Highlander to answer for his cheek, but the Highlander, full of Dutch courage, was undaunted. He felt up to any challenge that was offered him. After some debate, the devil and the Highlander agreed that they would hold a wrestling contest. If the devil won, he would infect the Highlander with the plague. If the Highlander won, the devil would have to put the plague in a bag and give it to the Highlander to dispose of.

The devil was strong, but the Highlander was a wily fighter. They wrestled with each other for some time without a clear victor emerging, both claiming to have won the tussle. In order to settle the argument, they hit upon the idea of a piping contest. The devil rustled up some pipes for them to play and the contest began. The devil, taking his turn first, played a fine tune, but when the Highlander picked up the pipes and began to play, the devil soon realised that here was a man who could play the pipes like no other. The Highlander's music was powerful and moving. It made the devil laugh, dance and weep in turn. The devil could not fail to be impressed and readily admitted defeat. He collected the plague together like a big black cloud in his hand, sealed it in a bag and gave it to the Highlander as promised.

The Highlander had gambled with the devil, a dangerous pastime if ever there was one. Now he was one of the fortunate few who won. He took the bag that the devil had given him to the abbot in Glenluce to see what could be done to get rid of the plague once and for all. It took all the powers of the monks in the abbey to subdue the dark spirits of the plague but at last they succeeded, and the dreadful disease was gone from Galloway.

Tam O'Shanter and the Devil

So we know that the devil was a gambler. He liked a game of cards, and he enjoyed pitting his wits against mere mortals. He was also a rogue with a liking for a good party. In whatever guise he appears in story or verse, as man or beast, the most frequent things associated with his appearance are music, dancing and wild times. Those who did choose to dabble in the occult and practise witchcraft may have traded their eternal souls when they did so, but they probably thought it worthwhile for the earthly pleasures of taking part in wild bacchanalian rites. Moreover, these pleasures did not necessarily come to an end with death. The ghost of Major Weir is said to haunt the West Bow in Edinburgh still. He was executed after confessing to witchcraft, but following his death, the sounds that were said to emanate from his house before it was ultimately demolished were not those of tortured wailing or lament – they were the sounds of wild merrymaking. His earthly demise may have been most unpleasant, but his ghost, it would seem, was still having quite a good time of it.

Robert Burns' famous narrative poem 'Tam O' Shanter' portrays the devil as:

. . . in shape o' beast
A towsy tyke, black, grim and large.

Burns' devil plays the pipes with gusto as the scantily clad witches dance around him with wild abandon. Tam fears for his life, and indeed his soul, when he comes upon the scene and sees the witches cavorting with the spirits of unchristened children and criminals. But in spite of himself he feels drawn to the sight. The devil and his entourage are having fun!

A Battle of Wits

Other stories of the devil and his encounters with mortals tell of the devil being outdone, not so much by piety or the power of God as by sheer ingenuity. One particular legend that has been told of such a battle of wits between a mortal and the devil has been associated in slightly different versions with Michael Scott (see page 221), the notorious thirteenth-century philosopher (some would say sorcerer), Lord Reay and another anonymous man. The stories differ only in detail; the essence is the same:

The devil has had encounters with the hero of the story before and is looking for a way to torment him. He gives the hero the use of one of his demonic servants to work for him at whichever tasks the hero chooses. The demonic worker is then set a variety of enormous tasks to carry out (bridge-building, barn-building, etc) and completes each task in record time, returning again and again for more work and giving the hero no peace. The hero finally hits upon a plan and instructs his tormentor to go down to the beach and construct a rope of sand. The demonic worker is then condemned to work forever at this impossible task. No sooner has something resembling a rope been made than the tide comes in and washes it away. The devil has been defeated once again.

The fear of the devil amongst the Scots, therefore, can be seen to have been counterbalanced by a certain amount of humour, and also, perhaps, a little envy. Nor is it always the case that those who have associated with the Evil One in life are seen to suffer for it after death. Ghosts with demonic associations are not necessarily unhappy ghosts, it would appear.

The Demon Crab

The devil appeared as many things. People saw him in the form of animals and strange monsters as well as in human form. Whenever something mysterious or sinister happened, signs of the devil were sought in case the events might be his work. One particular tale from Dundee in Scotland illustrates quite well that no matter how ready mere mortals were to see Auld Nick, they were not always right in what they saw.

A tragedy had occurred – a brave ferryman had been caught with his boat in a squall and the boat had gone down with all its passengers. Some time later, when the storm had finally subsided, the body of the ferryman was washed up ashore, just in front of the cottage where he had lived. The body was pulled into the cottage and laid out carefully in order that the locals might come and pay their respects. There was quite a crowd gathered. They stood in respectful silence as they looked at the bedraggled corpse of the drowned man.

Suddenly, someone saw a movement in the sleeve of the dead man's jacket. The crowd gave a gasp – the corpse was stirring! The corpse, however, lay quite still, and out of the sleeve crawled an enormous black crab. To the superstitious fisherfolk present, the crab could be only one thing – the devil himself! Everyone jumped back as the satanic beast scuttled across the floor of the cottage and made for the door. A path was quickly cleared to let the crab move on towards the sea – no one dared impede the progress of the devil!

At that moment an elderly fishwife stepped forward, scooped up the crab and tucked it securely in her pinny. Much to everyone's horror, she announced that it was a meal too good to waste. Stories flew here and there for many days afterwards about the terrible smells that issued from the fishwife's cottage as she cooked the crab. Some people even claimed to have seen a beastly black form flying out of the cottage as the fishwife put the crab in the pot to boil. In spite of the conjectures and rumours, however, no one could deny the fact that the fishwife ate the crab, enjoyed it, and came to no harm from the experience. People might have been reluctant to admit it, but it seemed that they had got it wrong about the Demon Crab.

Banshees

In various parts of Scotland, the sight or sound of a woman lamenting and washing clothes has for centuries been associated with doom and death. One such washerwoman was the banshee, who could be seen by streams and rivers, singing mournful laments as she washed the clothes of one or more people who were about to meet with a violent death. The banshee, it was said, could be approached with caution. If a mortal managed to sneak up to a banshee unnoticed, he or she could then take hold of her and ask her who was to die. Some people believed that, once caught, the banshee would also grant three wishes.

In Ireland, this harbinger of imminent death (literally 'fairy-woman) has a long history, which has been carefully examined by Patricia Lysaght in her book *The Banshee*. The unseen universe beyond our own, which can only be dimly perceived even by those who have some ability to sense it and communicate with it, contains beings that can present themselves in a variety of different ways.

It is said that a banshee was heard wailing in Glencoe shortly before the massacre of the MacDonalds by the Campbells. Some of the MacDonalds heard the noise and, realising that they were in peril, fled to the hills. This, so it has been said, is one of the reasons why the massacre, awful though it was, was not as bad as it might have been. Forty members of the clan perished, it is true, but given the facts that they were outnumbered by the Campbells and taken by surprise during the night, the numbers of the dead were not as great as might have been anticipated.

'Not for You'

It was not everyone whose death was presaged by the banshee. Once upon a time in Ireland in Dingle there were a lot of the Hussey family living in John Street, most of them merchants in a small way. One night, in the very middle of the darkest time, the banshee was heard wailing outside. In every house there were anxious faces and worried meetings. Some one was going to die – but who? But then to their surprise the banshee stopped her crying and they heard her voice outside, telling them in Irish:

Listen, listen, you hoarding traders,
You are not in danger,
A banshee never keened your kind.

The next day, they heard that a gentleman in the town, also of the name of Hussey, had died that night.

A Sceptic Converted . . .

In her scholarly book, *The Banshee*, from which the previous story comes, Patricia Lysaght also relates the story of a County Offaly man who 'did not believe in the banshee until it came home to me that there is such a thing as the banshee. I proved it. I was putting in the cows one evening. We had three cows and I put in a mash for one of the cows. When I was coming down with the cows, I heard a terrible cry, and didn't I run down. I thought someone was after meeting with an accident. But there was nothing wrong with any beast or human.

Now, when we seen that nothing happened, it kind of left our heads what occurred. But that same evening I heard the cry, Mary Anne (narrator's sister) had a letter in her pocket. She took out the letter which was from a brother of ours who was in North America. Martin was his name. And Martin said in the letter that another brother of ours had gone to hospital, he wasn't so well. About three weeks after, we got word that he was dead. So it would appear that at the time we heard the terrible cry our brother, Mike, was after dying. But I wouldn't believe such a thing unless it came home to me. And that's not such a terrible long time ago.

. . . and Another

In Rylands, Newtowncunningham, there once lived a family named Dunn, and the wail of the banshee was heard before the death of any member of it.

A local clergyman thought this was all nonsense, until he was called to the bedside of a dying Miss Dunn. Her friends sat around. He joined the company, and led a prayer. After it he was very surprised to hear in the distance a wail, as of someone in distress. The others heard it too. Shortly afterwards, Miss Dunn died. From that time onwards, the clergyman often told the story, remarking in slight misquotation of

Shakespeare's *Hamlet*, 'There are more things in heaven and earth than are dreamt of in your philosophy.'

Lament for the Harper

Although some sources claim that the banshee cries only for those born into old Irish families with the Mac or O' prefix, there are many accounts that challenge this. One tells of the Rev. Charles Bunworth, an 18th-century Rector of Buttevant, Co Cork. He had the unusual accomplishment – for a clergyman – of being able to play superbly on the Irish harp. Perhaps it was his sympathy for this traditional instrument that won him the attention of the banshee. The old man was ill, but not considered in a dangerous condition, when his herdsman, Kavanagh, who had been sent to Mallow to pick up some medicine, came back in a highly agitated state. He told the rector's daughter, Miss Elizabeth Bunworth, that all the way back he had been accompanied by the keening of a banshee, who had mentioned the rector's name many times. He described her as 'keening, and screeching, and clapping her hands, by my side every step of the way, with her long white hair falling about her shoulders'.

At Elizabeth's request he said nothing about his experience. But a few nights later, the old man, whose condition had got a little worse, was being watched over by an elderly female relation, when a sound was heard from outside, as of a woman moaning, close to the window. Some of those in the house went out, to identify the source, but nothing was to be seen or heard. Yet, when they came back in, those inside the house assured them that the moaning had gone on, with clapping of hands, all the time they were out. And when they were back inside, they heard it again themselves. Now the condition of the sick man grew rapidly worse, and late that night, just before dawn, he died.

The One Who Did Not Hear

It was commonly said the cry of the banshee was never heard by the person who was destined to die (there are some stories that dispute this). In one case the girls of a family named O'Casey were out working in the bog, near a big hole called the Poll Rua ('red pool'), and the banshee began to cry from the edge of the bog. They all heard it quite clearly except for one of them. They wondered why she could not hear it when it was so clear to them. But on the way home, when they stopped at the Poll Rua to wash, this girl fell in, and was drowned.

The Song of the Banshee

In Spicer's *Strange Things Among Us* is the account of a banshee in the Kenealy family, which was heard mourning at the deathbed of a child, a young boy. His brother told the story of how the family and the doctor were gathered round the bed. It was a beautiful day, the window was open on a prospect of fields and hills, and sunlight streamed in. As they stood, they heard a strain of music, more entrancing than any normal human music. Accompanying it was the sound of a woman's voice, melancholy and yet melodious, and expressive of profound grief. For several movements they listened, and then the sound diminished and fell away, and as it ceased to be audible they saw that the sick boy was dying. The nurse who was there exclaimed, 'That is the banshee,' and everyone who was present agreed that nothing physical could have produced that singing.

The Banshee at Bunratty

Rathlaheen Cottage, a house near Bunratty Castle, had been burned down in 1921 and later rebuilt. It had been haunted by unexplained knockings on doors and walls. In 1956 the banshee was heard here, immediately before a death occurred.

The Shane Castle Banshee

In Shane Castle, home of the O'Neills, there was at one time a room that was said to be the banshee's, and if her figure was seen to pace up and down inside it, crying and wringing her hands, then it was sure that some fatality in the family would follow. The banshee was described as a female figure of great beauty, tall, slender, dressed in green with a golden girdle, and with long golden hair and blue eyes.

The O'Donnell Banshee

In the course of several descriptions of the banshee, Elliott O'Donnell recorded a personal experience. He and his wife were awakened about midnight by a series of agonising and heartrending cries. If they had any earthly resemblance, it seemed to him that they were like the cries of a woman in the greatest distress. At length they died away in a long drawn-out sobbing wail. Then, hearing whispering outside the bedroom door, O'Donnell got up and opened it, and found all the other occupants of the house gathered there, talking in hushed and frightened voices about the sound which they had all heard. At their request, O'Donnell searched through the house and went out into the grounds around, but was not surprised to find nothing. He had recognised it as the cry of the banshee, and two or three days later heard that his aunt, also an O'Donnell, had died, on the day following the banshee's cry.

The O'Brien Banshee

In the seventeenth century, the Englishwoman Anne, Lady Fanshawe, with her husband, was visiting Lady Honora O'Brien, daughter of the Earl of Thomond. She described in her memoirs, published in London in 1907, how she woke up at night, disturbed by the sound of a voice. She was in a four-poster bed, and, drawing aside its curtains, found she was looking straight at the window. There she saw a woman's face, pale and with huge sad eyes, looking in at her. Surrounding the face was a mass of red-gold hair, clearly visible in the moonlight. For some moments the woman in the bed and the phantom at the window simply gazed at each other; then the apparition spoke. Three times it 'spake loud, and in a tone I never heard, thrice, 'Atone', and then with a sigh, more like wind than breath, she vanished, and to me her body looked more like a thick cloud than substance.'

Lady Fanshawe woke her husband, who had slept through it all, and told him what she had seen. He did not mock her story, and told her that such apparitions were well known in Ireland. In the morning, Lady Honora informed her guests that a cousin of hers had died that night in the castle, at about two o'clock in the morning. She herself had been up all night, but hoped that nothing had disturbed her visitors. Her reason for concern was that, whenever a member of the O'Brien family was at the point of death, the shape of a woman appeared, at the very room where she had inadvertently lodged her guests. According to Lady Honora the banshee was the phantom of a woman who had been seduced and then murdered long ago by the castle's lord. The body had been buried in the ground beneath that window.

A Banshee in Italy

Elliott O'Donnell gives the story of a banshee that came to a family on Irish extraction living in Italy. They were the Neilsinis, descended from one of the O'Neills, an officer who had served in the French king's Irish Brigade, and who had fled France after the revolution of 1789. In time he became a wealthy Count in Italy, and changed the family name to something more Italian-sounding. His great-grandson, who inherited the family's wealth and title, was cruising in his own yacht, with a party of friends, on one of the lakes in the Italian Alps. At one point, one of the guests asked him, 'Count, who is that strange-looking woman over there?' Puzzled, the count replied that there were only the guests' own wives, and his stewardess on board.

'Oh, no,' said the other man, an army colonel, 'I have certainly seen some one else.' Then he gave a gasp, and put his hands before his eyes.

'Oh my God, what a face!' he exclaimed.

'What is it?' asked the count, greatly concerned.

'It's gone,' replied the colonel. 'It was like nothing belonging to this world – a woman of no earthly type, with a queer-shaped, gleaming face, a mass of red hair, and eyes that would have been beautiful but for their expression, which was hellish. She wore a green hood, like an Irish peasant-woman.'

'That sounds like a banshee,' said one of the party.

'We are Irish,' said the count, and told them the story of his grandfather. 'It means the death of someone very closely associated with me. Pray God it is not my wife or my daughter.'

But it was he himself who was seized, two hours later, with an attack of angina pectoris, and died later that same day.

Superstitions on Death and Dying

Many superstitions survive to this day concerning the dead and the dying in Scotland. They have their origins in times when people were much more familiar with death, particularly premature death, than they are nowadays, when the country is no longer torn by war and internal feuding and when medical science is able to ensure that most of us survive into old age.

The custom of sitting up with a corpse before the funeral – the wake, or lykewake – has its origins in the belief that the body of the dead person needed protection from unwanted spiritual interference before it was given a proper burial. In the past there were several symbolic rites associated with the wake, intended to protect the spirit of the dead and send it safely to the afterlife, and also to protect those who remained living.

Those who sat up with the body at night were provided with a bible, a candle, whisky and food. In some parts of the country it was tradition that there was to be no fire lit in the room in which the corpse lay. The spirit of the dead person was in danger of being interfered with by the forces of evil and therefore no chances were taken with the corpse awaiting burial. Domestic animals were kept well away; if a cat or a dog passed over the body it had to be killed. Mirrors in the room were covered up, and if there was a clock in the room, it had to be stopped.

Those who sat up at night with the corpse had to remain there until daylight. If they left in the dark, it was believed that they might witness something fearful.

When the corpse had been laid out, a wooden platter was placed on its chest. On the platter was placed a small pile of earth – symbolic of the body – and another of salt – the spirit, which lived on after death. Sometimes only a small pile of salt was placed on the body.

In spite of all the precautions that were taken to ensure the safety of the dead person's spirit and the souls of those who had come to keep the corpse company, the lykewake was not always mournful by any means. It could be quite a social occasion. In some parts, the long night was whiled away with storytelling and singing – even dancing was not unknown.

Signs of Death

In Scotland, signs of approaching death were many. See, for example, the two stories associated with John Graham of Claverhouse (Viscount Dundee or 'Bonnie Dundee') on page 91. The gift (or curse) of second sight has often revealed itself for the first (sometimes the only) time when somebody has seen, or dreamt, of an imminent death. Many other stories record ghostly happenings or sights that then turn out to have been warnings of death. Some of these occurrences are very individual in nature, but there are others that have come to be accepted widely as death warnings, communications from the realm of the dead to the land of the living through a living medium.

Death Lights

Sightings of death lights, or death candles as they were often known, were quite commonly reported. These were lights that were seen in graveyards, close to the sickbed of a dying person or near the site of an imminent death or disaster. Thus an unfamiliar light seen on water was believed to foretell a drowning or a tragedy at sea, and a light above a house meant that death would take place therein before long.

Ghostly lights, similar to death lights, have often been reported shining at the sites of tragedies, in particular ancient battlefields. Rather than warnings of death to come, these lights seem to be markers or reminders of death that has gone before.

Ghosts of the Living

A ghostly figure of a person still alive might be seen alongside that person or sometimes in another place. This was taken to be an ominous sign. Death was not far away.

Dogs

Dogs are still widely believed to be able to see what many human beings cannot. They are thought to be sensitive to supernatural presences and will often show signs of fear and distress before any human being has realised that anything is amiss. Dogs can sense the presence of ghosts. In times gone by, a dog howling in the night for no other apparent reason would often be taken as a sign of approaching death. Some people believed that a dog howling like this should be able to indicate, by pointing, the direction in which the death would take place.

Birds

Birds, both domestic and wild, were believed be 'tuned in' to the world of the supernatural and were said to be able to foretell death. Poultry were observed with apprehension in some places in Scotland. A cockerel crowing uncharacteristically in the hours of darkness was thought to mean the approach of death somewhere in the vicinity. Hens showing signs of fear and panic in spite of the absence of any predator in the vicinity were often believed to be foretelling doom for someone close by.

If a raven flew in front of someone along the road that he or she was taking, it was believed to be a bad sign – death was not far away for that person. Birds tapping on the window of a house were an equally unfortunate sign, as was a seagull standing on one leg on the roof of a house.

Death in Foreign Lands

Oh, ye'll tak the High Road, and I'll tak the Low Road
And I'll be in Scotland before ye;
For me and my true love will never meet again
On the bonnie, bonnie banks of Loch Lomond.

The lines above, the chorus of a song nowadays more often sung raucously (or drunkenly) than mournfully, reflect another belief about the spirits of the dead. The song is thought to have been written around the time of the Rebellion of the '45. In 1745, some supporters of Bonnie Prince Charlie, retreating from England, were captured by the English. The words of the song are the words of one soldier who faces execution to another who is to be freed. The soldier who is about to die tells his friend that he will take the 'Low Road' back to Scotland. The Low Road was the name of a spiritual path that was believed to exist along which the spirits of those who died far from home could return to the place of their birth. The Low Road would speed the executed soldier to Scotland faster than his compatriot, who faced many miles of hard marching, but although he might return to his homeland swiftly enough after death, he would never meet with his sweetheart again.

Phantom Hordes

The dead were never far away. Whatever happened to their bodies, the spirits of those who had died had to go somewhere. Whilst some spiritual presences were believed to be benign, inevitably there were many fears about spirits of the dead who wished harm upon the living. Superstition about such malevolent forces was prevalent throughout Scotland.

The realm of the dead was seen in much the same way as the realm of the fairies. Living persons could be spirited away to either realm, either temporarily or permanently. Those who claimed to have gone through such an experience were usually greatly changed by it. In common with stories of visits to the fairy realm, tales of being spirited away by the dead indicated that time in the realm of the dead was different from earthly time. Great distances were travelled in no time at all, and although several hours, or even days, might seem to pass, the person who had been spirited away, once safely back in the land of mortals, would discover that his or her absence had been very brief in earthly time.

The Sluagh, or host of the dead, was greatly feared in the Highlands of Scotland. The sight and sound of their grim parades through the realms of the living struck terror into the hearts of those who witnessed them. The Sluagh could bring death to those in its path. Those of a superstitious nature would not leave a window on the west side of the house open at night. To do so was to court disaster, for the Sluagh could then enter and cause trouble.

The Phantom of Death

A strange legend is attached to the churchyard at Eringle Truagh in Ireland. The novelist William Carleton (1794–1869), author of *Fardorougha the Miser*, was familiar with the story, and wrote after a visit to the spot:

I have been shown the grave of a young person about eighteen years of age, who was said about four months ago to have fallen a victim to the phantom, and it is not more than ten weeks since a man in the same parish declared that he gave a promise and fatal kiss to the ghost and consequently looked upon himself as lost. He took a fever and was buried on the day appointed for the meeting, which was exactly a month from the time of contact with the spirit. Incredible as it may seem the friends of these two persons declared, at least those of the young man did, to myself that particulars of the meeting with the phantom were detailed repeatedly by the two persons without variation. There are several other cases of the same kind mentioned. . .

The spirit of the churchyard seemed able to take male or female form. It would appear to a solitary mourner, always as a handsome, but above all sympathetic-looking figure. It would talk softly, tenderly, to the grieving person, assuring them that their dead friend or relative was now in a far happier condition than before. With such consoling talk, they would sit down together in the porch of the church, or on the stone wall. Gradually the mourner would forget his or her grief and think only of the wonderful sympathy and irresistible attraction of the person beside them. The attraction would seem to be mutual, and soon there was intertwining of hands, kissing and caressing. When at last they knew they must go, inflamed by sudden love, the visitors to the churchyard would say, 'When will I see you again?'

'We cannot meet for four weeks,' would be the answer. 'But let us pledge ourselves now, that in four weeks' time we will meet again, in this very place.'

Eagerly the pledge would be made. Looking back from beyond the churchyard gate, they would no longer see the figure. As the trance of its charm gradually wore off, a cold fear would rise inside them. They had made a pact with the phantom of death. For all that they, their friends, even the priest, could do, they felt their days were numbered. Within four weeks they would catch a mortal illness, or simply decline and fade, until the fatal appointment was kept, to the day, by their own funeral.

Phantom Funerals

Phantom funerals, causing surprise and distress to those who witnessed them, were relatively common supernatural occurrences. Sometimes reports of such funerals record the witness as having merely seen and heard such a ghostly procession. However, there are stories of people who have been pushed aside in the roadway as the phantom mourners make their way past. To witness such an event was never a good sign. One story of a phantom funeral comes from the fishing town of Wick in the north of Scotland.

A Phantom Funeral in Wick, Scotland

The story tells how a crofter from Wick was visited every year by his cousin, who was a fisherman and came to the port for the herring run. While his fishing boat was based at Wick, he would spend his spare time at the crofter's house. The two men got along famously in spite of their different lifestyles.

One particular year, the fisherman was preparing to set sail for home after a successful season with the herring fishing. His cousin, although not a fisherman, still had a healthy respect for the sea and his farming experience had given him a keen eye for the weather. He felt that the weather was about to take a turn for the worse and urged the fisherman to stay a little longer in Wick. His time there had shown him a healthy profit – what was the hurry?

The fisherman brushed aside the concerns of his cousin and laughed off any suggestion that the weather was too dangerous to go to sea. He was an experienced seaman and his boat was sturdy enough to withstand any squall. He bade goodbye to his crofter cousin and set off.

During the day, the weather turned worse, just as the crofter had suspected it would. The crofter had spent the afternoon visiting a family some way from his own home and when he saw the skies darken, he decided he had better make his way back.

The weather turned very wild with alarming speed and a fierce storm was blowing as the crofter trudged home, battling against the gale. He was halfway home when he saw a strange sight – three men carrying a coffin in the direction of the graveyard.

It seemed a small number of people for a funeral procession – perhaps the bad weather was keeping the mourners away. Curiosity overcame the crofter, and he followed the sombre procession to the cemetery. The three men stopped and put the coffin on the ground for a moment or two. Approaching the silent group, the crofter leaned over the coffin for a closer look. He could just make out the name that was engraved on the brass plate on top. It was his cousin's name. The crofter then looked up at the three coffin-bearers. Their faces were all too grimly familiar – they were the faces of three other men from Wick who had been lost at sea within the last year.

The crofter made for home with dread in his heart. When the news reached him some days later that his cousin had drowned after falling overboard in the storm, he was not surprised at all. He had already learnt of his cousin's fate, the night when he had seen the phantom funeral.

Death Coaches

A number of other Irish families have experienced the phenomenon of the 'death coach' (see page 80 for the story of the death coach of Ballyduff).

The Death Coach of Derrymore

The death coach was also heard at Derrymore House, County Clare, in the late nineteenth century, when its owner, General Gore, lay dying. The doctor was awaited, and the general's wife, son and sister were at his bed. All clearly heard the sound of a coach drawing up outside. But then there was silence. No one got out. They hurried to the door of the house and looked out. There was nobody there; nothing to be seen. Receding down the avenue, however, they heard the crunch of wheels on gravel. Before the doctor arrived, the general was dead.

The Phantom Coach of the Vizes

The Vize family of County Cork were haunted by a coach drawn by headless horses and driven by a headless coachman. It was seen by Mrs Vize, in the late nineteenth century. With other members of the family, she was sitting in the drawing room of their house one evening, when they heard a vehicle approaching the house at a rapid pace. They sat up, expecting to find that some visitor had arrived. Gravel crunched as the carriage came up the drive; then the dogs in their kennels set up a howling and whining. Mrs Vize went to the window, to see who might be coming. As she looked out, she screamed, and fell fainting to the floor.

When she was revived, she said she had seen a great black carriage, like a hearse, pulling up at the door. But the black horses drawing it had no heads, nor did the coachman who sat on the black-draped box. The other members of the family were too busy employed in caring for her to look out themselves, but they recalled hearing the sound of the carriage as it went away. A family death ensued a day or so after the visit of the phantom coach.

Bibliography

Roger Boar and Nigel Blundell *The World's Greatest Ghosts* Hamlyn Publishing 1996

Eddie Burks and Gillian Cribbs *Ghosthunter* Headline Press 1995

Daniel Cohen *Encyclopaedia of Ghosts* Fraser Stewart 1984

Maggie Craig *Damn' Rebel Bitches, The Women of the '45* Mainstream Publishing 1997

Hilary Evans *Visions, Apparitions, Alien Visitors* Aquarian Press 1984

Joan Forman *Haunted Royal Homes* Harrap 1987

Joan Forman *The Mask of Time* Macdonald and Jane's 1978

Professor Colin Gardiner *Ghost Watch* Foulsham 1989

Michael Goss *The Evidence for Phantom Hitch-Hikers* Aquarian Press, 1984

Lord Halifax *Lord Halifax's Ghost Book* Geoffrey Bles 1936

Sarah Hapgood *500 British Ghosts and Hauntings* Foulsham 1993

Robert Jackson *Great Mysteries* The Apple Press 1992

C. G. Jung *Memories, Dreams, Reflections* Collins 1967

Dane Love *Scottish Ghosts* Robert Hale 1995

Nick McIver *Great British Ghosts* Longman Group 1982

Andrew MacKenzie *The Seen and the Unseen* Weidenfeld and Nicolson

C. A. E. Moberly and E. F. Jourdain *The Ghosts of the Trianon* Aquarian Press 1988

Elliott O'Donnel *Scottish Ghost Stories* Jarrold Publishing 1975

J. Aelwyn Roberts *The Holy Ghostbuster* Robert Hale 1990

John and Anne Spencer *The Encyclopaedia of Ghosts and Spirits* BCA 1992

John and Anne Spencer *The Poltergeist Phenomenon* Headline 1996

Colin Wilson *Ghost Sightings* Parragon 1997